THE
SERPENT
AND THE
BEES

"The serpent draws poison and the bee honey from the same flower."

—Armenian proverb

THE
SERPENT
AND THE
BEES

A KGB CHRONICLE

EDWARD ALEXANDER

UNIVERSITY
PRESS OF
AMERICA

Lanham • New York • London

Copyright © 1990 by Edward Alexander
University Press of America®, Inc.
4720 Boston Way
Lanham, Maryland 20706

3 Henrietta Street
London WC2E 8LU England

Library of Congress Cataloging-in-Publication Data

Alexander, Edward, 1920—
The serpent and the bees : a KGB chronicle / by Edward Alexander.
p.   cm.
Includes bibliographical references and index.
1. Soviet Union—Ethnic relations.   2. Armenian S.S.R.—History.
3. Alexander, Edward, 1920– .   4. Soviet Union. Komitet
gosudarstvennoi bezopasnosti.   5. Soviet Union—Foreign
relations—United States.   6. United States—Foreign relations—
Soviet Union.   7. Soviet Union—Foreign relations—1945–
8. United States—Foreign relations—1945–   I. Title.
DK33.A63   1990   305.891'992047—dc20   90–12482 CIP

ISBN 0–8191–7820-9 (hard : alk. paper)

*For
Roseann*

Acknowledgments

Certain past and present colleagues have been generous with their time and counsel in helping to shape my manuscript. Some knew it as it progressed, others at later stages, but all contributed in myriad ways to its final version.

While everyone to whom I am indebted could not be named, David Binder, Robert Byrnes, James Critchlow, Nathan Glick, Paul Goble, Elinor Green, Ysa Kapp and Walter Roberts must be singled out—all of them from the worlds of public affairs, diplomacy, journalism, academia and international broadcasting.

In the experience itself, no one played a more palpable role, especially in its early stages, than Francis J. Meehan, former United States Ambassador to the German Democratic Republic (and earlier to Poland and Czechoslovakia), whose distinguished Foreign Service career brought us together initially in West Berlin where his wisdom and guidance served me immeasurably.

The greatest debt, however, is to my family: Mark, Scott and Christian, whose young lives were often burdened by these events, and to Roseann, who was a partner in every sense and whose gift of never confusing the trees for the forest has been a stabilizing factor in our lives.

* * * * * * *

CONTENTS

Preface

The story about to unfold is not exclusively about Soviet Intelligence and its methods, nor about the Foreign Service and diplomatic life, nor about behind-the-scenes insights into American-Soviet relations, nor about the modern-day survivors of a three-thousand-year-old cultural heritage. It is about all of these things but with a special emphasis on two central themes, in actuality two seductions.

The first, rooted in ethnicity, concerns the primal instinct which goads us into knowing more about our origins in order that we may look deeper into ourselves. As an ethnic Armenian I focused my interest on that nation which in the twentieth century happens to be one of the fifteen republics of the Soviet Union.

The second seduction, linked to the first but more esoteric by far, concerns my experiences with agents of the Soviet Union's Committee for State Security, known far and wide by its more evocative initials KGB.

How these two seductions, working in confluent ways, sought to exercise their influence over me is the heart of the story, which begins in the city of the two Berlins, that microcosm of the tensions and conflicts between East and West, between the United States and the Soviet Union.

* * * * * * * *

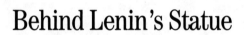

Behind Lenin's Statue

L ENIN SQUARE WAS AS SILENT AS A TOMB.
I emerged from the *Hotel Armenia* into the cool midnight air. The expanse of the square was rimmed by a stonehengian circle of government buildings which hovered ominously over the scene like some mute audience to the unfolding drama in which I was playing a central role.

There was no way I could deceive myself into thinking this was going to be just another casual Soviet encounter. Perhaps I was about to commit a blunder, I told myself, perhaps needlessly endanger my wife and myself. And both of us without our diplomatic passports, in fact, without any passports at all!

Only moments before, the phone had rung at that late hour as we were almost asleep. A mysterious unidentified voice had bade me, urged me, to meet him behind the statue of Lenin on the square on this, our last night in Yerevan before the flight back to Moscow. All we had ever wanted was to simply visit Soviet Armenia, where we had just enjoyed four exhilarating days meeting fascinating people and admiring its antiquities.

Seen through Soviet eyes, we were not, I had to admit, the usual Armenian-Americans who visit there. I was obviously a curiosity—a Foreign Service Officer stationed at the American Embassy in Budapest, an American diplomat who needed no interpreter and whose visit appeared to have no official purpose.

But I also knew that certain malevolent forces were at work, as the phone call indicated, and as I approached the towering statue to the right of the hotel, my conscience prodded me into facing some stubborn facts which I could not erase from my mind.

Four years earlier in West Berlin, Soviet Intelligence officers had zeroed in on me, singled me out, cultivated, flattered, cajoled me and had sought to awaken inchoate ethnic instincts about nation and heritage. Time and time again I had been offered a free trip—with escort—to Soviet Armenia, and every time I had refused.

Now, here I was on my own, deep in the Caucasus in the southernmost republic of the Soviet Union, having left my wife alone at midnight, walking to a rendezvous with a total stranger as though Berlin had never happened.

But Berlin had happened, and because the climax of that daunting experience flashed suddenly before my eyes, my steps became smaller as I moved more slowly towards the monument. Although I was by now but a few yards away, the mystery of this midnight tryst was momentarily driven from my mind by a surge of memories—memories of a chain of events which had begun in a dynamic city divided by politics, ideology and the most infamous wall of modern times . . . .

PART ONE

West Berlin
1959–1964

I

I T WAS THE BEST OF YEARS, IT WAS THE WORST OF
years—for treason.

But 1963 may well have been, as it was for me, the most memorable
year in view of everything that happened.

When the Soviet news agency TASS announced on May 16 of that
year that Colonel Oleg Penkovsky had been executed, the CIA and MI6
lost their most successful penetration into Soviet Intelligence. Then,
when the Swedish Government announced on June 20 the arrest of
Colonel Stig Wennerstroem, Soviet Intelligence lost a major source of
NATO secrets. But when on July 1 the British Government belatedly
announced that Kim Philby had been a Soviet agent, the notorious British traitor who had operated for three decades within the upper ranks of
Anglo-American Intelligence had already escaped some six months
before to the Soviet Union.

These sensational events, coming against the backdrop of political tensions in Berlin, where I was stationed on my first assignment in the
Foreign Service, had come to have a special significance for me because
in that same year I was becoming embroiled deeper and deeper in a
unique adventure with the KGB. Although initially and on the surface an
intelligence exercise almost classical in its evolution, it was in time to
become for me something far more fundamental—a search for identity,
touched not a little by a subliminal fear of finding it.

The true genesis of that adventure had been two major events some
years before: one involving the capture of a Soviet master spy in Brooklyn, the other the shooting down of an American plane from Soviet
skies. For had these two seemingly unrelated events and their aftermath
not occurred, I would not have had the fateful encounter in Berlin whose
consequences were to affect me for the next two decades of my life.

Rudolph Ivanovich Abel, a colonel in the KGB, was arrested on June 21, 1957 in New York City on charges of espionage against the United States. He was tried in the United States Court House in Brooklyn and on November 15, 1957 sentenced to thirty years imprisonment.

Francis Gary Powers, a U-2 pilot employed by the CIA, was shot down on May 1, 1960 near *Sverdlovsk* deep inside the Soviet Union. He was tried before the Military Division of the Soviet Supreme Court in Moscow and on August 19, 1960 sentenced to ten years imprisonment.

Eighteen months later in East Berlin, an American lawyer and a Soviet Embassy Second Secretary began negotiations for the exchange of Abel and Powers, an exchange which took place in the early hours of February 10, 1962.

On that dank, misty morning, the lawyer, James B. Donovan, and the Soviet diplomat, Ivan A. Shishkin, stood at opposite ends of the *Glienicker Bridge* connecting West Berlin and Potsdam. With Donovan escorting Abel and Shishkin accompanying Powers, the four walked towards each other and at mid-point on the bridge made the exchange, thereby consummating one of the earliest and most sensational spy deals in post-war American-Soviet Intelligence operations.

So secret had the negotiations been that only a tight circle of American diplomats in West Berlin had known of them. Although I had access to the classified messages between the United States Mission in Berlin and Washington, the cables dealing with the negotiations had obviously been in another channel.

Consequently, eleven months later when I was introduced to Shishkin at a social gathering, I did not know of his role in the Abel-Powers exchange. But more importantly, I did not know, as Donovan himself had not at first known, the true identity of Ivan Alexandrovich Shishkin.

For in the book which Donovan later wrote describing his experiences in defending Abel at his trial and then negotiating his exchange, there is the following passage: ". . . our people (in the U.S. Mission) had informed me that in their judgment I had been negotiating not with the Second Secretary of the Soviet Embassy in East Berlin but with the chief of the KGB in Western Europe."*

---

*James B. Donovan "Strangers on a Bridge" (The Case of Colonel Abel) Atheneum, New York, 1964 p. 418

II

M Y ASSIGNMENT IN WEST BERLIN WAS TO *RADIO IN the American Sector,* known far and wide by its acronymic call-letters RIAS, an American-sponsored radio station broadcasting around the clock in German to a huge audience in East Germany. Financed by the United States Information Agency (USIA), which was my employer, it was staffed by seven American Foreign Service officers supervising some 500 German programmers and broadcasters. Each of the Americans had his own department and mine was the cultural, which fed a voracious audience a steady diet of commentaries, features and interviews laden with political views and information which the East German regime had either distorted or suppressed. Because of their subtlety and variety, the cultural programs were often more effective than the political broadcasts.

The Soviet Union regarded RIAS as the voice of the enemy, inimical to everything for which the communist world stands, and, therefore, dangerous not only to Soviet interests in East Germany but throughout Eastern Europe—where RIAS had yet another audience of German-speaking intellectuals. Soviet diplomats and officials never hesitated to pursue a contact made at RIAS, whether it was German or American.

And so it was on January 23, 1963 when my wife and I attended a cocktail party at the West Berlin home of Associated Press correspondent Carl Hartman. Carl and I had known each other as graduate students at Columbia University's School of Journalism and were delighted to have found ourselves on concurrent assignments in the same city. It was a full house with many segments of Berlin society rubbing shoulders in the throng. As it turned out, not everyone there was from the Western sectors of Berlin.

Over the heads of a nearby group, Albert Hemsing, the top USIA official in Berlin, beckoned to me and when I reached him discovered he had been talking to a tall, distinguished, intellectual-looking gentleman who peered at me with interest.

Hemsing said—"I'd like you to meet Mr. Shishkin of the Soviet Embassy," then turning to him—"Mr. Alexander is one of the American staff at RIAS" and left us.

Shishkin and I struck up a conversation. He was certainly not the first Soviet official I had encountered and proved to be of that special category—the Germans have an excellent word for it, *salonfähig*—wherein one could carry on a stimulating conversation. Shishkin, as I discovered, was relaxed, somewhat business-like but pleasant, and certainly curious.

"So you are at RIAS," he began, "then you must be of German extraction." His English was excellent. I shook my head. He examined me with mock seriousness, attempting to ascertain my ethnic origin by appearance. I laughed at his efforts and said I would spare him the trouble since it would take all night. When he heard me say 'Armenian,' he displayed astonishment, then as though shifting to a higher gear, his eyes intent through his rimless glasses, he fired a series of questions about birth, background and language capability.

When he seemed to have finished, I in turn asked if there were any Armenians attached to the Soviet Embassy, as is sometimes the case, the Soviet Foreign Service representing one sector where Armenians have attained status and rank. Shishkin responded immediately by saying that a good friend of his was a 'commercial agent' who liked to meet Armenians.

Shishkin took out a small address book and asked for my home phone. I suggested my office phone. He looked at me sharply—"At RIAS? No, no. Your home phone is much better." I gave it to him since he could have easily gotten it anyway. While he was writing it down and almost as an aside, Shishkin said his friend's name was Aghayan. We shook hands and parted.*

---

*I cannot resist the temptation of noting an unusual coincidence, namely that on this same night, the British traitor Kim Philby, on the verge of exposure, disappeared from Beirut, escaping to Soviet Armenia. From Lebanon he traveled through Eastern Turkey and finally crossed over on foot into the Soviet Armenian Republic. See Page, Leitch, Knightley—"The Philby Conspiracy" Doubleday, Garden City, 1968 pp. 256–263

III

M Y DUTIES AT RIAS WERE FAR TOO FORMIDABLE TO afford me leisurely moments in which to speculate on the nature of Shishkin's Armenian friend. But in the weeks that followed, whenever the thought of the imminent contact would occur, my mind would almost automatically revert to the few Soviet Armenians I had known.

Three had been my colleagues at the "Voice of America," where we worked in the newly-organized Armenian Service, broadcasting daily to the Soviet Socialist Republic of Armenia, alongside similar programs in Georgian, Uzbek, Tatar and Azerbaijani.

Captured by the *Wehrmacht* in its invasion of the Soviet Union, the three former Red Army soldiers had worked as slave labor in the Third Reich, had been liberated by American forces, refused repatriation to Soviet Armenia and came to the United States. When I had been asked to form the Armenian unit at VOA in 1951, following the State Department decision to recognize the multi-national aspects of the Soviet state, these three were among those I recruited, and they proved to be invaluable founding members of a VOA element still in operation and enjoying a considerable following both inside and outside the Soviet Union.

One had been a school teacher, the second an engineer, and the third a poet-translator, and all three were the first Armenians from Soviet Armenia I got to know intimately. I often studied them as they worked so diligently at their typewriters—a skill newly-acquired at VOA— hunched over their machines, seeking the most hard-hitting and effective word in their Cold War vocabulary. All three were physically dissimilar and none of them looked anything like the Armenians one encountered on Manhattan's East Side—Little Armenia. Two were blue-eyed, one was very tall, all were fair, none was hirsute, thereby contradicting the stereotype image of Armenians held in the United States.

Beyond their common ethnic heritage, all three had psychological and emotional characteristics which made them very unlike one another. But on one issue they were always united, and that was political injustice, especially when it concerned relations with the Soviet Union. Nothing aroused their heightened sensitivity to injustice, of which they had all been victims, more than the failure of their adopted country to react to Soviet initiatives, and on that gloomy Sunday of November 4, 1956 when Soviet tanks returned to Budapest to crush the historic Hungarian revolt, the mood of all three was tragic. For in Hungary they saw Armenia, and it was with heavy hearts that they trudged to the studio to broadcast the melancholy news.

With them I began an initiation into Soviet Armenian culture—its society, mores, literature, history and traditions—supplemented by a daily reading of the Soviet Armenian press which through early familiarization with the unique Armenian alphabet I was able to comprehend. All of this kindled the first sparks of intellectual and personal curiosity about the Armenia my colleagues came from.

Nevertheless, even after I made a lateral entry into the Foreign Service for assignments anywhere in the world, I never realized that those nine years of total immersion in Soviet Armenian affairs were to be the prelude to encounters and confrontations filled with excitement, suspense and intrigue which would eventually lead to the very reality itself, Soviet Armenia, with its own passions and problems.

But beyond my three VOA colleagues, there had been two others from Soviet Armenia, the encounters with whom were of greater dramatic impact, not only because they were world-renowned personages, but also because the occasions were my first contacts with those cold-eyed escorts who accompany all such travelers beyond the borders of the Soviet Union.

One afternoon in June 1954, while I still worked at VOA, *The New York Times'* Soviet affairs expert Harry Schwartz phoned to invite me to the Hotel Roosevelt that evening to attend the opening matches between the United States and Soviet chess teams. It was the first visit of a Soviet chess team and included among its eight members the Armenian champion Tigran Petrosian, already becoming famous as a Grand Master. As Harry put it to me—"Here's your chance to talk to one of your more famous compatriots in the mother tongue."

Inside the grand ballroom more than 1,000 people fought for seats with an advantageous view of the stage. Advocates of closer U.S.-Soviet relations mixed with chess fans in the bucking crowd, while towering over everyone like a floating sculptured ebony bust were the powerful head and shoulders of Paul Robeson.

Applause greeted the two teams as they walked out onto the stage which was flanked by the American and Soviet flags. There was a certain incongruity in the display of the stars and stripes and hammer and sickle in the hall, for in the world outside, the Cold War was in full swing, the airwaves between East and West thick with invective. Flashbulbs popped now as Petrosian, looking uncomfortable, frowned at the outstretched arms begging for autographs.

Harry leaned over to me—"Now's the time. And while you're at it, maybe he'll tell you as one Armenian to another, why Botvinnik didn't come." Indeed, there had been huge speculation surrounding the absence of the top Soviet player who had led the delegation everywhere else, but would Petrosian deign to give me an answer—much less talk to me?

Now he was scowling as I approached the stage and stood between him and the first row of chairs behind me. Welcoming speeches had begun as I looked up at him and said—*"Parev, Hayrenagits!"*

There is no Armenian anywhere in the world, especially when far from home as I have discovered, who is impervious to the greeting in his native tongue—"Hello, compatriot." The dark scowl disappeared and was replaced by a big smile as Petrosian arose from his chair, bent down and extended his hand.

"Parev," he replied, "are you really Armenian?" his voice incredulous.

"Of course, and happy to meet you."

I studied the chess master close-up. His visage was more conventionally Armenian with its strong nose, heavy beard, dark complexion and dark curly hair. Petrosian was only 25 but he looked older.

"You are the first Armenian I am meeting in the United States. Are you from here?" Then, he suddenly looked past me as he spoke.

I explained that New York was my birthplace, and when he asked how come I spoke Armenian, I told him my father had taught me Armenian before I could speak English. He liked that and nodded full approval, but again he looked past me, uneasily. This time I turned and looked directly at several occupants of that first row of chairs who stared right back. From their haircuts and clothes I recognized them to be Soviets, and in fact later I established that they were non-playing members of the Soviet chess delegation.

There was polite applause now as a tall, elderly white-haired gentleman with a hearing aid approached the microphone. Petrosian asked his identity and when I said he was Bernard Baruch, he shook his head, but when I mentioned the Baruch plan for the international control of nuclear energy, Petrosian said—"Oh, I know who that is," and his frown reflected his government's position on that plan. I asked Petrosian if he understood English and whether he wished me to translate for him. He said No to both questions but leaned closer as I began anyway and twice stopped me when he had missed a phrase.

Finally, the 84-year-old elder statesman made a concluding remark which evoked heavy applause, Petrosian wishing to know what it was. I quoted Baruch—"May the best man win" at which Petrosian joined in the prolonged applause. As I watched him, only inches away, he looked over my shoulder again, but now I knew why.

I asked him if he were uncomfortable and he nodded but ascribed it to the new pair of shoes he had just bought in New York. I asked him if he liked it here and when he looked curtly at me I realized my question had an implication I had not intended. My God, I thought, how near the surface are their sensitivities, and could only imagine the kind of briefings the team had been subjected to in preparation for the trip to the great ideological enemy.

I quickly changed the subject—"Why hasn't Mikhail Botvinnik come?"

He took the question in stride—"You know, just before the trip, Botvinnik played a long match against Smyslov which tired him very much. But on top of that, Botvinnik is very busy with his regular work as an engineer."

It was not very enlightening, after all Smyslov had not been too tired to lead this team, but I left well enough alone.

"How are conditions in our Armenia?" I asked, emphasizing the 'our' to ease the atmosphere and establish common ground. Although no one else could have understood our conversation, he looked quickly at the first row again and replied—"I've been in Moscow most of the time. I'm not living in Armenia now."

"Are you aware that Armenians in the United States follow your career because of their pride in your achievements as an Armenian?"

"I am grateful," he replied modestly, but now looked past me with a startled expression just as I felt something brush against my arm. Turning, I looked into the hostile eyes of a burly Soviet 'delegate' standing directly before me, his companion by his side and appearing equally unfriendly. I looked up at Petrosian whose sad smile and apologetic eyes told me all.

"Goodbye," he said, and I replied "Good luck."*

"You created quite a stir among the boys in the first row," Harry Schwartz said teasingly as I rejoined him.

As predicted by the experts, the Soviet team won beating the Americans 20-12 and left the United States two weeks later. For me it had been a vivid experience, not only in meeting the moody Armenian genius of the chessboard but in my first brush with Soviet security agents.

That had been in New York. The next remarkably similar experience had taken place in West Berlin and was just as vivid. First, a word of explanation.

The most neglected department in RIAS was Music and because all six of my fellow American officers had deflected any overtures to supervise that department, its vast resources became an essential part of my responsibilities. And what resources! I had under my control two symphony orchestras—the already famous RIAS Symphony Orchestra, at that time led by Ferenc Fricsay, and the gifted RIAS Youth Orchestra; recordings with every major musical artist who visited Berlin; an ongoing agreement with the Berlin Philharmonic Orchestra to broadcast all their concerts to East Germany which required meeting periodically with Herbert von Karajan and all the other famous conductors and soloists who performed with that great ensemble; and finally, a huge budget for special broadcasts and concerts of virtually unlimited potential.

It was an enormously gratifying task to which I had not come totally unprepared. The career I had chosen as an undergraduate at Columbia before the outbreak of World War II had been music criticism and musicology, but subsequent events had drastically altered the considerable study and preparation I had invested in such a career. But somehow, by chance and circumstance, perhaps even by what Armenians call *jagadakir* (literally "written on the forehead," figuratively "destiny"), this Foreign Service assignment, the only one of its kind in the world, fell to me. In the five years that I worked this assignment, I lived and participated in Berlin's musical world virtually as a professional.

---

*Petrosian died in August 1984 in Moscow.

Consequently, when the Soviet Armenian composer Aram Khatchaturian crossed over from East to West Berlin for a reception in his honor in
1961, three months before the Wall was erected, I was among the invitees. The reception at the West Berlin Academy of Arts was hosted by
Gerhart von Westermann, President of the Academy and a former director of the Berlin Philharmonic Orchestra when Wilhelm Furtwängler
was its conductor. Having heard that Khatchaturian was conducting concerts in East Berlin, von Westermann sought to bridge the ideological
gap dividing the city by this magnanimous gesture. Khatchaturian
accepted and came over with his wife and a large Soviet entourage, also
bringing with him Hanns Eisler, East Germany's most famous composer
and brother of Gerhart Eisler, East Germany's infamous director of propaganda and former spy.

The room was packed, the air opaque with tobacco smoke and the
dense constructions of German and Russian. Getting close to Khatchaturian seemed too formidable a task for the time being so I sipped my
drink, chatted with H.H. Stuckenschmidt, the brilliant Berlin music
critic, and Hans Scharoun, the great architect who was building the
Philharmonie, the new home of the orchestra. When they had passed
on, I turned to find myself face to face with the rotund Eisler.

I greeted him in German and when he replied in English, we continued in that language which, as it emerged, he had improved while in
exile in Los Angeles during the war. Our conversation was civilized and
free of the bitter animosity which characterized the then non-diplomatic
relations between the United States and East Germany. Most striking
was the nostalgia with which Eisler reminisced about his years in Hollywood and his association with that singular colony of European exiles
and expatriates—Thomas Mann, Arnold Schoenberg, Bertolt Brecht,
Aldous Huxley and Charlie Chaplin.

But always I kept watching for an opportunity to approach the guest
of honor. It finally came some moments later as he moved closer, being
introduced by von Westermann to all within reach. And then, we stood
face to face.

As Von Westermann opened his mouth to introduce me, I pre-empted
him with the magical—*"Parev, Hayrenagits!"* Khatchaturian's fleshy lips
opened, his eyes popped and he stared in disbelief. I repeated the greeting and now the questions poured out of him as he gripped my arm,
questions about identity, background, parents as a thoroughly confused

von Westermann looked at us non-plussed. Just as suddenly, Khatchaturian stopped, looked over my shoulder and seemed amused as he said to me with a broad smile—"Wait here, I'll be back shortly."

Within a few minutes he circulated back and was again deep in conversation asking whether I had ever visited "the homeland." I replied that it was too expensive from the United States, to which he replied that he would discuss that problem with friends in Moscow. Our conversation understandably was now attracting the attention of not only the German invitees but members of the Soviet entourage who were openly putting their heads together and muttering to each other while watching me. Khatchaturian said almost conspiratorially—"Stay where you are, I'll come over again," and walked away. He was introduced to several senior members of the Academy but looked over at me twice, nodded with a warm grin, and then returned.

As he came up to me I was jostled several times and saw behind me some of his escorts who had accompanied him from East Berlin. This time the Armenian composer addressed me without amusement, for he was clearly irritated. "You see the problem of talking further. No one can understand us and so everything appears to be different than it really is. I hope you understand. I look forward to our meeting again. If you ever get to Moscow, call me," and extended his hand. Two of his escorts now had their heads only inches from ours as they attempted to penetrate the barrier of the unique Armenian language. But as Khatchaturian walked away he smiled once again, somewhat sadly, I thought.

Those encounters with Tigran Petrosian and Aram Khatchaturian had lingered in my mind. Certainly not just because they were famous. I had met famous Armenians before—Rouben Mamoulian, for instance, who had talked so nostalgically about Greta Garbo, or William Saroyan, so suffused with his ethnicity. But the film director and the writer were creatures of our own familiar civilization, while the chess master and the composer came from that wholly disparate set of values known as Soviet society, from an arid patch of land in the Soviet Caucasus they called "the homeland."

And now, Shishkin's friend. How would he be? I wondered and waited.

IV

FOUR MONTHS LATER TOWARDS THE END OF MAY THE phone rang at home and an abominable connection distorted the voice of someone speaking in urgent tones. Unable to make out what he was saying, I kept asking in German who he was, until I suddenly realized that the person at the other end of the line was not speaking English or German but Armenian, and with an indescribable accent.

The line cleared inexplicably and the voice said—"My name is Rafael Aghayan. A mutual friend of ours, Shishkin, suggested I call you. Can you understand me?" On hearing my reply in Armenian, he said with enthusiasm—"Ah, then you really are Armenian. We must meet."

We began to dicker about the day. Could he make it two days later on Friday? Yes, he could. Did he know West Berlin well? Yes, very well. Then how about the *Berlin Hilton?* The what? I repeated it clearly. Never heard of it, he said. I said he could clearly see the *Hilton* from his side of the *Brandenburg Gate,* but he professed not to know it. How about the *Kempinski Hotel,* I asked? Where was it? On *Fasanenstrasse,* I explained. Where is that?

At this point, I gave up, concluding that anyone who did not know the two best-known hotels in the city was not only a stranger to West Berlin but perhaps even to East Berlin. I suggested that he phone me the following Monday at 11 AM at RIAS from somewhere in West Berlin to ensure a good connection, tell me where he was, and that I would meet him.

On Monday at 10:55 AM he phoned, asked if I were free and said he was very anxious to meet. He was in a phone booth, he said, in front of the Ford dealer on West Berlin's main street, the *Kurfürstendamm.*

I arrived there twenty minutes later and saw a tall, darkly complexioned male walking up and down somewhat aimlessly in front of the showroom. As I approached him, he stopped and for a few seconds we examined each other, then extending his hand and with a broad smile exposing flashes of gold he said in Armenian—*"Parev, Hayrenagits!* You are Mr. Alexander," pumped my hand warmly many times, adding "it is good that Armenians seek each other out."

We decided to lunch at the Copenhagen Restaurant within walking distance to which I led the way and where we sat in a corner. When I asked what he wished to eat he pleaded that I do the ordering, explaining "I can't make any progress in this damned German language." When the orders had been taken, we began a conversation which lasted two hours.

He asked some basic questions about birth date and place, as though filling in the vacant spaces of a questionnaire, but reciprocated with information about himself: he was born in 1923—therefore three years younger than I—in Baku, the capital of Soviet Azerbaijan, which neighbors Armenia, but raised in *Karabagh*—which explained his strange accent—a mountainous region within Azerbaijan.*

Aghayan said he was married to an Armenian woman and had two children, a girl and a boy. He said he worked in the Soviet Embassy's Consular Section and was concerned primarily with visas and passports. (Shishkin's description of him as a "commercial agent" was not clarified, even when I raised it.) Aghayan maintained that his assignment to the Soviet Embassy in East Berlin was his first in a foreign country; that he had already been there for two years and was due for a vacation in the Soviet Union that summer.

"Since my son's name is Edward (which he pronounced *Yedvart*), the same as yours, let's address each other by our first names," he proposed just as the beer arrived, upon which he made a toast—"To friendship of the Armenian kind," and continued—"You work for RIAS. Tell me, what do you there?"

So now the interrogation was to begin. I described the cultural and musical programs of my department, the need for informing the 17 million East Germans of a thriving vibrant cultural world beyond their borders, the knowledge and experience of which they were being denied, and that together with political programming was filling the enormous vacuum which existed in the loyal satellite of the Soviet Union. Aghayan toyed with his food silently, then finally said—"This should be one city."

Karabagh was ceded to Soviet Azerbaijan in 1921 even though 80% of its population is Armenian. It lies but ten miles from the Armenian border and is the source of continuing violence between the two Soviet republics.

"It was one city until you put up that Wall," I responded.

Abruptly he changed the subject and asked if I had ever been to Armenia and whether I knew anything about "the homeland." I said the pleasure of visiting Armenia was still unknown to me, but that I was aware of the rather large role played by Armenians in Soviet life and achievement. I began with the obvious name of Anastas Mikoyan, who at that time was First Deputy Premier,* then mentioned the Alikhanian brothers, both nuclear physicists, former Soviet Minister of Heavy Industry Ivan Tevosyan who had died while serving as Ambassador to Japan, and the UN economic expert Hamazasp Harutiunian.

I asked what had ever happened to former Soviet Armenian Communist Party Chief Suren Tovmassian? Aghayan looked at me curiously for a moment, then after pointing out that Tovmassian was now Soviet ambassador to Vietnam, asked—"How is it that you are so well informed on Soviet Armenian affairs, an American-Armenian born and raised in New York?" I replied that for eight years I had been chief of the "Voice of America's" Armenian Service, in which capacity it had been my business to know such things.

Aghayan showed what seemed to me genuine surprise, saying—"So it was you who directed the hostile propaganda against Armenia and the Russians! Why are you so anti-Russian? Don't you realize that if it hadn't been for the Russians, there would be no Armenia today?"

We now engaged in one of those back-and-forth debates on the Soviet Union and its early history in which neither side concedes anything and the only escape is to change the subject without decorum—a tactic Aghayan was to employ often in such situations.

Suddenly brightening, he bent close over the table and asked—"Isn't it marvelous about Petrosian?" The Armenian chess master had just defeated Mikhail Botvinnik in Moscow in twenty-one games to become the new world champion. I agreed that it was indeed marvelous and described my encounter with Petrosian in 1954 when he had come to New York with the Soviet chess team.

"I know Petrosian too," he beamed, "and when I heard here in Berlin that he had won the championship, I immediately telephoned

---

*Some months after this conversation Mikoyan was elevated to the post of Chairman of the Presidium of the Supreme Soviet, that is, President of the Soviet Union, and retired two years later with honors. He died in 1978.

friends in Yerevan who told me that the whole capital had gone wild. In Yerevan they are saying that it took an Armenian to beat a Jew." He looked to me to match his own amusement at his little joke but on seeing my frown added quickly—"Don't misunderstand. This has nothing to do with nationalities. In our country they say it takes ten Jews to equal one Armenian."

This time I changed the course of the conversation and asked if Nikita Khrushchev—still Chairman at that time—had changed conditions very much in the Soviet Union. "Oh yes, he has corrected the mistakes made by Stalin and raised the standard of living. Of course, we cannot live as well as Americans, but on the other hand, you have never experienced a major war in your native land. We, however, hadn't yet recovered from World War I when World War II broke out. You must come and see for yourself what we have accomplished."

We agreed that war had no victors, to which I added that this was especially so if we had to face up to the Chinese together. When he didn't react to that, I tried the old joke about the difference between an optimist and a pessimist: the optimist studies Russian and the pessimist Chinese. Aghayan had not heard that before and laughed heartily. Then, not to be outdone, he told one of his own, about a NATO meeting in which the various countries were discussing which language should be adopted as the common language of NATO. As each went on record pushing for his own, a voice in the rear was heard to call out—"You'd all be smart to learn Russian. When you become prisoners of war, it might help out." Aghayan laughed loudly at his own joke, while I merely smiled.

"Tell me about your father," he said. When Armenians of our generation talk about their fathers, it is always a harrowing story of terror and persecution that begins deep in Turkey, and Aghayan knew very well what he was asking. I reviewed my father's early years, orphaned at the age of six when marauding Turkish troops slew his father as both walked to the well in their native village of *Palou;* of the kidnapping of his mother and sister, whom he never saw again; of the imprisonment of his younger brother whom he eventually got out of prison with money he earned in America; of his years of anguish in an American missionary orphanage until he emigrated to the United States in 1910; and of his determination to avenge his family's tragedy by enlisting in the U.S. Army when America entered World War I because it was the only way he could fight Turks.

Aghayan listened very attentively and sympathetically. It was a story which every survivor of those horrific years knew well and one which had been given literary prominence in Franz Werfel's superb novel "The Forty Days of Musa Dagh." Aghayan said—"Next time, I'll bring you a book for your father," and as he lit another cigarette—he proved to be a chain-smoker—he gesticulated with it—"It's from Armenia, I'll bring you some, and Armenian cognac, the best there is."

We ate silently for a few moments, I still under the spell of the tragedy which had befallen grandparents I had never known. Aghayan tried a new tack now—"Tell me about those men at the 'Voice of America' you worked with, those Armenians. We know they are from Armenia." That surely was no secret, I replied, since the scripts they wrote and announced were in the accents and syntax of Soviet Armenia.

"We also know they were prisoners of war of the Germans."

I shrugged and said since emigration from the Soviet Union was not permitted, the war had provided thousands of former Soviet citizens in similar straits to find new lives in the West. While almost all have forgotten their past, I continued, a handful, such as those at the "Voice" have not and are trying to do something about it. This did not sit well with Aghayan and he grimaced, but recovered to ask why I had never been to Armenia. I said it was too expensive and recounted my conversation with Aram Khatchaturian only two years before.

Looking now at my watch I said it was getting late and that I had to be getting back to RIAS. "Can you come over to our side?" he asked. When I said of course, he insisted that next time I bring my wife and that he would as well. We agreed to meet on the third of June in front of the *Cafe Sofia* on *Friedrichstrasse* in East Berlin at 3 PM.

As we shook hands he said—"By the way, to avoid getting into trouble, don't tell your people about meeting with me. My people don't care about such things but your people don't approve of your talking to Russians (sic), so be careful."

There was something about this admonition which struck me as monumentally naive. As I drove back to my office I wondered whether Aghayan truly believed that I would keep our meeting secret from personnel in our Mission whose business it was to know and follow such matters. "My people" as he had put it. In any case, he may not have known of the requirement placed on all U.S. Government personnel to report the nature and substance of such contacts, which of course I did and subsequently as well. The detailed descriptions of events and conversations in the pages to follow attest the extensiveness of my notes.

Thus, following the report of this first meeting and in reviewing its many aspects, "my people" arrived at a consensus that Rafael Aghayan, by virtue of the circumstances of our meeting—his style, questions, manner and general demeanor—was not in diplomatic consular or commercial service but by profession a Soviet Intelligence officer not with the Soviet Embassy in East Berlin but assigned directly from the KGB Center in Moscow, which also explained his unfamiliarity with West Berlin and why it had taken four months for him to make the first contact.

The immediate question following this initial contact was whether I should continue seeing him, in view of the nature of Aghayan's true identity. There was the negative argument that it was not all that relevant to my own assignment, namely supervising cultural-political broadcasts to East Germany, and therefore consumed time and energy I could better devote to RIAS.

But the more adventuresome of my colleagues argued that the opportunity to engage at first hand a genuine Soviet Intelligence officer whose national origin was not Russian and with whom I could communicate in his native language was so uncommon that the chance should not be forfeited so readily. One even said with open envy—"God, I'd give anything to have a contact like that!"

The fact is, as I suspected, that Intelligence Services like occasionally to make direct contact with each other, and although I was not in that clandestine brotherhood, in the view of some I could serve just as well as a surrogate. Given the nature of the Soviet mentality, it had to be assumed that Aghayan considered me an opposite number. In any case, the second argument prevailed, but the final decision was left to me—and I made it.

Thanks to Ivan Shishkin, I was entering the arcane and, as I was to discover, convoluted world of the KGB.

V

MY WIFE ROSEANN AND I WERE FIFTEEN MINUTES late. We had walked from Checkpoint Charlie across *Unter den Linden* when we spotted Aghayan in Front of the *Cafe Sofia*. He looked pleased as we approached, was gracious to Roseann and said his wife was waiting around the corner, where we then joined her.

Kohar Aghayan was nervous with us and it took a long time before she became relaxed. Aghayan waved to a man in an empty lot across the street who drove up to us in a black Mercedes sedan with a diplomatic license plate. As we climbed in, Aghayan said he had reserved a table at the *Cafe Budapest* on *Karl Marx Allee*.

Once there, after he had instructed the driver in Russian when to return, I selected a table which overlooked the main street, ignoring the reservation. Aghayan asked me to order the food as he ordered the drinks so that before I had even finished, the table was covered with bottles of Czech beer, Hungarian wine, German lemonade and Armenian cognac. True to his word, Aghayan—and his wife—came bearing gifts. He opened a briefcase and handed me a book in Armenian describing the mass repatriation of Armenians from the western world in 1947–48, recommending I read it to learn of their new life.*

That done, Kohar, a plumpishly pretty woman, opened her bag and took out three small medallions wrapped in tissue paper, two of them commemorating the 1600th anniversary of the invention of the Armenian alphabet by Mesrob Mashtots, all 36 letters included on one of them, and a third depicting a female figure representing Armenia. Then he took from his briefcase two packages of Armenian cigarettes, the first called *Massis* (the Armenian name for Mt. Ararat) and the second *Sassountzi*

---

*Several hundred thousand Armenians, primarily from the Middle East and France and about 150 from the U.S., settled in Armenia only to encounter unendurable economic and political conditions. Those who complained were sent to the Soviet Far East.

David (a legendary Armenian hero). Although I had brought nothing, my wife had and reciprocated with a bottle of French cologne which brought a quick bright smile to Kohar's face and effusive thanks.

Lunch on this day, the first in which our wives participated, was to last almost four hours, followed by a pleasant diversion that would carry us late into the evening.

Aghayan got right down to business, the wives meanwhile fumbling for conversational openings. Soviet Armenia, he said, has prominent sons throughout the country in every branch of Soviet life, thanks to the Russians. Every true Armenian must visit the homeland, he insisted, and asked that I begin thinking seriously about a date so that he could make the arrangements.

Next, he expressed irritation with the "Voice of America's" Armenian broadcasts. "They are very hard-hitting and seem to know what is going on in Armenia," he complained, "but those people cannot be counted as true sons of Armenia." He sought to find out more about the personnel, even asked for their names. I laughed at his brazenness and asked if VOA was that much of a problem for his government. He waved it aside as unimportant, replying rather loudly—"Certainly not, absolutely not," as heads turned in our direction at the odd-sounding language. "We know much about them and where they come from. One is from *Karabagh*. Kohar and I recognized the accent since we are also from there."

Aghayan now raised RIAS, about which he directed his most persistent questioning: Were the programs prepared in Washington? How much control was exercised by the Berlin Senate? Was policy suggested by the Bonn government? These were all easy questions to which a negative reply sufficed to cover all three.

"Why is RIAS so aggressive, so much against us, against Ulbricht?" he went on.*

I delivered a small lecture on the basic objective of RIAS—to inform the population of East Germany about events in their own country and in the world—and pointed out that if in the process harsh words were spoken, it was because of Soviet policies and Ulbricht's regime, concluding—"You don't expect kind words from RIAS about the Berlin Wall, do you?"

---

*Walter Ulbricht was the veteran East German communist boss who since 1950 headed the most Soviet-oriented regime in East Europe. He was replaced in 1971 by Erich Honecker and died two years later. Honecker in turn, was forced to resign in 1989 when the Wall crumbled.

He ignored my question and asked for my candid opinion of Ulbricht. After describing the East German Party Chief as a ruthless demagogue, I commented that while neither the U.S. nor the West German government respected him, the population of the Soviet zone of Germany had nothing but contempt for the communist leader whom they had nicknamed *Spitz-bart* (because he sported a pointed beard in emulation of Lenin).

I asked how it was possible for Moscow to be replacing Stalinists in the other East European countries and still retain this hard-liner? It struck me now that Aghayan was somewhat out of his depth. He mut-tered lamely about Ulbricht being 'the people's choice,' looked over at his wife as though for support, and then, in one of the innumerable *non sequiturs* I was often to experience with him, he blurted out—"Why is your president coming to Berlin?"*

"Why does Khrushchev have the right to come to Berlin and our president not?" Smiling at my reply he continued—"Can you tell me if your president will go to the border?"

I explained that President Kennedy's route would not be a secret since all newspapers in West Berlin would announce it, and besides, RIAS would carry every moment of the entire visit. Satisfied with that, he asked about visits to Berlin of the new U.S. Ambassador, George McGhee, did I know him, would he visit RIAS? I said the ambassador was not yet known to me, but that he could be expected to come to RIAS when I certainly would meet him.

Meanwhile, the two wives were in deep conversation as well, and Roseann established that in addition to the boy and girl living with them, there was a third child, a daughter, living with her grandmother in Baku, even though he had earlier said they had only two children. Kohar, it emerged, was an eye surgeon unable to practice her profession; she missed her third child, was extremely unhappy in East Berlin and disliked the Foreign Service. Her Armenian was difficult to understand through the heavy *Karabagh* accent and she mixed many Russian words in her speech, often interrupting her husband for an Armenian equiva-lent. She spoke no German, thought East Berlin "an ugly village," and missed no opportunity to praise Moscow. She finally admitted at one

---

*The White House had just announced the one-day visit on June 26 of President Kennedy to West Berlin as part of his travel to the Federal Republic of Germany.

point, to her husband's dismay, that she bore no love for the Germans, upon which he quickly inserted—"You know, they killed 20 million of our countrymen."

VI

WE LEFT THE *CAFE BUDAPEST* AND WHILE WALKING to the car which had been waiting, Aghayan asked—"Why didn't you let the Secretary of the Treasury go through with his idea? That was a good idea and a good solution."

Did he mean Henry Morgenthau and his plan to convert Germany after World War II into a potato patch? "That's it, he's the man," he replied excitedly, "He knew what he was talking about. You know why? Because the Germans cannot be trusted."

In the car he turned around in his front seat and asked if we had ever been to the *Müggelsee,* and when we said we hadn't, without asking if we wished to go—it was now 8 o'clock at night—he instructed the driver to proceed.

As we drove down *Karl Marx Allee* with its workers' apartments on both sides, Aghayan waved at the buildings, explaining—"They've tried to recreate Moscow here. By the way, have you been to Potsdam? I'll take you there also. That's where Truman came for the conference with Stalin and Churchill. But we loved Roosevelt. You know, that was naive of Eisenhower to admit he knew about the U-2 flights."

He said many things, made many asides which, while vulnerable to counter-argument were frequently pointless to engage in. But that last comment intrigued me, so I said—

"If you are talking about spying, Rafael, admit that your country spies more than any other. We are catching them all the time, unless," I paused and looked at him drolly, "they voluntarily defect, as many do."

He turned around fully in his seat and watched me intently as I continued—"I wondered whether you would show up today."

Aghayan shook his head—"I don't understand. Didn't you believe my invitation was sincere?"

"Yes, of course I believed you, but in the meantime *Pravda* has run an editorial after the Penkovsky trial warning all Soviet citizens to keep away from foreigners."*

Aghayan's face reflected consternation at mention of Penkovsky, and he shot back—"What *Pravda* was talking about does not pertain to diplomats," turned his back to me and pointed to Ernst Thaelmann Park which we were just passing and said surely I knew who he was. I said the head of the German Communist Party in the 1930s was known to some as a victim of the Soviet-Nazi pact who was later killed by the Nazis in *Buchenwald*. Aghayan preferred to ignore my comment and after some silent driving we came to a stop. We were at the *Müggelsee*. The four of us got out of the car, he and I walking on ahead.**

I asked Aghayan what he had done professionally prior to his Berlin assignment. He said he had been employed by the Soviet Ministry of Foreign Affairs to which he hoped to return. Why wouldn't he go to another foreign country, as was customary for career foreign service personnel?

"Not if I can help it. I don't like the Foreign Service, nor does my wife." Then, perhaps in response to my questioning look, he made the surprising admission—"We both of us miss our other child" in tones so solemn that I felt a surge of pity.

As though anxious to dispel this sudden change of atmosphere, he stopped me and asked—"If I arrange a trip to Armenia, can you go?" I shrugged my shoulders non-committally and he continued—"Do you have to inform your superiors when you leave Berlin or can you just take off for a few weeks?"

I explained that my whereabouts always had to be known in case of emergency, but in any case I wouldn't want it any other way. He nodded and continued.

---

*Oleg Penkovsky, a colonel in Soviet Military Intelligence, had just three weeks before been convicted in Moscow of having worked for American and British Intelligence. He was condemned to death and according to a Soviet announcement shot. His British contact, Greville Wynne, himself imprisoned in the Soviet Union and later exchanged, claims, however, that Penkovsky took his own life. Wynne has given a detailed account of his involvement with Penkovsky in "Contact on Gorky Street" (Atheneum, New York, 1968)

**In fact, we were at one of the extremities of East Berlin beyond which Americans could not go, as a sign in Russian, English, French and German informed us. After we established diplomatic relations in 1974, Americans accredited to our Embassy in East Berlin could go anywhere.

"Listen, if you wish, I can arrange it so that no one will know you have been to Armenia. I will travel with you. It takes only five hours by Soviet jet from Berlin to Yerevan. There, we will spend five or six days, then one or two in Moscow, and nothing will be stamped on your passport. The Americans will not approve your going and I don't want you to get into trouble with your government. Can you make it in autumn when Armenia is at its most beautiful?"

I said I would think about it.

"Good. I and my family go to Baku on July 15 on vacation and must be back by September 1 for the children's school. We can talk about it then."

We continued walking, watching little motor boats on the lake, with a scattering of East Germans also taking evening walks.

"I brought you here away from the crowd so that we wouldn't be seen by your people. American soldiers like to tour our part of Berlin but never come this far. Your government does not look with favor on contacts of this kind. You and me, you know."

We returned to the car and as we were driven back to the center of East Berlin, Aghayan and I continued the game we played last time of identifying prominent Armenians in the USSR. I particularly wanted to pursue this with him, suspecting that his knowledge was superficial. We named Marshal Ivan Bagramian, hero of World War II, Viktor Ambartsumyan, the USSR's foremost astronomer, the Orbelian brothers, one a chemist, the other a philosopher, and the Shakespearean actor Vahram Papzian, famous throughout the Soviet Union for his portrayal of Othello. All of these were highly publicized Armenian figures, known inside and outside the Soviet Union.

But then I asked Aghayan about three literary scholars and confirmed my suspicion when he shook his head at their mention: the philologist Stepan Malkhasian, whose four-volume dictionary of the Armenian language is a lexicographical monument; the historian Manoog Abeghian, who has written a superb two-volume history of Armenian literature; and the grammarian Hrachia Adjarian, author of a seven-volume study of the Armenian language as well as an exhaustive etymological dictionary tracing the origin of over 5,000 Armenian words.

Aghayan appeared annoyed at his ignorance, wanted to know how I could know about them and when they had achieved these things. I said that all three had begun their researches long before the advent of a

Soviet regime in Armenia but that their work had been published later and that I owned some of those books.

Attempting to convert the information he was ignorant of to his advantage, Aghayan asked if the United States could match such a record, quickly adding to the scholars the names of those mentioned earlier. I recited a list of the most prominent Armenian-Americans, headed by writer William Saroyan, composer Alan Hovhannes and film director Rouben Mamoulian, explaining that the arts were full of Armenian musicians, painters, choreographers, as was most every facet of American society.

"By the way," he said with sudden enthusiasm, "I called Yerevan again and was told that Tigran Petrosian, our new chess champion, had received a hero's welcome and addressed 15,000 Armenians in the Stadium, giving them a play-by-play account of his victory over Botvinnik."

We had now reached *Bahnhof Friedrichstrasse* where we got out, thanked them for their hospitality, and Roseann promised to reciprocate it at our home. She suggested a Saturday so that they could bring their children, at which the Aghayans became uncomfortable, looked at each other quickly, then he said—"We'll meet your children in your home and you'll meet ours in our home, when you come over again."

We discussed the date of our next meeting and agreed on Saturday June 15 in front of the Ford dealer on *Kurfürstendamm* as the pickup point. Now, Aghayan took my arm and led me aside as the women shook hands, and said—"It is in your interest not to inform your superiors of these meetings. Believe me, I know," as I smiled.

It might have been more in our interest not to have dined at the *Cafe Budapest* on that or any other occasion because we began to feel ill after getting on the *U-Bahn* to *Kochstrasse* in West Berlin where a U.S. Mission car had been waiting for us, and by the time we got home, both of us were retching badly.

VII

RAFAEL AND KOHAR AGHAYAN WERE WAITING IN FRONT of the Ford showroom when we drove up and both reflected warmth and pleasure. Kohar in particular seemed a different person; she was far better dressed and had apparently paid a visit to the hairdresser. Her manner was friendly and relaxed and she looked one in the eye when she spoke, frequently carrying the conversation when her husband seemed at a loss for words.

Roseann explained that since it was somewhat early for dinner, perhaps we should drive around West Berlin; for instance, had they seen the *Hansaviertel?** "Many, many times, both of us," Aghayan said with great emphasis, but Kohar, seated behind him next to Roseann, asked her many questions discreetly, displaying a curiosity which belied his claim.

Instead we drove to the Academy of Arts where an exhibit of 20th century French portraits was in progress and which we thought might generate some amusing reaction. It did, Aghayan revealing a predictable aversion to the nightmarish visions of the human countenance which surrounded us. His final comment as we departed—referring to Picasso—was—"Well, it doesn't matter what the artist's convictions are. If he has big enough name, he can paint this kind of nonsense and the public will be impressed."

We then drove around the *Gedächtniskirche*** and when Kohar asked what it represented, Roseann explained and suggested we all go in, whereupon Aghayan said with a big smile—"Oh come now, what would

---

*A residential quarter of West Berlin devastated by Allied bombers and reconstructed in the 1950s into a stunning showcase of dwellings.
**The Memorial Church, actually the Kaiser Wilhelm Church, kept in its gutted state as a permanent reminder of the war, but around which have been built two contemporary church structures in use.

a good communist be doing in church," adding that he was getting hungry. Kohar shrugged in a hopeless gesture.

Because it was still too early to dine, we drove to the *Berlin Hilton* and sat at the bar, whose appointments evoked admiring comments from Kohar. Roseann took out photographs of our three sons in our Berlin home. Kohar said matter-of-factly that the pictures were, of course, taken in America in view of the furnishings and was surprised when Roseann corrected her.

Aghayan nursed his drink quietly as the conversation centered on the children. Roseann and I, as we later discussed between ourselves, sensed that something was not quite right with respect to theirs. My wife again established that the smallest, a girl, was living with Rafael's mother in Baku, Azerbaijan, and that they would visit her when they took their leave in July.

During this phase of the conversation we distinctly heard Kohar sigh whenever the girl in Baku was mentioned. The talk turned to the attitudes of children as they grew up and Roseann said that after marriage young couples should live separately from their parents. Kohar agreed vociferously but Aghayan disagreed and looking pointedly at his wife said—"All families should live together. The state takes good care of children, and besides, it gives the wives a chance to go out and work." Roseann said she did not believe in having our children raised by anyone else and that nothing could replace parents' love and care. Kohar's sighs became even more audible earning her a reproachful look from her husband.

It was now 5 PM and the drinks had opened all our appetites, so we got back in the car as my wife explained that she had intended to have them to our home in *Zehlendorf* but that she had not found the time to prepare some Armenian dishes. Consequently, we were taking them to one of the finest restaurants in West Berlin. As we entered the *Zlata Praha* (Golden Prague), he exclaimed that of course he knew it well, but once we were inside it was obvious from his demeanor that he had never been in the small Czech restaurant.

After we had ordered, which again he left to me because of his poor German, we continued to talk of children and of educational problems in the Foreign Service. Aghayan said both of his children attended the Russian school which had teachers from Moscow and which he considered an excellent facility. The East German schools, on the other hand, he said were disrupted by too many German holidays.

I couldn't resist the temptation, and asked—"Such as two days from now?"

His brow wrinkled and he looked quizzically at me as I went on—"Our children will be home on Monday except for the one hour of solemn observance we shall all note." This did not clarify the occasion for him— "I don't understand, Monday is June 17. What happened on June 17?"*

I explained and as I went into some detail his displeasure increased, and most of all when Kohar asked him to explain. He did, in Russian, and as she began to fiddle with her napkin avoiding our eyes, he said to me—"Now I remember, that was when those West Berlin hooligans came into our part of the city and started trouble. There are always two sides to every question. Look, things can never improve until the two Germanys are brought together, and that can't happen until the two Berlins are re-united."

"Then why did you put up the Wall? Doesn't that make re-unification all the harder?"

"We had to," he shot back, "things were getting very bad. Otherwise, the GDR** economy would have gone bankrupt. Our Germans, those on our side, were going over every day and taking advantage of the East-West exchange rate to buy everything. We could not tolerate that. So we built the Wall to stop them."*** I did not outwardly take note of his seeming candor—or was it an impetuous slip?—and listened with courteous indifference until he abruptly changed the subject.

"Is it firm now that President Kennedy will visit Berlin on June 26?" he asked, repeating the date several times for confirmation, then—"Will RIAS programs be changed?" I gave affirmative replies to both questions and said I was consequently very busy. He said almost abstractedly that Khrushchev was also a very busy man and devoted much time to his work, which made me wonder how I should regard this curious comparison. Roseann noted that some Soviet leaders such as Mikoyan

---

*Workers in East Berlin, then in other parts of the country, went on strike protesting low wages and higher work norms, leading to violence and bloodshed, which was finally suppressed by Soviet tanks in what was to be the first major uprising in East Europe against Soviet rule.

**German Democratic Republic, the official name for East Germany

***While it must be assumed that the GDR makes no move without prior consultation with the Soviet Union, it is also public policy to affirm GDR autonomy in all matters. Hence, it came as a surprise to hear this admission of Soviet responsibility for the decision to construct the most visible symbol of ideological failure by a communist country.

seemed to place work above personal affairs, and looking at Kohar who appeared to be reacting to this sympathetically, added that she found it odd that the Soviet leader had remained in Cuba when his wife had died. Aghayan looked at his wife sharply and commented—"One's duty to one's government comes before one's duty to one's family."

Seeking to ease the slight tension which had developed, I asked if they had much contact with East Germans. Aghayan, relieved, replied with some exuberance—"Yes, quite a lot. But they are very curious about us. Once, we invited a neighbor to have dinner with us because I had made some *shashlik** in the backyard, and I knew the neighbors could smell it. This one neighbor came over and throughout the meal kept asking me questions about why we were here and what I did. Can you imagine? Instead of enjoying the delicious *shashlik* I had made, he was more interested in being nosey."

The propaganda war between the People's Republic of China and the Soviet Union had already become very intense in these days and so I decided to make a foray into this as yet uncharted territory with the simple question whether a reconciliation was possible. Aghayan gave the standard Marxist reply that the two peoples were the closest of friends. When I pointed out that I wasn't speaking of the two peoples but of the governments, he looked displeased but made no further comment. I suggested that while in the past relations between the two communist countries had seemed to be correct, I could now see why the Soviet Union never gave the secret of the atom bomb to its ally. He agreed with that, nodding vigorously.

"Do the Americans know very much about that situation?" he ventured. I laughed, replying that in the absence of an embassy in Tirana, we found the Albanians no source at all of information about their great Asian protector. He merely smiled at my allusion to one of the strangest alliances of the day.

For dessert my wife ordered strawberries for herself and Kohar, trying to explain what they were. For a moment, neither of us could think of the Armenian word, so I asked the waiter if he spoke Czech, explaining that since our guests spoke Russian, they might understand the slavic root. Aghayan became agitated, seized my arm and in a low angry voice said— "Don't tell this waiter we are Russians! Don't, Edward, please."

*Barbecued lamb on a spit

As I tried to assure him that I had not said they were Russians, the waiter suggested Aghayan write the Russian word down on a piece of paper in case they wished to order strawberries again, and spoke the word. As Aghayan hesitantly picked up the proffered pencil, Kohar snatched it impatiently away from him and wrote down the word for strawberries as he sulked. He and I then ordered one last Pilsener Urquell, "the finest beer in the world" I had said to him on previous occasions, which he repeated mimicking me, and we left the restaurant.

"Next time, you are *our* guests, of course," he said as we got back into the car, "so let's agree now on time and place."

Until President Kennedy came and went, I explained, I would have no free time but if he gave me his phone number I could let him know after the visit. Aghayan gave me a number and said they lived in *Karlshorst** and that Kohar was usually at home. Roseann asked if before we lunched next time in East Berlin we could visit the Pergamon Museum** and Aghayan responded "Of course, of course, we have been there many times," which meant to me he had never been there. As though on the same wavelength and to our utter astonishment, Kohar turned to her husband and said she also wanted to visit the museum because she had never seen it. Annoyed, Aghayan now began to openly argue with her in Russian as we drove down *Kurfürstendamm* until, unable to dominate him, her mood changed and she stared silently out the window. He asked that they be dropped off at the S-Bahn station at *Bahnhof am Zoo* and we arrived there in silence, Roseann and I somewhat uncomfortable, but then he reached into his briefcase and presented me with a bottle of Armenian cognac.

This broke the ice to a degree and even Kohar now smiled, aware we would be parting. Roseann asked if Armenian films were ever shown in East Berlin. Rising to the occasion Aghayan promised to arrange a special showing for us on our next visit.

Driving back to our house I reviewed the themes we had touched on and realized that in this, our third, time together, he had made no men-

---

*About thirty minutes from the center of East Berlin, *Karlshorst* is the district where Soviet troops are garrisoned and where Marshal Zhukov accepted the surrender of the defeated *Wehrmacht.*
**One of the world's great museums devoted to Greek, Roman and Middle Eastern antiquities and named after its most treasured exhibit, the Pergamon Altar.

tion of a trip to Armenia or tried probing into VOA, and had asked only
one question about RIAS. Perhaps, I thought, he had new instructions.
Next time might tell.

VIII

O N JULY 6 AGHAYAN PHONED ME AT HOME TO SAY HE and his family were departing on leave for the Soviet Union in six days and whether we could squeeze in a meeting before then. We set the date for July 10—"remember to bring your wife" he said strangely— and of course in front of the *Cafe Sofia,* which was apparently as convenient for him as it was for me. As it happened, my wife was not well that afternoon so I went to East Berlin alone. When I arrived ten minutes early, the Aghayans were already there and visibly upset that I was alone but accepting my explanation. Aghayan waved to his driver across the street in the parking lot and Ivan, as I learned his name to be, drove up in the same Mercedes limousine. Once inside, I became aware of why their disappointment had been so pronounced as Aghayan said that in response to Roseann's inquiry, he had arranged a private screening of several Armenian films. Until the car stopped, Kohar kept repeating the phrase—"what a shame Roseann couldn't come."

Ivan drove us to the *DEFA** offices near the center of East Berlin where we walked upstairs to a screening room on the second floor. When we had taken our seats Kohar opened a shopping bag that I had noticed her holding in the car. On an improvised table she spread an oilcloth which was soon covered with a large tray of peaches, a dish of candy from Leningrad, she pointed out, several bars of chocolate, two bottles of East German lemonade and a bottle of Armenian cognac.

Aghayan plunked himself down as Ivan also joined us, and said— "And now, Edward, my surprise for you. I've gotten three films from Armenia for you and Roseann and it really is a shame she couldn't

---

*The East German film studio which was formed in 1947 as a Soviet-German company but which became a solely German undertaking in 1953. It inherited many of the facilities and personnel of the great old UFA studios of pre-war Germany.

come. But we'll make up for that in September when we return. So now, let's sit back, eat and drink and enjoy the beauties of Armenia."

The lights dimmed as drinks were downed and the first of three films began—a cultural short about an Armenian painter named Arpenik Nalbandian. The second was much longer, lasting a full hour, and entitled "Poem of Armenia," commemorating the 40th anniversary of the founding of the Soviet Armenian Socialist Republic. Its purpose was obviously to arouse emotions of pride and joy but despite its succession of ebullient scenes—children happily attending school, adolescents happily collecting fruit on collective farms, artists happily painting, scientists happily working in their laboratories—I felt a severe depression setting in. The only interesting moment came unexpectedly when in a long shot of Yerevan, Aghayan pointed at the screen exclaiming loudly—"Look, when they made this picture, Stalin's statue was still standing on that hill overlooking the capital."

Finally, and mercifully, it ended and as another round of drinks lowered the level of the cognac, the third film flashed on the screen. This was a feature-length picture made only two years before entitled "Born to Live," about an Armenian-American who returns to the homeland in search of his brother and two nephews. The story was told in flashbacks from which it eventually emerged that the brother was a partisan who together with his wife was brutally killed by the Nazis. The two nephews, however, had disappeared and the protagonist pledges to continue searching for them as the film ends. Although less propagandistic than most Soviet films in this genre and quite well acted, it was very slow and all in all a mediocre film. Nevertheless, I thanked Aghayan for his effort in trying to please us and said I was sure my wife would have been pleased.

Aghayan, Ivan and I had by now just about killed the bottle of cognac and although there was very little left, Aghayan called up to the projection room loudly and incoherently, waving the German operator down. Within minutes, as ordered, he joined us, looking glumly from one to the other. Aghayan offered him a small cognac with the word—"Schnapps." The German took it, looked coldly at Aghayan and downed the drink.

"Ask him how he liked the film," Aghayan said to me in a low voice even though no one else could understand him. I stared at him wondering whether his objective was to needle the German for amusement.

How else could the German feel about the film other than shame: every German in the film was portrayed as a sadistic SS murderer who enjoyed gunning down Soviet Armenian men and women with machine guns at close range. "Ask him, ask him" Aghayan prodded me.

I turned to the German and said—"My host here who invited me to look at these films has asked me to ask you how you liked them, especially the third one." I wanted no part of this and hoped he understood that. He did, and replied—"Tell him I understand that he was showing a film about us. Tell him . . . ." and did not finish what it was he wished to convey, though his voice and eyes spoke for him. He left us walking rapidly.

"Obviously he didn't like it," I said, and Aghayan laughed bitterly— "Germans! We lost 20 million in the war. Can we ever forget?" He seemed strangely elated at having rubbed one German's nose in the dirt.

Almost four hours had gone by and I said it was time to rejoin my wife but they both protested so vehemently that I was compelled to agree to dine with them. Ivan drove us to the *Warsaw Restaurant* on *Karl Marx Allee* and then went home to eat.

There was only one empty table with three vacant chairs; the fourth chair was just being occupied by a German. As is the custom in Germany, I asked if we could sit at the table with him and he nodded. I murmured to Aghayan that when this poor fellow heard our strange language he would be utterly confused, thinking to myself that Aghayan's antics would not only confuse but irritate him the more. Aghayan laughed and said since it was a German, the more confusion the better. I looked at Kohar and asked why he was in such an anti-German mood, to which she shook her head and rolled her eyes.

Since our last meeting, the main event in Berlin had been President Kennedy's one-day visit and I was not at all surprised when Aghayan concentrated on that and related matters. "We are rather disappointed," he began, "that what your president said at American University and what he said in Berlin are contradictory. We liked what he said in Washington, but in Berlin he was back in the cold war again."*

---

*On June 10, 1963, in a commencement address at American University, Kennedy made an impassioned plea for peace, citing the horrors of war, acknowledging sympathetically the huge Soviet losses in World War II and expressing the need for greater contact and communication between the U.S. and USSR. One of his proposals was the hot line between Washington and Moscow.

I explained that the American University speech was a serious attempt to surmount the obstacles created by the cold war, while the now famous *"Ich bin ein Berliner"* speech had a totally different purpose.

"You were there, weren't you?" he asked.

"Of course I was. RIAS is only a short walk from the *Rathaus Schoeneberg*. You know, Rafael, those people have put up with an awful lot from you. You've blockaded them, cut off their food supply, cut off their electricity, you've shot their relatives and you've built a Wall separating them. Could you expect the President of the United States to talk to these people, these Berliners, about peaceful co-existence with the Soviet Union? Come on now, be realistic."

Both of them were silent. I suggested that if they wanted to hear a more dispassionate and objective view of where matters stood between the U.S. and USSR, they should study the speech President Kennedy made the same day at West Berlin's Free University.*

Aghayan's frown changed to wide-eyed delight—"But that is the speech we have been studying at the embassy! So *that* is really the correct policy."

Kohar said very little, every now and then looking with amusement at the German at our table who, as predicted, seemed utterly confused by his table companions. She did react once, however. When I criticized Ulbricht at one point, Aghayan defended him saying the Soviet Government fully approved of the East German leader, and Kohar burst into laughter and got a visual rebuke.

Another event which had taken place in the interim between our meetings had been a visit by Khrushchev to East Berlin as a counterweight to Kennedy's.** Complaining that he had caught a cold and missed several receptions, Aghayan asked what I had thought of Krushchev's interpreter. By my look I indicated awareness of the point of his query, but said only that at times he seemed better than Khrushchev. "He is an East German who has lived for many years in the Soviet Union."

---

*While calling for the cooperation of the great powers, Kennedy gave a hard-hitting, realistic appraisal of the situation in the Soviet Union, East Europe, East Germany and East Berlin, referring to all of them as police states which were oppressing their populations.

**Khrushchev arrived in East Berlin two days after Kennedy departed and stayed for six, ostensibly to celebrate Ulbricht's birthday but, in fact, to offset the American President's visit, as attested by his much publicized speeches and travel inside East Germany, which exceeded the occasion.

"What you really want to say is that you know who President Kennedy's interpreter was, don't you?"

Aghayan laughed—"He is your chief, isn't he?"*

Kohar broke in—"What chief? What are you talking about?" Just as I was about to inform her, Aghayan said sharply—"Chief of *that place,*" looking cautiously at the German who now appeared totally unsettled by the company forced upon him and the provocative names that were being dropped. He left within minutes and after he did Aghayan snickered—"I hope we gave him a hard time." (I was to become increasingly aware that when others were within earshot, Aghayan always referred to RIAS as "that place" or "the place where you work," avoiding the widely-known acronym.)

"I have a favor to ask of you," I said, words which were as music to his ears. In fact, the favor concerned music. He gesticulated as though to say—anything at all. I continued—"My chief and I know from the East German press that David Oistrakh, your great violinist, will perform in East Berlin. We cannot possibly get tickets. Can you?"

His reaction was so violent that I was taken aback. He leaped to his feet and cried out—"You've told your chief you know me?"

"You must be joking, Rafael. I certainly wouldn't be coming over here this often without telling him. Anyway, he has no objections. None of my chiefs do. Well, can you get those tickets?"

He didn't pick up on my reference to other chiefs and sat frowning, his face a picture of confusion. Then, as though resigned to this new turn of events, he said he would do what he could and be in touch after returning from his leave. I said there was plenty of time since the concert was still three months away.

It was now 9 PM and we left the *Cafe Warsaw,* Ivan driving us to *Friedrichstrasse* where I got out. Standing by the car, Aghayan asked if there was anything he could bring back from Armenia (although he had said he was going only to Moscow and Baku). I asked if he knew the name of the Armenian poet Yeghishe Charentz and when I saw the smile disappear from his face it was obvious he did.

"Bring me back a book about Charentz," I said, "and I wish you and Kohar a happy reunion with your little girl in Baku."

*Robert H. Lochner, Director of RIAS, was selected personally by Kennedy to interpret for him during the visit. Lochner was totally bilingual, having been brought up in Berlin in the 1930s when his father, Louis Lochner, was bureau chief for the Associated Press.

His expression mellowed and when I bent down to take leave of Kohar, her eyes spoke their appreciation as well.

I pondered the day's unusual events all the way home and once there related what had happened in detail to Roseann, especially about the three films and the incident with the East German film operator. I also told her that we would not be hearing from the Aghayans for the next few months because they would be in the Soviet Union on vacation.

With her customary prescience, Roseann guessed—"And no doubt he offered to bring back something for you."

"He did and I asked him for a book about Charentz. I think the request had its effect on him."

"You've mentioned that name before. Why would Rafael be upset?"

"Charentz is not someone Soviet officials and especially the secret police would readily discuss."

"Why is he so special? Tell me about him."

I had been fascinated by this poet and his fate for some time and could supply the major details of his rise and fall. When the Red Army invaded the two-year-old Independent Republic of Armenia in 1920 and established Soviet power, some intellectuals were immediately attracted to the new ideology. Foremost among them was the 23-year-old Yeghishe Charentz, already a writer of promise who in the next fifteen years would emerge as the most gifted, the most brilliant poet not only of his generation in Armenia but of the entire crop of survivors of the Turkish massacres as well.

Charentz published essays, novels and poetry and was hailed and celebrated even in Moscow for his championing of the new order. But as the years went on, as Lenin passed from the scene and the mantle of leadership was seized by Stalin, the period of terror began to take its intellectual toll. Charentz was already beginning to have second thoughts about the grandiose and seemingly humanitarian ideology he had so early espoused and with such enthusiasm. By the early 1930s a new theme began to creep into his work, the theme of nationalism.

Charentz was warned officially, both in the press and verbally, to relinquish such dangerous trends else he be charged with being a class enemy—the most egregious of communist heresies.

Word of the by-now famous poet's difficulties reached Stalin's ears and in a famous exchange in January 1938 with the head of an Armenian delegation attending a Moscow Writers Conference which *Pravda* and

Izvestiya both reported, Stalin asked about Charentz's well-being, adding—"I believe they are giving him a hard time."

Overlooking the cynicism inherent in this comment—for the 'they' of reference could only have been his own NKVD, the KGB's earlier name, the fact that the Soviet leader had taken note of the Armenian poet's plight came as a bombshell. This brief inquiry, published in the two major Soviet newspapers, was enough to elevate the harassed poet, at least temporarily, to an unexpected honor.

It was announced in Moscow that in observance later that year of the 100th anniversary of Alexander Pushkin's death, in Russia the chairman of the commemorating committee would be Maxim Gorki, and in Armenia Yeghishe Charentz. Posters appeared in Yerevan with pictures of Pushkin and Charentz. But that was the last anyone knew of his involvement, for he was not heard from thereafter.

Roseann had been following my narration closely—"And that's the end of the story? There's got to be more. I still don't see why he is so very special. Many Soviet writers suffered the same fate."

"The best part comes now," I assured her and continued. Charentz's growing disillusionment with communism could not be stemmed by charges of nationalism and the threat of being labelled a class enemy. He was too shattered by what he saw happening around him in his beloved Armenia and too principled a human being not to act, in the only way a poet can act.

In May of 1933 Charentz wrote a poem entitled "Message" *(Batkam)*. It was not long, only 47 lines, and remarkably innocuous for the poet known for his penetrating thought and linguistic bite. The poetry-loving Armenians were mystified and wondered what the 'message' could be of a poem which began—'New light dawned on earth/Who brought the sun?' Its content was obscure, its thought muddled.

Sometime in 1936, despite the prominence he enjoyed at Stalin's inquiry and the subsequent Pushkin honor, Charentz was arrested and imprisoned in Yerevan. He was never heard from again, but the word spread like wildfire throughout Yerevan that Charentz had done something astonishing.

Roseann couldn't wait for me to continue—"Obviously it's got to be in that poem. What was it?"

How it was discovered is still not clear, I continued. One theory has it that Charentz confided in a friend who betrayed him; another is that

Charentz himself, in an unguarded moment of conviviality—for he loved wine, women and song—gave it away.

However the means, three years after he wrote his "Message," the NKVD discovered that reading downwards at the second letter of each line spelled out the poem's secret message—*"Armenian people, your only salvation lies in your collective strength."*

"Perhaps you expected something more startling, more bombastic," I said, "but you have to look at this message through Soviet eyes. Charentz was saying to his people—forget the Soviet system, forget communism, your only hope for survival as a nation is in sticking together, in uniting all of your efforts inside and outside the Soviet Union, forgetting all of your private and public differences and acting as one people.

"You see, it was not directed just to his fellow Armenians inside Soviet Armenia but to his compatriots all over the world. In the eyes of Soviet officialdom, Charentz had now committed the ultimate sin: he had rejected the system and ideology which he had embraced and which had embraced him."

Roseann nodded in understanding—"That's one damned good story. But for God's sake, how could you ask Rafael to bring you a book about Charentz. He must be absolute anathema over there?"

"He was, of course, for almost twenty-years, but not any more. Stalin had to die in 1953 for the final chapter to be written. Even before Khrushchev in 1956 delivered his historic speech denouncing Stalin and his crimes, the Armenians apparently got word earlier and rehabilitated their favorite poet. In 1956 they published a large volume of his *Selected Works* about which I read in a Soviet Armenian newspaper a few years ago."

"Surely, it would not contain 'Message,' would it?"

"Absolutely not, but it will be interesting to see what Rafael does bring me."

IX

THREE MONTHS WENT BY BEFORE I WAS AGAIN TO hear from Rafael Aghayan. He was in the Soviet Union and any new instructions would be reflected in the direction of his questions, added to the vagaries of his own curiosity, in which I had not thus far found much depth.

For my part, I had just come to the end of a difficult but highly rewarding series of visits by famous American composers which had taken almost two years to arrange. I had invited Aaron Copland, Virgil Thomson, Henry Cowell, Elliott Carter and Gunther Schuller to West Berlin to conduct the excellent RIAS Symphony Orchestra in concerts, to record some of their most famous works and to lecture, in what proved to be the first festival of American music in Berlin. (They were later joined by Roger Sessions, French composer Darius Milhaud and British composer Michael Tippett.) While this was to be the culmination of my efforts on behalf of American culture in Berlin, it had also exhausted me.

But then had come the Berlin Film Festival, which had a nervous and jittery Joan Crawford as the official American representative, and a host of other film personalities, such as a rather haughty Satyajit Ray and a delightfully modest Alec Guinness.* There was also an endless round of dinners and receptions such as the one at which I had first met Shishkin, but centering around cultural activities. At RIAS we always received these invitations and often I gratefully split such responsibilities

---

*Everyone alighting at Tempelhof had been saying to reporters in English how happy he or she was to be in Berlin until it became a joke. Guinness slipped quietly into town avoiding the press and at the major ceremony in the huge Deutschlandhalle, I found myself backstage standing next to the actor who was waiting to be introduced. He turned to me for suggestions on what to say to the audience. I told him of the gag and suggested he say it in German. He learned it on the first try, strode out and won the audience over.

with my American colleague Walter Engel, who by virtue of his rich
Viennese background, embodied splendidly the major trends in American and European culture.

I was also writing and announcing a regular jazz program for RIAS
which required a great deal of preparation. I mention these various pre-
occupations, having omitted the more routine but equally demanding
business of running my departments at RIAS, merely to emphasize the
countless problems, themes and continuing activities which my Soviet
interlocutor could have explored, but didn't. His interests lay elsewhere.

I took my family on vacation to *Berchtesgaden* where we played tennis and golf during the day and almost every evening attended the
Salzburg Festival, just thirty minutes across the German-Austrian border. We returned to Berlin late in August, tanned, refreshed and ready
to plunge into the new cultural season beginning in September. It was
going to be a busy schedule, beginning with Pablo Casals, moving on
to Count Basie, and working up to a great climax with the opening of
the Philharmonie, the astonishing new home of the Berlin Philharmonic Orchestra, where Herbert von Karajan would conduct the Beethoven Ninth Symphony.

The last thing on my mind was my Soviet inquisitor, so that when one
evening in early October I came home and my wife greeted me with—
"Guess who's been calling you?" I didn't think of him at all.

"Rafael Aghayan has been phoning here since late afternoon even
though I've told him every time to call you at RIAS. He just refuses to.
Once he even talked to Mark . . . ." Our son had been attending an
excellent German school, the *Luisenstiftung,* and was now fluent, han-
dling Aghayan's pidgin German with ease.

Within fifteen minutes the phone rang. I picked it up to hear Aghayan's raspy voice greeting me jovially and asking when we could meet.
After some fencing we finally agreed to have lunch in West Berlin at
the *Bristol.*

I now found Aghayan more aggressive in his questioning, and far
more blunt. He bombarded me with questions about RIAS, our embassy
in Bonn, our Mission in Berlin: why had Ambassador McGhee come to
Berlin; had he visited RIAS, brought new instructions, provided new
guidance and policy; what could I tell him about McGhee's personal life.
I responded casually with bland replies, freely available in the media, to
the public matters he asked about, the rest I sloughed off. Before every
one of our meetings, I always studied the *International Herald-Tribune*

from Paris and *Der Tagesspiegel* of West Berlin with more than usual care, especially on bilateral issues which I knew interested him such as between East and West Germany, West Germany and the USSR, and most of all between the United States and the Soviet Union. Then abruptly, he asked—

"How sincere is the desire of the United States to have better relations with the Soviet Union?"

I mocked him by asking why the Soviet Government was at that very time blocking a U.S. military convoy trying to enter *Babelsberg* on the outskirts of Berlin. Aghayan at first professed ignorance of the incident, which was hardly possible, but when I questioned his own sincerity, he admitted having known all about it, and smiling slyly, jibed—"So what's wrong with our counting your troops?"

He switched to the offense now and probed even deeper—

"What happened yesterday between President Kennedy and our Foreign Minister (Gromyko)?"

I shook my head, only to hear him say, in an untypically quiet voice—

"But you see all the cables," as he watched me carefully.

I realized with a start that he had asked an especially searching question, one which, as events developed, advanced his mission and would prove to be a portent of the future. He was looking steadily at me now and nodding, as though he had me cornered. I decided to make my own move.

"Rafael, do you particularly enjoy this kind of work that you do?"

He remained silent and picked at his food. He inclined his head to indicate he had heard me, but did not appear in any hurry to reply. Then finally—

"While I was in Moscow, I asked to be relieved of these foreign service duties and to be returned to more normal foreign ministry work. Quite frankly, Edward, I am not happy in Berlin"—it was an oblique reply to my question but nevertheless frank, and he continued—"and my wife is losing touch with her field, which as you know is eye surgery. I may be transferred next year. What about you?"

I said it will have been five years in Berlin the following year and time for a transfer.

"Any chance of being assigned to Moscow?"

Just to egg him on I said Moscow was not out of the question, and he quickly responded that he knew the embassy staff there, consequently in what capacity would I be going and whom would I be replacing? That was jumping the gun, I told him, Moscow was only an idea, but that wherever I went, it would be in a press and cultural function.

"Do you know your ambassador in Moscow, Mr. Kohler?"

Of course, I replied, from 1951 when Foy Kohler had been Director of the "Voice of America."

Aghayan now mused for my benefit about East European capitals: Prague was beautiful "but you get tired of it in three months"; Sofia, Bucharest and Belgrade were "dull and boring." He made no mention of Warsaw and Budapest, presumably because he had not been to either. I prodded him slightly—

"Although Berlin is your first assignment, according to what you have told me, you seem to have travelled widely," but he spiked that by praising Moscow as "the only good place to serve as a diplomat."

On parting I reminded him that the Oistrakh concert at East Berlin's *Staatsoper* was but two days off and that he had agreed to get me four tickets. He immediately promised to have them the next day and said I should meet him at *Savigny Platz* in West Berlin at 1 PM. I was struck by his certainty and precision and couldn't help wonder what strings he was going to pull to get tickets to a concert I knew had long since been sold out.

Driving back to work I realized that with our mutual questioning, we had swum into deeper waters. For one thing, I had no doubt that he had returned from Moscow with new instructions, hence the sensitive and revealing question about access to diplomatic cables. It was clear that after examination a decision had been reached to move forward—a decision made where and by whom? Could it have been Shishkin?

In his book, Donovan had said that the several times he had met with Shishkin at the Soviet Embassy, it had been not in the Chancery but in the Consulate, in a separate wing. At our first meeting Aghayan had said he was a Consular Officer. It all fit. Although I was not to meet Shishkin again, I felt his presence, his control over his operative. And there was that curious comment about wanting to return to "more normal foreign ministry work."

The next day, a Saturday, taking Scott, my six-year-old, along for company, I drove to *Savigny Platz* and saw from afar that Aghayan was already there. When I pulled up to him, he saw that there was someone beside me and froze, until he realized it was a little boy. He opened the door and picking Scott up hugged him, and said he wanted us to spend the afternoon together. Scott replied in German that it was his smaller brother's third birthday and that we had to return home. Feigning anger, Aghayan turned to me—

"What a friend you are! Your smallest son has a birthday and you don't tell me so I can bring something. Well, next time."

He reached into his pocket and produced two tickets—

"Edward, I am truly sorry, but two are all that I could get. Everyone seems to like Oistrakh. Let me ask you something. Do you know what *Regierungsplätze* are?

I said of course I knew what government seats were, why did he ask?

He explained that he had had to go to great lengths to get the two tickets but that he wanted to get the very best seats for me.

Would this mean, perhaps, that we would be sitting with East German officials? Aghayan said that would be very possible. He departed after we agreed to next meet on October 24.

* * * * * * * *

With only two tickets for the concert and both our wives indisposed, Bob Lochner and I decided to attend the Oistrakh concert together.

On the evening of October 13, we drove through Checkpoint Charlie, unhindered in a U.S. Mission black sedan, onto *Unter den Linden* and in five minutes were at the *Staatsoper*. When the doorman saw our tickets, he first stared at them, then at us—we were so obviously not East Germans—then directed us towards the Middle Loge.

It was, of course, exactly as Aghayan had said. We were sitting in the government box situated directly in the middle of the famous old opera house, one level above the orchestra.

When we entered, all eyes in the loge turned in our direction. We recognized a number of East German officials, most notably the President of the *Volkskammer* (the East German Parliament), Johannes Dieckmann; the propaganda chief, Gerhart Eisler, who had been branded by the House UnAmerican Activities Committee as 'America's No. 1 communist' but escaped capture by stowing away on the Polish ship *Batory*;* and finally, the notorious Minister of Justice Hilde Benjamin, known to

---

*Eisler returned to the GDR as its propaganda chief and chairman of the State Committee for Radio and Television. He died in 1968.

the people of East Germany as 'Hanging Hilde' because of her severity. Their faces, and most of the others', some of which we couldn't readily identify, were familiar from East German TV and *Neues Deutschland,* the party paper.

Lochner and I thoroughly enjoyed the program of all-Russian music and especially Oistrakh's emotional performance of the Tschaikovsky Concerto.

But we also enjoyed the great irony that we, two American officials of RIAS, were sitting in the official East German loge, surrounded by senior representatives of a government which so abhorred and feared RIAS that it jammed all of its broadcasts.*

*East Germany stopped jamming RIAS in 1979, as a trade-off for reciprocal rights in international agreements for its own use of certain wavelengths.

X

A GHAYAN AND I MET AS PLANNED IN FRONT OF THE *Sofia* and Ivan drove us to the *Hotel Newa* where we lunched. I tried to have our table changed because, as I told Aghayan, the portrait of Ulbricht I had to face was making me lose my appetite, but despite his sympathy for my plight we remained in the absence of any other free tables.

I thanked him for the concert tickets, described who had been seated around us and joked that the only member of the government who seemed to be absent was the man whose portrait I faced. Aghayan was amused by this—"I told you they were government seats. How did Roseann like it?" I told him what had happened and that my companion had been the director of RIAS. He paid no heed, as though he had known it all along and which I assumed, and expressed concern at my wife's illness—"If it is something special, perhaps I can order medicine from Moscow, even special equipment. After all, my country is closer than yours."

He closed in on me now, his questions coming hard and fast, mostly about Ambassador McGhee and RIAS. Then he asked whether the East German elections which had just taken place had not proven acceptance of Ulbricht and his regime by the people. "You know, 96% of the people voted yes," he pointed out. "Wrong, Rafael," I corrected him sarcastically, "the precise figure is 99.87%, which strikes me as preposterous."

This did not sit well with him and he shifted his attack—"de Gaulle is giving you trouble, isn't he?" "Mao is giving you more trouble," I responded, "with the difference that we'll patch up our troubles while yours will become larger." "They are both alike, both want war." "Nonsense" I said, "de Gaulle doesn't want war, merely independence for France."

Since we were on a French-Chinese track, I teased him—"What do you think of the idea of France recognizing Red China?" The mention of this jolted him and he stared at me—"Does the U.S. Mission know that for a fact?"

"Of course not," I shot back, "but it is a major rumor in the western world. My God, man, don't you follow our media at all? Everyone is talking about it." Aghayan said that he read *Pravda* and *Izvestiya* every day, some West Berlin newspapers which he didn't understand well, but listened "of course" to "Radio Volga."*

He asked me about the Kennedy-Gromyko meeting of two weeks ago and I asked why he hadn't asked Gromyko himself when the Soviet Foreign Minister had visited East Berlin a few days ago. "You saw him, I am sure," I said, looking at him dubiously. Aghayan merely said that Gromyko had been to the Soviet Embassy.

On this occasion he succeeded in angering me although I don't think it was deliberate. He asked for signs that the United States was sincere in its attitudes towards the Soviet Union. I pointed to the recent sale of wheat to the USSR, as well as corn to Hungary, as evidence of good will towards countries of completely different political and social systems. "I don't think so," was his rejoinder, "because you received gold in payment. So much for American aid," he said, almost spitting out the last two words.

That got to me, I seized his arm suddenly as his eyes widened in alarm and said sharply—"You don't know what you are talking about. For the moment forget the Russians. Don't you as an Armenian know what America did for the Armenian nation in 1919, when the phrase 'starving Armenians' became popular? The American aid you sit there and ridicule came to $11,000,000 and thousands of your generation, orphans from the Turkish massacres, are alive today because of American generosity."

He was taken aback by my intensity, reached over to me and said quietly and remorsefully—"I have made you angry when I only wanted to express a political view. I am sorry, Edward. Please accept my apology." When I did, he reached down into his briefcase and took out

---

*A Russian-language station broadcasting for the 400,000 Soviet troops stationed in East Germany. It was always tuned in on Ivan's car radio. Although situated in Potsdam, a suburb of Berlin, it frequently carries Russian-language programs direct from Moscow.

several books. "Here is the one you requested about our poet Charentz. I hope it will be a surprise to you. By the way, if you need any other books," he added as though to mollify me further, "I can telephone Yerevan directly from Berlin. It costs only 4.50 marks."

Despite this brief truce he got a second rise out of me by maintaining that there were many Armenians in the West who still wished to return to their Armenian homeland, some of them working at the "Voice of America" and "Radio Liberty." He insisted that "Radio Liberty" was, like VOA, part of USIA, and said that I knew it, he knew it and the Soviet Government knew it.*

This was patent claptrap and aroused me again. At first patiently but with increasing irritation I tried to explain the difference and to clarify the relationships, concluding—"What I can never understand about you people, Rafael, is why you persist in believing obvious untruths, because the facts in this instance are so easily substantiated. What do you gain by drawing the wrong conclusions, or is it your intention to be provocational?"

He had provoked me, no question, but I also had the feeling he was searching for something. We got no further but agreed on our next meeting as Ivan drove us to *Friedrichstrasse.*

I held on tightly to the package he had presented to me, wrapped in pink paper, anxious to see the book on Charentz. As soon as I reached the West and got into my parked car, I ripped off the paper and felt a surge of pleasure. As Rafael had said, it was indeed a surprise, for he had brought back the one volume *Selected Works,* the very edition I had mentioned to Roseann.

That night, comfortably at home, we riffled through the almost 500 pages of Charentz's poetry which, as the title implied, was only part of his huge output and obviously only those poems which were not controversial or problematic. The volume consisted exclusively of Charentz's writings and was totally devoid of foreword, commentary, or even the years of his birth and death, which is reliably thought to have occurred in December 1937 when he was 40.

---

*Radio Liberty was never part of USIA and at that time was funded, as Aghayan surely knew, by the Central Intelligence Agency. In 1971, the CIA association ended with funding coming from Congress. RL broadcasts in Russian and fifteen other languages of the Soviet Union, including Armenian, from Munich.

The poems, however, do all bear dates, including some before the Soviet takeover of Armenia, while one of the very last is dated 1936, the year of his arrest, and is prophetically entitled 'Epitaph.' Although dedicated to the Armenian choral composer Komitas, who had just died in Paris where he had fled Turkish persecution, it is tempting to speculate whether while composing 'Epitaph,' Charentz did not have his own impending fate in mind.

If ever there was untranslatable poetry, it is Charentz's, whose every line has been described by Armenian critics as poetic compression of Armenian history and philosophy. Daunting as that may be, this translation of the four impassioned lines of 'Epitaph,' while admittedly inadequate, will perhaps convey something of this remarkable poet's spirit:

> "Here rests Komitas, forever earth and clay,
> The ashes of his heart, once vessel of song, now earth,
> O man, o mortal, in this world he was composer, priest,
> Immortal master—monarch—scribe of sound."

XI

O N NOVEMBER 14 WE MET ON *KURFÜRSTENDAMM* AS agreed for lunch and I took Aghayan to the *Maison de France* within walking distance and with the best French cuisine in Berlin.

When he began to pursue the business about Ambassador McGhee and new instructions for RIAS, I turned on him—

"Rafael, you are becoming a nuisance. Just think, will you—even if I knew about the Ambassador's meetings, could I relay what he talked about to a Soviet . . . official. (I had almost said something else.) Pure and simple, it's none of your business."

My reprimand had a friendly tone to it which he appreciated, but he shot right back—

"Why not? Whatever he says concerns Berlin and we are all responsible for Berlin, aren't we?"

"You are incorrigible!"

While he studied the menu, little as it meant to him, I studied him. Here we were, I thought, Armenians both in every fibre, he born in the ancestral homeland, and I, the son of a refugee fleeing oppression, born half a world away. Yet, despite this chasm separating us, I wondered how much he could know about Armenia and the Armenians—who they were and what they had endured.

If he had studied Armenian history, as he must have, it would have been projected through the prism of Karl Marx, which struck me as amusing. How could the illustrious habitue of the British Museum explain those early bloody centuries when the Armenian plateau was transformed into the camping ground and battlefield for hordes of Greeks, Persians, Arabs, Khazars, Huns, Mongols and eventually Turks; when famous and infamous military adventurers with evocative names such as Xenophon, Alexander the Great, Lucullus, Hannibal and Tamerlane filled the serene country air of Armenian villages with the sights and sounds of whirring arrows, the ringing clash of armor, the cries of the maimed and the shrill trumpeting of elephants.

Armenia before and especially after Christ was the crossroads for invaders from East and West. The turbulence and disruption of the Armenian people drew the attention of historians from the earliest times and in many languages, but no one has described this more succinctly than Edward Gibbon in his monumental work where, in looking back on 2000 years of Armenian history, he concludes: "The helpless nation has seldom been permitted to enjoy the tranquility of servitude. From the earliest period to the present hour, Armenia has been the theatre of perpetual war."*

I looked at my luncheon partner who, under his thick eyebrows, was squinting, trying to decipher the meaning behind the strange wording on the placard. In a slight fit of temper, I blurted out—"Rafael, did you ever hear of *Avarair?*"

Taken aback by my abruptness—for which I couldn't blame him—he put down the menu and asked—"What is *Avarair?* I don't know what you mean."

"You don't know what I mean? Shame on you, shame on your Soviet schooling that you don't know about one of the glories of Armenian history. Even more shame that you in Armenia don't know it and I in America do."

I then gave him a brief history lesson to which he listened with visible reluctance. In the fifth century when the Armenians had already adopted and practiced Christianity for one hundred and fifty years, the fire-worshipping Persians attempted to impose their pagan beliefs on the small nation to the north. In 451 on the plain of *Avarair* in sight of *Mt. Ararat,* 220,000 battle-ready imperial Persian troops fought an ill-equipped untrained citizen army of 66,000 Armenians. Outnumbered four-to-one, the Armenians led by Vartan Mamigonian were of course decimated, but by their valiant defense of their Christian faith, they won the respect of the Persians who eventually allowed them religious freedom and granted them home rule.

Aghayan looked at me with a bored expression—"What has that got to do with me?"

---

*Edward Gibbon, "The History of the Decline and Fall of the Roman Empire," Methuen and Co., London (1898) Vol. V, p. 158

I laughed in disbelief—"You call yourself an Armenian, you speak so proudly of your homeland, and you don't really know its history."

"That is not history. That is religious mythology."

"Is it mythology that you are the oldest Christian nation in the world? Since 301, Rafael. No other nation can match that."

He replied phlegmatically—"So they say."

This irritated me further—"Rafael, I suppose it means nothing to you that art historians consider Armenian church architecture unique."

"Edward, Edward, all that happened 1,500 years ago. Today is what matters, not the past. Ah, here's the waiter, so let's now enjoy ourselves."

As usual, I did the ordering, he agreeing to eat anything I suggested. It was clear he had disliked the conversation so far; it was probing depths in him which did not exist. In fact, Rafael's lacunae were becoming increasingly evident, and realizing the impasse we were reaching, I switched to the present.

I asked why the American scholar Professor Fred Barghoorn of Yale had been arrested while in Soviet Georgia, adding—"If he isn't released, those U.S.-USSR relations you're always worrying about won't be worth very much."

"Come, come, Edward, you know this man is no ordinary professor. Innocent people are never arrested in the Soviet Union."

My laughter embarrassed him for he added quickly—"not any more, anyway."

"I'm glad you said that because after what Krushchev said about Stalin and his era, you wouldn't want to make a liar out of your party chairman."*

He asked again about my next assignment, hoped it would be Moscow and if it was, he would introduce me to Anastas Mikoyan. On the other hand, he said, if Mikoyan were to come to East Berlin, a meeting with him was assured. I welcomed the idea. He then raised the possibility of a trip with our wives to Potsdam to visit the famous palace of *Sans Souci,* built by Frederick the Great, proposing that we fix a date later.

He expressed annoyance with Berlin as he had on earlier occasions saying it was not an interesting life he led there and that he wished to leave the Soviet Foreign Service. He intended to request a transfer to Moscow next year where his wife would also be happier.

*Barghoorn was later released when President Kennedy intervened with Krushchev.

"And where she could be with your other daughter?"

He looked at me soberly for a moment and then said in a hollow voice—"Yes, the girl in Baku."

The lunch was brief and we both made claims to being busy. He asked me to bring an empty spool of tape next time so that he could have friends in Armenia dub native music on it. A strange request but I agreed to it. In turn I asked if he liked Scotch whiskey; yes indeed, he did. We agreed on November 26 for our next lunch in East Berlin, shook hands and went our separate ways on busy *Kurfürstendamm,* both oblivious of the shattering event which would intervene before our next meeting.

XII

IN MID-NOVEMBER WE HAD TWO PENDING ENGAGEMENTS for later that month: the first was an invitation from West Berlin's leading composer Boris Blacher for November 23 when some of his students from the *Hochschule für Musik* would gather at his home for an informal discussion of contemporary American music; the second was my appointment with Aghayan in East Berlin on November 26.

On the evening of November 22 my wife and I were having a dinner party with some diplomatic friends of Hungarian origin to celebrate my just-announced assignment next year to Budapest. Everyone was in high spirits at my expense as I trembled in mock terror at the impenetrability of the Magyar language which I was to study in Washington. Around 8 PM the phone rang and I was informed that President Kennedy had been shot in Dallas. I excused myself and while speeding through Berlin's suburbs to RIAS heard in direct links from Dallas on the Armed Forces network that the president had died.

We were a doleful crew that night at RIAS as we tried to bring order out of the chaos 5,000 miles away that was coming over the news tickers, seeking to separate rumor from fact for our East German audiences. When finally I returned home at 3 AM, my wife was waiting up for me, her face a mask of grief.

The next morning, remembering our engagement for that evening, I phoned Blacher and said he would surely understand if I regretted his invitation. He did and expressed deepest sympathies.

But that evening, our home silent with even the children not communicating, Blacher phoned back, apologized profusely, and said he hoped I would understand the spirit in which he wished to make a special request: if my wife were not up to it, could not I go because his students who were already gathered there wished to spend the evening with an American. Blacher said—"They know you are in mourning and want to share their mourning with you."

I realized they were asking me to represent more than myself, and although the U.S. Mission had ordered that all social functions be cancelled, I considered this to be more ceremonial than social. So I went.

Blacher and his wife, the talented pianist Gerty Herzog, were immensely grateful, as were the fifteen young Berliners, their emotions teetering on the brink. It was an unforgettable evening, its original purpose lost, and the whispered conversations not of music but of their love for the first world leader with whom they related, the memory of his visit to their beleaguered city where he proclaimed himself one of them still fresh in their hearts and minds.

As each in turn talked with me in hushed tones, I felt a profound solace in their affirmation that the loss of our president went far beyond being an American tragedy. If Germans felt as these students did, so would Greeks, Nigerians, Chileans . . . even Russians and Armenians. That night I decided to keep my appointment with Aghayan three days later.

He and I arrived at the *Sofia* at the same time. He walked up to me, seized my hand firmly and expressed condolences, labelling it as a barbaric act which had taken the life of the president. Once in the car, I told him I had almost not come, and he said he was glad I had although he would have understood. Ivan drove us to the *Bucharest* Restaurant near *Alexanderplatz* as Aghayan promised to chase away my depression.

The first half hour in the crowded restaurant turned into a silent demonstration as East Germans, recognizing me as an American, shook their heads, smiled sadly, closed their eyes nodding knowingly, clasped their hands and did the many things people do to convey sympathy and sadness. On leaving, some walked past our table pointedly brushing against the only American to whom they could communicate their true feeling. It was the most poignant of experiences and was having an obvious effect on me, as Aghayan noticed with increasing annoyance.

It became a greater source of irritation when the waitress, ignoring him, addressed me as "Sir" and displayed a degree of solicitude uncommon to her occupation in East Europe. Contrasted to the studied indifference, bordering on scorn, more normally practiced in restaurants in that part of the world, this East German waitress kept returning to our table and addressing only me, asking if the soup was warm enough, if I wanted more bread, advising of the better entrees. Aghayan, fed up with this attention from which he was being excluded, suddenly bellowed at her—"Bring me some vodka, some Soviet vodka," so loudly that she was stunned while everyone at surrounding tables turned to glare at the source of the angry outburst.

Now in a bellicose mood Aghayan shocked me with his initial comments after downing the vodka—"Is it not generally suspected that Vice President Johnson is behind the assassination?" I debated hard with myself whether I should get up and leave, which he must have sensed for he reached over touching my arm and said he did not want to offend me but merely to discuss the realities. "You should also be interested to hear what is being said on our side."

Incredulous, I asked—"You mean to say that your people actually think that? If so, then I can only assume it is because such things do happen in the Soviet Union, but believe me, not in the United States." He didn't like that but seemed to appreciate that I had a right to snap at him, and smiling raised both palms towards me.

"Can we talk about it at all?" he asked timidly and when I nodded, continued—"How can any reasonable man really suspect from what strikes me as lack of evidence that Oswald was the assassin? You don't know this but I studied law, and I go by hard evidence. Until now, I do not know of any." I asked where he got his information, from the Soviet media? "No, actually I have studied the Soviet Embassy's summary of the western press. You know, it is a very shady business involving power groups. How could the president have been so inadequately protected? How could Oswald have been approached at such close quarters by Ruby and shot in a room full of policemen?"

Indeed, these were questions every American was asking, I said to myself, at which point I heard Aghayan say—"Such things do not happen in the Soviet Union." Anticipating my reaction he quickly went on— "No, please listen to what I am saying. There are many diabolical ways to kill a famous man, without killing him directly. For instance, when his enemies wanted to kill Maxim Gorki,* at the time a very sick man, they

---

*The pen name of the great Russian writer who was at first sympathetic to the aims of the Bolshevik Revolution but soon realized its true direction. He died in 1936 at the age of 68 when the terror reached its peak.

didn't attack him, they killed his son who was so dear to Gorki. Soon thereafter, he died unable to survive the tragedy."

This was truly so diabolical that I indicated not wanting to hear it further. Aghayan asked if there had been any ballistical evidence; I said it was probably too soon but that I didn't know. He seemed preoccupied with Oswald, kept repeating his name as he drank one vodka after the other. Enough had already been reported on Oswald that it was general knowledge he had defected to the Soviet Union and then returned. Could that be the reason for Aghayan's seeming obsession? I reminded him that the State Department had issued a statement to the effect that no foreign power was thought to be behind Oswald. Aghayan said he had heard that.

I asked if he had read the Red Chinese reaction to the news of the assassination: a series of vicious attacks on the late president, and one report by the official news agency that Chinese schoolchildren had applauded the news.

"The Chinese are savages," he cried out, "we can't trust them, believe me."

"But *we* have never trusted them, *you* have," I responded, "they were always your comrades. First you had to be awakened to Stalin's crimes, and then to Mao's. Why has it taken you so long?"

"I want to return to Moscow," he said demanding more vodka of the waitress, "and it can't be soon enough. We are miserable here." His eyes were becoming bleary. I remained silent for a moment, watching him, and looking from time to time at the Germans at nearby tables who stole surreptitious glances at my demonstrative Soviet companion. As though reading their minds, I said quietly—"It must be difficult to serve in a country where you are so unpopular."

Caught off guard momentarily, Aghayan replied—"Yes it is, yes it is." Realizing his admission, he looked at me, his eyes bloodshot, and went on—"It is not so much that we are unpopular here. It is just that these people, these Germans, can't be trusted. You should understand that. It is a mistake of both our countries to want German reunification. Anyway, we want to go home where my wife can resume her eye surgery and the children will be back in their homeland. Besides, I've dreamed of my mother lately, more often than ever before. It is a sign that she wants me back."

Now he wanted to know when I was being transferred and whether it would be to Moscow. It was too soon to know, I told him. "In Moscow,

I'll make your life very interesting. I can find work for your wife, especially with her English and Armenian. She could work at Intourist or at
some Institute."

As he switched to RIAS and whether there were new instructions
from Bonn and the American Ambassador, I cut him off and said nothing had changed in East-West relations to warrant new policies. "Oh but
there has, Edward. Didn't you see that Ulbricht sent a message of con-
dolence to the United States on the death of President Kennedy?"

"Rafael, sometimes your sense of humor escapes me. I've got to go."

He agreed on December 6 for a visit to Potsdam with our wives, that
we should meet at the *Sofia* and then drive in his limousine. I said if
anything came up I would phone him.

As we left the restaurant, the German waitress whispered to me that I
was always welcome at the *Bucharest.* Aghayan glowered.

XIII

I T WAS ANOTHER TWO MONTHS, ACTUALLY ON JANUARY 27 in the new year, when we again resumed contact. Aghayan phoned me at home on that day and asked why I hadn't been in touch with him. We agreed to meet on January 30 at the *Sofia* in the East. I arrived bringing a bottle of Scotch as I had promised which pleased him very much, and Ivan drove us in the Mercedes to the newly-opened *Cafe Moskva* on *Karl Marx Allee*.

Aghayan asked why my wife and I had not shown up on December 6 for the trip to Potsdam. I apologized explaining that Ambassador McGhee had come at that time and as Aghayan probably knew also met with the Soviet Ambassador, thereby keeping us all busy. As he also knew, I said, there were no telephone lines to East Berlin.

"We waited for you for two hours," he said, his voice free of any acrimony, "and Kohar even prepared a basket lunch because we are all sick of German food." I tried to imagine those two hours, the impatient looks Kohar must have rained on him, her growing irritation as she realized that her efforts and time were not to be rewarded, the tension between them as they drove back home, perhaps even a final quarrel about the nature of his work.

Though Aghayan did not raise the subject again he went on to rail against the Germans: their arrogance, their habits, their difficult language, their love of militarism. "Ours are as bad as yours and neither should be re-armed," he argued, his face flushed, "because they can't be trusted." I wondered what kind of day it had been for him to be meeting me with such anti-German feeling so near the surface. He finally desisted and asked what I had done since our last meeting. He became interested in the details of a ten-day trip I had made in early January to Yugoslavia.

The Directors of the Zagreb Music Festival had invited me as a RIAS official in the belief that I was a German and when they discovered from my passport that I was an American diplomat, they treated me royally. Aghayan asked if any representatives of the Soviet Union were there. I said there were several from the recording industry, one or two soloists, but most notably the great Soviet composer Dmitri Shostakovitch. This seemed to get no rise out of him at all.* It is difficult to believe that Aghayan had never heard of the composer, but even if he had, the subject did not appear to be worth exploring.

We discussed Christmas passes granted by East Germany for West Berliners to visit relatives over the holidays which Aghayan thought a major turning point in German relations. I snorted at that, pointing out that as long as the Wall stood, progress would be at a standstill.

He noted that France had indeed recognized Red China since our last meeting and acknowledged that I had alerted him to the possibility. I in turn noted that the Soviet Union had purchased wheat from the United States "no matter what you or your government thinks of American aid."

Aghayan laughed somewhat sheepishly. "By the way I have just seen a wonderful American film that I enjoyed very much entitled 'To Be Or Not To Be' (he spoke the words in English), do you know it?" I said of course, that it starred Jack Benny and Carole Lombard. "I don't know those names but it was superb." I showed surprise that it had been shown in East Germany since I normally scanned the East German press for such items and had not seen the film mentioned. "Oh it was not in a German theatre," he explained, "it was a special performance, synchronized in Russian, for our Soviet personnel in *Karlshorst.*"

He asked for a favor: a friend of his in Moscow owned a Russian translation of a book entitled "One Thousand Questions About America and One Thousand Answers"; could I get him a copy too? I promised to try. (I ordered it from USIA but it never came and eventually he forgot about it.)

"Speaking of questions about America, Rafael, how about a few on Armenia? You never seem interested in telling me anything about Armenia, even though you always want me to go there."

---

*Shostakovitch presented a pathetic sight, his hands trembling constantly to the degree that by the time a spoonful of soup reached his lips it was almost empty. Although sitting mostly in silence, he made one lapidary comment when told he did not look well: "It is difficult to appear healthy when one's children have been killed one after the other"—a reference to the suppression of symphonies and operas in the Stalinist era.

"Seeing it with your own eyes, especially if I'm with you, is better than talking about it."

"Yes, but I am a long way from going there. What can you tell me about Mardiros Saryan's latest paintings?"

Rafael fidgeted and looked uncomfortable—"I don't know about such things."

"How about Sylva Gaboudigian? Surely you have heard of her. Armenians love poetry and she is the best-loved poetess in your native country."

"Maybe you can ask her yourself!" he shot back.

"How often does Aram Khatchaturian go to Yerevan?"

"All right, enough with your questions, Edward. Why should I know such things?"

"Because you are always extolling the virtues of the homeland and I am interested in your cultural life."

"But you are a political person, you were at the 'Voice of America,' now RIAS. Why don't you ask me political questions?" His tone seemed defensive.

"Fine, let's talk politics. How do the Armenians feel about the Russians?"

"They are like brothers. The Armenians love the Russians."

"And does that mean they love the Russian leaders too?"

He did not reply, but his narrowed eyes were response enough.

"Tell me about Stalin, Rafael. Do the Armenians feel a nostalgia for Stalin's times? And for Beria's?"

"Edward, you are trying to provoke me. Listen, in the Soviet Union, there is a strong fraternal bond among all peoples, including the Russians and the Georgians. Let's change the subject. By the way, next time remember to bring that tape so I can have it dubbed with Armenian music. Now, tell me when we can meet again."

His abruptness annoyed me. I was irritated at his dismissal of the matters I had raised, cultural and political, and wished to retaliate with stubbornness. I said maybe we could meet in a month but it would have to be in West Berlin. We agreed on February 13 and Ivan drove me to *Friedrichstrasse* and the *U-Bahn*.

In the subway my thoughts were jumbled more than usual, and once again I ruminated over this—for me—novel and bizarre relationship. Those in the U.S. Mission who followed it, however, were fascinated with my experience and one senior colleague again said he envied me the contact.

Of course, I could have stopped at any time, but my reasons, my own personal reasons, for not breaking it off were not sinister: I was getting around East Berlin—the target of our RIAS broadcasts—and absorbing its atmosphere, courtesy of my Soviet host; I enjoyed speaking the rare language I had learned as a child; I did not find Aghayan's company unpleasant, and, it was intriguing to expose the areas of his limitations.

But beyond these personal reasons, there was one other factor which guided my continuing—and future—decisions to meet with Aghayan or anyone else from the KGB, and it became the most overriding factor of all: it was impressed upon me that what I was doing was in the best national interest. As I have indicated, this relationship was far from being merely a social arrangement between two chatting representatives of East and West, and the fact is that little transpired throughout its fifteen-year duration which was not immediately made known to interested elements on our side. Among the many aspects of the relationship pointed out to me, some were recondite, but one which I understood very well was that we were gleaning more from him than he from me because his questions bared the focus of current Soviet interests while my replies were largely public information.

Meanwhile, evidently my value had increased for in underlining his government's interest in Red China's improving relations with the West, he had seemed impressed with my 'prediction' of France's recognition of the Chinese. This had seemed to establish my credibility as a contact for him in the United States Mission and palpable confirmation that I did indeed have access to diplomatic cables.

It must have stood him in good stead with his superiors, either in the Soviet Embassy on *Unter den Linden* or at KGB Headquarters on *Dzerzhinsky Square.* Or both. I got out of the *U-Bahn* in West Berlin and then into my parked car.

Driving back to RIAS, I was overcome with the realization that something must be developing, something about which I should be cautious, national interest or not. Aghayan had been dispatched to Berlin at Shishkin's command on my account, I had no illusions about that, and as long as I remained, so would he. But what was his game, what was the KGB's game, and how would it all come to light?

XIV

W E MET AT *SAVIGNY PLATZ* ON FEBRUARY 13 and I suggested *Pero's* on *Kantstrasse* for lunch. Aghayan was bursting with questions about RIAS: pending changes in long-wave frequencies, in short-wave, staff dismissals, the future of its programs, and as always about Ambassador McGhee—had he made another visit, had he brought new instructions?

I looked so reproachfully at him that he switched to the current topic of concern, passes for West Berliners to visit East Berlin or *Passierscheine:* what was the official U.S. view? how far were we prepared to go? what were our conditions? I made the general comment that so long as East Berliners were not allowed access to West Berlin, there was little hope for progress. (This was a safe response inasmuch as the important *Passierscheine* issue was still under negotiation—a process of which I had no part. Besides, I had given him the same response at our last meeting.) Aghayan accepted this but said my reply was in fact more a criticism of the Wall than a reply to his question, and went into a long and tedious defense of that concrete obscenity. He finished slightly breathless and looked at me meaningfully.

"You may wonder why I ask you so many questions about the American position on Berlin and on Germany in general." I responded with an indifferent shrug of my shoulders. His answer to his own question had little impact on me then but I could not know that it was preparatory in purpose: "I am something of an expert on these subjects and write articles for a journal which is distributed internally by our Ministry for Foreign Affairs. I write the articles in Russian and they are later translated into Armenian for the Armenian Ministry for Foreign Affairs.* I

---

*One of the facades created by the Soviet Government to support its claim of independence for each of the fifteen republics. Later in Armenia I had an excellent opportunity to puncture that balloon.

am always grateful for the information you give me and for any further
information you can get for me."

He then put to me two matters which he said were "more official,"
and on which the Soviet Embassy needed information. (This was a curious differentiation to make and suggested that the Embassy at some
level was aware of Aghayan's mission and had decided to let him
explore the channel for its own purposes, which were quite different
from his.)

"Our Embassy is confused about a procedure over here in West
Berlin. As you know we control the Russian Church on *Hohenzollern-
damm,* and we also have a rest home in *Tegel.* By the way, something
you might know, our composer Mikhail Glinka is buried there. To go on,
our people often come over and spend the night there. Until recently the
Allied Travel Office was the competent authority in these matters, but
lately the West Berlin police intervened to say only they could issue a
residence permit. Now, our Embassy doesn't know how to handle this,
and I would appreciate your looking into it."

Matters such as these were, of course, totally outside my area of
competence and I told him so, but I did pass them on to the responsible
officers in the Mission.

He asked if I had brought the tape for dubbing. I said, truthfully, that
I had been engaged elsewhere in the city, in fact in a long conference
with William Steinberg, conductor of the Pittsburgh Symphony Orchestra, who had come in advance of the Orchestra to discuss his program in
Berlin. Aghayan said it was just as well I had not brought the tape
because it would probably have been a blank. I looked questioningly at
him. He smiled—"I have a personal favor to ask for my friends in Armenia. They would be very happy if you could put some American popular
songs on the tape which they could then copy before dubbing Armenian
music on it." I was amused by his request and agreed.

He asked if I knew any of the Armenians in West Berlin and whether
any were interested in visiting "the homeland." I said a few were known
to me but that from my brief conversations with them had determined
that none of them ever wished to see the homeland so long as it was in
its present status. He listened soberly then addressing me with determined sincerity said—"You know, Edward, I have special authority to fly
Armenians free of charge to Armenia. I think every Armenian who has
never been there should have a chance to see the homeland." When he

saw that I did not react, he dropped the subject as though even if not wishing to pursue it, he wanted to plant the seed in my mind.

Then abruptly—"My wife and I want to invite you to our home for dinner on February 23. That means the children, too, of course. I shall make *shashlik* in the backyard. Will you come?" I accepted his invitation and asked if we could bring anything. "Yes, yes, if you would, please bring some eggplant. On our side, we have no eggplant and as you know without it *shashlik* is not the same. In fact, bring several."

We agreed that on February 22 he would phone me at home since that is where I would be because of the holiday. He would phone in the morning early because Kohar had to get to the stores before they closed at 2 PM; we might even include Potsdam on that day, and if not, while the women prepared the food, we and the children could go ice-fishing. We left it at that.

XV

I N 1964 GEORGE WASHINGTON'S BIRTHDAY FELL ON A
Saturday. Instead of taking the family on an outing, I stayed home
waiting to receive Aghayan's phone call confirming the invitation for the
next day. I waited until mid-afternoon; then because there were no civilian phone links with East Berlin, I made a laborious effort through the
British military switchboard, which was reserved only for emergencies,
and finally reached the Soviet Embassy.

Someone picked up the phone at the other end, speaking German
with a thick Russian accent. I tried to explain who I was and why I was
calling. I asked that he phone Aghayan at home and gave him the number Aghayan had given me. The man said he knew no one by that name
in the Soviet Embassy, but when I insisted there was indeed someone,
he said he would try and for me to hold on. A few minutes later he
returned, now curiously and suddenly enthusiastic, to say that the plans
already agreed upon were to be followed and that Aghayan would pick
us up in his limousine on Sunday at 3 PM in front of the *Sofia*. He also
apologized "for not knowing the comrade."

The next day was bitterly cold—the Berliners say *nass-kalt* (damp-
cold)—and traffic was light as Roseann and our oldest son Mark, then
11, and I drove to the *U-Bahn* at *Kochstrasse* near Checkpoint Charlie
which let us out at *Friedrichstrasse* in the East.

Aghayan was already there, stamping his feet to keep warm, overjoyed to see us and making a fuss over Mark whom he at first took for
his younger brother Scott.

He said he had called me several times on Saturday. I said obviously
we had crossed signals and wondered if it had been awkward for him
that I had phoned his embassy directly. Aghayan waved it aside and
explained that the person who had answered was one of the embassy
interpreters "who doesn't know me."

Ivan pulled up, opened the doors as he greeted me, and drove us to *Karlshorst,* the residential area in East Berlin for Soviet military and civilian personnel. The streets on this Sunday were deserted and as we turned this way and that and I tried to get our bearings, Ivan stopped at 79 *Koepenickerallee* in front of a wooden gate, which Aghayan unlocked with a key. The gate led to a dirt driveway on which we walked then turned behind a house on to another small house. It was one of many houses in which, he told us, Russians and Germans lived. There was no one in sight as we approached the entry but suddenly the door opened and Kohar Aghayan greeted us with warmth and effusion, and inside introduced us to their two attractive children, Edward 12, and Ina, 14. We were ushered into a small dining room, bare of everything but the essential table and chairs, and then into a small living room whose sparseness was equally striking.

Roseann went into the kitchen and took out some of the edibles we had brought, noting the bare cupboards when she sought some serving bowls. Kohar began to set the table with no end of cold dishes whose rich variety included beans, cold cuts, salad, chicken, pickled garlic, cabbage and other delicacies.

"And this is for *us,*" Aghayan bellowed at me, his arms laden with Russian vodka, Armenian cognac, Georgian mineral water, Hungarian wine and Czech beer, elbowing me in the ribs as he held up the Pilsener Urquell. He insisted we down two vodkas right away "to battle the cold," which we did, helping ourselves from the richly-laden table whose profusion of colorful food contrasted with the museum-like starkness of the walls around us.

With western dance music playing in the background on the radio, our host and hostess excused themselves and went into the kitchen, as Mark went upstairs with young Edward. Roseann and Ina were chatting in Armenian when the music program ended and I recognized the voice of RIAS' most popular announcer signing off. My wife and I exchanged winks and were amused to hear immediately thereafter the regular Sunday afternoon direct broadcast from the "Voice of America" in Washington.

It was such a bizarre experience being on the receiving end of a live VOA report over RIAS, deep in East Berlin and in a Soviet home, that I couldn't restrain myself. I called out to Aghayan in the kitchen that it was very thoughtful of him to have RIAS tuned in for our benefit. The reaction was startling. He came charging in with what at first appeared to be a stiletto in his hand but which proved to be a skewer on which he was arranging chunks of lamb already marinated for *shashlik*. He glowered at Ina who was cowering in mild fright. His voice rising, he asked— "Why is that station on?" Ina kept silent, not repeating her remark to Roseann that she loved American popular music.

He went to the radio and with his greasy fingers tried at first unsuccessfully to twist the dial, eventually finding what he sought, as he told us—"Radio Volga." A Russian voice now droned on and the contrast to the snappy rhythms of before must have turned him off as well. He switched off the radio and said nothing could take the place of Armenian folk music. Aghayan went to a large chest, opened a drawer and took out a phonograph record with a Soviet label and several large picture books about Soviet Armenia. He left us for a moment, returning with a small portable phonograph on which he put the record, made by the Altounian Song and Dance ensemble of Soviet Armenia. He then retreated again to the kitchen where he resumed skewering the lamb as we turned the pages of the now very greasy picture books.

Some fifteen minutes later Aghayan emerged from the kitchen and asked me to join him in the yard. I helped him carry out the meat and vegetables and saw he had already prepared a good fire in a portable brazier. Once the skewers were in place on it, he re-entered the house and returned with a full bottle of cognac "from the homeland." I did not object; it was now 5 PM, freezing cold and getting dark as it does early in Berlin and the cognac only partially alleviated my discomfort. The cooking took only half an hour whereupon, with the skewers of sizzling broiled lamb raised high in the air, we made a triumphant entry into the house, Aghayan bellowing everyone to the table.

The seven of us were ravenous, the food was delicious, and we all complimented Aghayan for his culinary excellence. The talk was solely about families, school, food and the jumbled cross-conversations back and forth over the table were far above the sound levels of normal discourse.

The house itself was very much a curiosity. It did not strike us as a home. At one point I recalled something Aghayan had once mentioned casually, and asked—"Rafael, I thought you told me you lived in a villa where you only had the bottom floor, and that two Russians lived above you?"

"We've just moved into this house," he came right back at me, as though prepared for the question.

I have already noted Roseann's awareness of the bare cupboards in the kitchen. Meanwhile, eleven-year-old Mark was making observations of his own about other parts of the house. He had brought a plastic model of an American Sabre Jet as a gift to Edward and the two of them assembled it upstairs in a sitting room. I saw this room once when I went upstairs to use the bathroom. It had a table, chairs and a sofa and nothing else. Next to it was the only other room—the children's bedroom where both slept apparently in the one bed in it. Mark saw it briefly several times when Edward was not quick enough to douse the light and close the door. It was a room barren of furniture, and the small accoutrements which lend personality—pictures, books, lamps, and the knick-knacks which teenagers accumulate. Mark and Edward communicated in German in which Mark was already fluent having attended a private Berlin school for the last four years, while Edward's was minimal. On occasion, when Edward couldn't find the right word, Mark would come down to consult with us and on returning upstairs would discover that Edward had retreated to his room. It was on those occasions, when Edward would come out that Mark would have his quick peeks into that bedroom.

The bathroom which we had to use upstairs was forbidding. It was devoid of a single mirror, but did have a toilet bowl, sink and bathtub—all of them indescribably dirty. There was also one wet towel, crumpled between a water pipe and the wall. It was most assuredly not the kind of bathroom that Kohar Aghayan, Armenian mother and eye-surgeon, would have in her home.

The house was quite cold and whenever this was mentioned, Edward was asked to go down into the cellar. Once Mark went down with him uninvited and discovered that Edward was shovelling coal into a small stove with pipes leading into the wall. Mark also noticed another room which was pitch dark and when he tried to peer into it, Edward shouted excitedly that he should go away. Later, the boys played checkers and when I noted that Mark played a good game of chess, didn't Edward perhaps, Aghayan said of course he did but his chess set was "back home."

Ina was a sweet girl who spoke very little and spent most of her time staring at us but mostly at Roseann, her eyes filled with wonder. Kohar noticed our awareness of her daughter's fascination and excused it with a shy smile by noting that we were the very first Americans the children had ever seen. Both children attended the Soviet school, spoke fluent Russian and very good Armenian. Ina said she took German lessons twice a week.

There was no end to the drinking and eating as the discarded empty bottles and dishes attested after three hours at the table. Aghayan observed that our appreciation of his hospitality represented the most characteristic and best Armenian traits, "therefore, it is unthinkable that you should not have the opportunity to see Armenia." After five hours together for the first time he had raised one of his ongoing themes. I said jokingly that until now he had always proposed that I go alone, but I did want him to know that going without my wife was out of the question.

"That settles it," he shouted as his family all looked at each other, "I'll arrange everything. I need twenty days' notice. You like music, opera and theatre, leave that all to me. We'll have two days in Moscow, one in Leningrad and the rest of the time in Yerevan. Just tell your superiors you are going to Munich for ten days." I said that was out of the question because I always wanted my superiors to know where I was at all times.

"All right, that's your affair, if you insist. But remember, you've got to give me twenty days."

We were less than one month away from the opening of the annual Leipzig Fair, he pointed out, and it was customary for a leading Soviet official to attend. "This year, dear Edward, it might be none other than our compatriot, Anastas Mikoyan, and if he comes to open the Fair, I promise you will not only be my guest there but I shall introduce you to him. He is a superb fellow and a very patriotic Armenian, and I know he'll like you immensely."

It was well after 8 PM now and I said it was time for us to leave.

"Impossible!" he cried out, "and certainly not before you and I play a game of *tavlu*."* We played on the obverse side of Edward's checker-board which reduced what is normally a battle-like game of rattling dice and crashing checkers on wooden boards to a polite parlor pastime. Nevertheless it was fun and Aghayan played expertly and won.

But now it was 9 PM and when I again arose, this time with greater effort because of additional helpings of dessert, to our amazement

*Backgammon

Aghayan insisted that he return outside to the brazier and broil some more *shashlik*! He didn't seem to want the evening to end. We engaged in a mock struggle as I tried to restrain him and finally won out. We got our hats and coats from a closet, otherwise bare, and Roseann said they were all invited to our home in West Berlin.

"No, no, no, out of the question," Aghayan protested categorically, "when we meet like this with our families, it will always be here in our house."

We agreed that when the weather was more pleasant, we could all perhaps still make that trip to Potsdam and *Sans Souci*. Hearty farewells soon had us outside where Ivan was waiting and within half an hour we were back at *Friedrichstrasse*—with Aghayan who, at the last moment, had forced himself into the car arguing that he could not allow us to ride all that way alone.

But apparently there was more to his forced company than mere courtesy. He wanted to know about Easter passes for West Berliners, visits of American officials to Berlin, residence permits for Soviet citizens visiting the Russian church and the *Tegel* rest home. I wearily sloughed off all his questions advising his Embassy to inquire directly of the Allied Travel Office. As we left the car we made a quick agreement to meet on March 5 at the *Sofia*.

Frozen to the core we took the *U-Bahn* to West Berlin and got into our car and turned on the frigid heater. As we drove slowly home to *Zehlendorf*, a distance lasting about half an hour, the three of us were at first silent. Roseann was the first to voice her feelings—"What a strange experience, and in some ways sad. You know, she's not such a bad sort. I know what you think he is and I'm sure you're right, but somehow, I have the feeling she is a reluctant party to it all." I confessed to having the same feelings.

Then Mark described his impressions, especially of the cellar and the upstairs, adding—"And another thing. I noticed the telephone had no number," looking at me for approbation. I commended him on his perceptiveness and said that the telephone number Aghayan had first given me was not a *Karlshorst* exchange.

"The fact is," I said in measured tones to impress my family, they listening to me attentively as we drove through the deserted streets, "we have spent this day in a KGB safe house."

"What's a safe house, Dad?"

"A house that is totally controlled by an intelligence organization, such as the KGB or even the CIA. Which means that in all probability, everything we said today is on tape."

I saw Roseann's features tighten as Mark, sitting between us, muttered an awed "Gosh."

XVI

AGHAYAN WAS LATE FOR OUR APPOINTMENT ON March 5 in front of the *Sofia*, running up breathless with apologies—"I had to meet 300 Soviet tourists at the railroad station, guests of East German youth organizations. They have hundreds of questions I'll have to take care of later."

We walked to the empty lot where Ivan always parked but he was nowhere in sight. Aghayan offered no explanation outside of saying that today he would drive us, in his Volkswagen. I sorely missed Ivan as Aghayan drove maniacally through crowded streets, East Berliners shaking their fists at us, my mind anticipating a frightening return drive later, when suddenly he careened onto *Karl Marx Allee* and finally stopped in front of the *Budapest*. Although breathing a sigh of relief, I had misgivings when I saw where we would lunch, recalling the last experience there. I also felt a curious twinge as we walked in, wondering if this might by Aghayan's subtle way of indicating that he knew the place of my next assignment.

After we were seated Aghayan said he could not take any alcohol because of his meeting later with his 300 Soviet countrymen. I was more than happy with just plain mineral water. He began by relaying his family's pleasure at our get-together in *Karlshorst*. He said Mark had made a big hit with young Edward, who spoke of little else since Mark was the first American boy he had ever met. I apologized that Mark had brought Edward a military toy, but Aghayan laughed with obvious amusement: "Edward loves the Sabre Jet, just as he loves guns, knives and other weapons. He always wanted a knife when we were in the Soviet Union, but couldn't have one because there it is against the law, but here in the GDR it is possible."

Aghayan also spoke of his wife's pleasure at seeing her two children enjoy Mark's company and that it had given her a big lift: "You see, she is so anxious for the arrival of our other child who will be coming shortly. She will exchange places with Ina, who is finishing the 8th grade of the Soviet school and then go to join her grandmother in Baku."

Intense strife on the island of Cyprus was very much in the news and we discussed the bitterness dividing Greeks and Turks, between whom the sizeable Armenian community on the island was trapped. Aghayan said that a large number of Cypriot Armenians had been repatriated recently, sailing to the Soviet Black Sea port of Batumi on a ship called "Soviet Armenia." "They have now settled in several cities of Armenia," he said, "and when they arrived they were given the keys to brand new homes."

"What lucky people," I said so drily that he changed to German problems and the usual questions about relations between Americans and Germans, Bonn and Berlin.

He said he had just returned from Leipzig after the opening of the Fair and that Mikoyan had not come, which had been disappointing. "Of course, had he come, I would have phoned you."

I asked if my calling him through the Soviet Embassy had been embarrassing or even awkward. He replied that phoning him directly was always preferable, and gave me the reason that it would be unpleasant for me if "my people" found out. "You should either send me a telegram or come over to East Berlin and phone me at home."

When it came time to arrange the next lunch he refused my invitation, to the West: "No, I cannot. I must insist. I realize it is a matter of honor with you because then in the West you pay. But you should know that I make a great deal of money and it is no drain on me." Amused at his intransigence I gave in and agreed to March 19.

I suddenly remembered the tape I had had dubbed for him and handed it over. "American music?" he said expectantly. I nodded.

In the car I cringed as a sober but reckless Aghayan returned me to *Friedrichstrasse.*

XVII

THE IDEA OF CANCELLING OUR NEXT LUNCH descended on me several days before the date but out of the blue the East German press announced the arrival of Deputy Premier Mikoyan, and while he was late for the opening of the Leipzig Fair, he was very much in presence. Recalling Aghayan's pledge to arrange a meeting I thought it worth a try, especially as a test of his authority and influence. On March 19 I went over, was met as usual by Aghayan and Ivan, who drove us to the rooftop restaurant of the *Berliner Haus* near the *Frankfurter Tor.* I was relieved to see Ivan.

We had hardly sat down when, as though his conscience troubled him, Aghayan began to apologize profusely: "I didn't do it, I didn't arrange a meeting with Comrade Mikoyan and you. Let me explain why. First of all, Mikoyan came not to participate in any Soviet Embassy activities but as a guest of the GDR. Second, because of the absence of our Ambassador, Comrade Abrassimov, no Soviet-hosted receptions were arranged. Third, Mikoyan did not want any Soviet functions for him." He then downed two vodkas one after the other.

"How is it possible," I asked, "that a Deputy Premier of the Soviet Union visits East Berlin and the Soviet Ambassador is absent? Why wasn't Abrassimov at the arrival ceremonies at *Schoenefeld* Airport?"

Aghayan looked ominously around at the tables near us, as though everyone understood the rare language we were speaking, then bent close and revealed his secret: Abrassimov had had an attack of angina and was in the Soviet Hospital in East Berlin, adding—"And Comrade Mikoyan visited him there."

Having cleared that up, I set out to clarify another minor mystery which had puzzled our Mission: "Can you also tell me why Ulbricht wasn't at the airport to greet Mikoyan?"

Frowning, Aghayan replied curtly—"He didn't come."

"Come on, Rafael, you said Mikoyan came as a guest of the GDR. How can it be that the GDR's most important and senior party official was not at *Schoenefeld* Airport to meet this most important and senior Soviet guest?"

As though to shut me up once and for all, he spat out angrily—"I guess he had more important things to do!"* Several heads turned in our direction.

He now ate in silence, perturbed, but gradually snapped out of it, aware perhaps that communication was at a minimum because of his outburst. He thanked me for the assistance on the residence permits for Soviet citizens, said his Embassy was in direct touch with the Allied Travel Office and that even the West Berlin police were satisfied.

"Have you ever visited the Soviet rest home in *Tegel*," he asked, "I ask only to remind you that Glinka is buried there. I thought that might be of more interest to you than most Americans."

He again raised the Easter passes for West Berliners but with a twist: "What do your Chinese say to the problem?" I searched his face for meaning which provoked laughter from him—"I mean the French, I mean de Gaulle, your Mao Tse Tung." I let that go by as he tried a few other probes about West German internal politics, then suddenly raised a speech that Ambassador McGhee had made earlier in the month in which he had said that West Germany must not deal with the problems of both Germanys without paying heed to the security of the Soviet Union.

"Does that especially interest your Embassy?"

"Yes, very much," he replied immediately, then—"Actually, it interests only me. You know, those articles I write. I've already told you about them." He seemed to be watching me.

I shifted attention back to the Chinese and asked how the dispute between the two communist super-powers was going.

"The Chinese are out of their minds," came the quick reply, "But don't think it has anything to do with their love of Stalin. It is a national

---

*In his later years Ulbricht displayed increasing dissatisfaction with the subjugated role forced on him by the Soviet Union, symptoms of which were gestures such as not greeting prominent Soviet guests because, as in the case of Mikoyan—the USSR's top trade authority—he had not honored the opening of the GDR's top trade event, the Leipzig Fair.

problem—Chinese nationalism trying to dominate the international scene, that means us, you, everybody."

I suggested he was making that more of a racial than a national argument which didn't fit in with the curious alliance of Red China and Albania.

This seemed to enrage him and he now railed against the Albanians. He claimed that it was not the Albanian party chief Enver Hoxha who was the cause of the problem but Premier Mehmet Shehu who had forced the enmity with the Soviet Union. Then with what to me was comic relief he cried out—"Some gratitude! Do you know, we even equipped the Albanian Army with uniforms."

He preferred to drop that thorny matter, for now he mentioned the children. Ina would be finished shortly at the Soviet school and, as he had told me last time, returning to Baku, whence his third child, whom he now identified as Alla, age 10, would join the family in Berlin, to Kohar Aghayan's joy.

"We also had a slight misfortune," he continued, "Edward injured his leg and we had to take him to the hospital. In fact, the same hospital where Comrade Abrassimov is. Unfortunately, Comrade Mikoyan did not visit Edward," he said with an ironic little laugh.

"How much do you know about Mikoyan?" he asked me, and I said his early years as a divinity student and then a revolutionary with Stalin were known to us. "No, no, I mean the great figure he is now. For instance, let me tell you about Mikoyan the father. A good parent but a stern father. Two years ago, in 1962, Comrade Mikoyan visited the Leipzig Fair, and there to greet him was his son, a Soviet general stationed in our part of Germany. "Can you believe that the father berated his son for leaving his post for personal reasons? Even so, he allowed his son to remain for the reception. But at the reception the father's influence was still evident. Think of this, Edward, here is the son, a Soviet general, who did not dare drink vodka in front of his father!"

"He sounds like a stern parent," I continued on the same subject, "but what kind of image does he have in Armenia? Stalin was a Georgian and from all that we hear, the Georgians seem to have forgiven him his sins and still revere him. But Mikoyan—is he as good to Armenia as Stalin was to Georgia?"

Aghayan cared as little for that line of questioning as he had earlier when I had raised similar questions. He shook his head, his lips thinned in disapproval, and asked about my next assignment and when I would leave Berlin. I shrugged my shoulders, he persisted, I resisted, finally he gave up and we took the elevator down to where Ivan performed his regular duty.

Aghayan set March 31 as our next luncheon date and I automatically agreed, but inwardly determined not to keep it. In the West again, I turned the entire affair over in my mind as I drove back to RIAS and decided there wasn't much point to seeing him again. While I did indeed pick up bits of information, they were not matters of life and death.

On the other hand I had noticed that the tempo of our meetings had accelerated to just about every ten days, accompanied by a sense of urgency in his manner. Before, he had been more relaxed, on the surface anyway. I realized that the change had taken place in the fall when he had returned from the Soviet Union.

Had he received new instructions? Mulling this over and curious about his next move, I changed my mind and decided to keep the appointment for lunch—courtesy of the Soviet Government.

XVIII

I HAD INTENDED TO MAKE THIS ONE A SHORT LUNCH and was therefore annoyed when after meeting Aghayan and Ivan we drove for some time past the center of East Berlin and kept on going. Seeing my concern Aghayan said we were going to the *Müggelturm* near the lake for lunch. As it was, it turned out pleasantly.

We reviewed major events since our last lunch. Aghayan asked if I had followed the Khrushchev visit to Budapest? Budapest again! Could he know? But he didn't keep at it. (Neither of us could know that Khrushchev would be deposed in seven months.) After a few forays into German affairs, he looked at me calmly.

"I have often told you of my reasons for asking these questions. Twice a month I write an article for our Foreign Ministry which is re-published in Soviet Armenia. I am regarded as the Berlin expert and my opinions are highly valued. That is why I ask you so many questions. Believe me, if you were to go to Armenia, it would be very interesting for you.

This gave me an opening: "Rafael, you have told me you see summaries of the western press. Perhaps then you have read two articles in *The New York Times* on the despair of repatriated American-Armenians in Soviet Armenia."

He stared at me, asked when the articles had appeared. I told him only last week. What did the articles say? I mentioned some of the themes: homesickness for the United States, lack of the freedom they had given up to return to the homeland, vain attempts to get exit visas, obstacles put in their way to prevent contact with the American Embassy in Moscow.

To all this, his only retort was—"Western newsmen are always distorting the facts. I'll find out about that."

I cut the lunch short saying it would be a longer trip than usual back to the *U-Bahn*. En route he tried a few questions about RIAS and its future operations, explaining that his readers were very curious to know about the radio station.

"I would assume your readers are interested in everything you write about our meetings, whoever they are," I said cuttingly, but which he chose to ignore.

After asking once again about my departure from Berlin, he said he had just been asked to extend for one more year, which had made his wife very unhappy. It appeared to weigh on his mind for he mumbled it several times—"one more year, one more year"—throughout the return ride.

As I was getting out at *Friedrichstrasse,* he told me to keep April 6 free when we would be together with our wives in East Berlin. I turned on him angrily and asked for an explanation.

"I have four tickets for us to see the African Ballet from Guinea, and Kohar is looking forward to seeing your wife. She misses her."

Exasperated at being coerced in this manner I told him that I couldn't know what was on my calendar for that day but that I would let him know.

That evening at home we discussed the invitation. In fact, we had nothing for April 6 but in view of my wife's health we agreed that a long night at the theatre would be strenuous for her. The next day I sent a telegram to the Soviet Embassy regretting that we could not attend the performance but that I could see him on April 16. I initiated the lunch-eon date largely because I didn't wish us to appear ungrateful, and I must admit to a slight pang of conscience that Kohar was being deprived of a diversion she apparently enjoyed.

XIX

AGHAYAN HAD OBVIOUSLY RECEIVED MY TELEGRAM for he was waiting at the *Sofia* on April 16. As Ivan drove us to the *Bucharest* for lunch Aghayan stressed again that it would always be better if I phoned him directly at home rather than try through the Soviet Embassy, even with telegrams. "For your sake, you understand," he said in avuncular tones, "your authorities would not approve."

That ticked me off and made up my mind that this day would be the last on which we would meet. The game, the facade had gone on long enough and I no longer wished it to continue. I had about two months left before departure in which I would be bringing five years of work and cultural contacts to a close. These time-consuming excursions to the East were becoming dispensable.

I told Aghayan I had brought my 8 mm movie camera and wanted to see the Soviet War Memorial in *Treptow,* which was much preferable than sitting in a stuffy restaurant for several hours. He agreed, but soon thereafter began the usual questions. I cut him dead: "That's enough, Rafael. No more questions. For one year I've tolerated them and enough is enough."

He seized my wrist across the table—"Agreed, enough is enough. When is your transfer? I shall miss you very much."

"I'm still in the dark about when or where," I replied and feeling mischievous on the occasion of this, our last lunch, added—"Who knows, perhaps I'll be sent to Albania."

I was unprepared for his reaction. He sat upright, his jaw dropped, and as I realized how he was interpreting this, I laughed—"For God's sake, Rafael, we don't even recognize Albania. You know that."

"But you predicted that France would recognize China, and it did. You're sure this isn't a joke?" I laughed, just plain good-natured laughter, at his innocence.

Cautiously, he asked if we could discuss the articles about Armenia in *The New York Times* and when I nodded, he began to refute them point by point, and lost my attention. I chatted with the waiter and looked around distractedly at other diners. When I again tuned into Aghayan he was citing *Izvestiya's* "exposure of the articles as figments of the journalist's imagination."

I was anxious to visit Treptow and soon we were in the car and heading down *Frankfurter Allee* toward the Berlin district. Just before arriving there, Aghayan reached into his briefcase and handed me the tape. His friends had enjoyed it, he said, and in exchange had dubbed it with Armenian folk music "from the homeland."

At *Treptow* we walked around the impressive monuments to the Soviet war dead, the names of the fallen inscribed on marble. As I panned around the memorial, I trained the camera on Aghayan, but he stopped me, saying—"I'm not dressed for pictures today. Perhaps next time."

"There will not be a next time, Rafael. This is farewell."

He ran up to me excitedly—"But I've already made plans for next time, special, different plans. I want us to get away where I can make *shashlik* and we can drink good Armenian cognac. Edward, please, you must come, you cannot deny me this pleasure."

I looked at this curious man, usually so self-confident, now so distraught. I had no illusions about his motives, after all he was an Intelligence officer of the KGB. Yet, there was that nagging curiosity to know more about him, about his method and about his next move.

He looked at me now so entreatingly that I thought: a common ancient blood flows through our veins, and still we are so different; why? Is it perhaps our different levels of compassion? Because we are products of the vastly different societies from which we stem? Or was it something deeper, something too complex or difficult to define?

In any case, I told myself that to meet him one more time would be a final gesture, and so I relented and agreed. Relief flooded his face—I later knew why—and he proposed April 29, a date on which my curiosity was finally to be satisfied.

XX

I FELT LIGHT-HEARTED DRIVING TO CHECKPOINT
Charlie, parking my car and taking the *U-Bahn* to East Berlin. This
was to be the last time. Spring was already in the air. My next assignment to Budapest was exciting and I had just been informed I would
first be transferred to Washington for one year where I would spend all
my time studying Hungarian at the Foreign Service Institute. I
approached the *Cafe Sofia* with a spring in my step and greeted a
smiling Aghayan with a heartiness which surprised him. "I hope you
have a good appetite today," he warned, "because we are going to have
an Armenian feast. I'm going to make *shashlik* in the country." I
assumed he meant at *Müggelsee* or one of the other forested suburbs
on the perimeter of East Berlin. He waved to Ivan who swung the
Mercedes around to the curb and we began what turned into a journey
of some length.

At first enjoying the green fields and trees, I soon felt a growing sense
of uneasiness as I realized we were well outside of East Berlin and in the
Soviet Zone of Germany. This was forbidden territory for us; even with
diplomatic passports Americans were prohibited from exceeding the city
limits of East Berlin. In fact, we were now on the *autobahn* and shortly
arrived at a *Kontrolstelle* manned by uniformed East Germans. I started
to tell Aghayan that he had to turn around and take me back. "We're
going to have some fun today, don't worry about it. You're with me,
remember. This is *our* part of Germany," he sought to reassure me. The
East Germans took one look at the Soviet diplomatic plates and waved
us on as we never even came to a full stop. Aghayan smiled confidently
at me, noting "No identification necessary, see?" But I wasn't smiling,
for I felt a prisoner in the Mercedes.

"What's that?" I asked, pointing to a field filled with innumerable radio antenna towers. *"Radio Volga,"* he replied tersely. Ivan slowed down and turned off the *autobahn* coming then to a major crossroad. A sign said *Schoenefelder Kreuz,* which meant that we were south of Berlin and heading in the direction of Leipzig. My heart sank. Ivan turned again and I saw another sign, this one read *Pätz.* I had never heard of this place and before I could ask about it, Ivan took yet another road and we began winding our way into a forest. "We'll soon be there," Aghayan said rubbing his hands, "I hope you're as hungry as I." Ivan slowed down and within minutes came to a small lake and shut off the engine. I looked reproachfully at Aghayan—"Did we have to come this far to have a barbecue? Where are we anyway?" He laughed—"I'll tell you where we are. Have you ever heard of *Königswusterhausen?"*

"Is that where we are?" I replied casually. The town was well-known at RIAS because it harbored a nest of jamming stations. I also realized that we were some forty miles from Checkpoint Charlie, the nearest U.S. Army outpost.

Ivan went to the trunk of the car as we got out and withdrew several bags of food, drink, charcoal and a grill. It was now one hour from the time we had left *Friedrichstrasse.* Aghayan said it might take an hour to cook the food and suggested we begin killing time with vodka, pouring the three of us a generous first drink. Ivan remained with us, silent but industrious, helping Aghayan grill the skewered meat which had been marinated. When it was ready some half dozen vodkas later, we all pounced on the food, the brisk air and alcohol having made us all voracious. Ivan had only one helping with us, then grabbed a handful of lamb chunks and bread, excused himself and went some fifty yards from us toward the lake. There he busied himself with a fishing rod and soon made his first catch. We in the meantime were just relaxing as Aghayan now turned his attention to "cognac from the homeland." After the first, he looked at me suddenly with a fixed stare.

"I'd like you to read something," he said, and as he did I knew we had reached the focal point of this elaborate maneuver. There was something in his voice, firm and purposeful, which triggered an alarm within me. He took out of his pocket several folded sheets of paper and handed them to me. "Please read this letter before we talk any further." I looked at the top sheet. It bore the seal of the Armenian Soviet Socialist Republic and under it the name of the Soviet Armenian Ministry of

Foreign Affairs. The typewritten letter was addressed to him, "Comrade Aghayan," was four pages long and written on a Royal.*

I began reading the letter. It complimented Aghayan on a series of articles it said he had written on the situation in Berlin and in Germany. The first three pages were filled with the contents of those alleged articles and I recognized a great deal of material which he had raised in questions to which I had given replies available to all readers of the *International Herald-Tribune* and to listeners of RIAS. As I reached the end of the third page, Aghayan, who had been smoking a cigarette and silently observing me, said—"Edward, read that fourth page very carefully." I did.

It began with the comment that Aghayan's articles had been of great interest to the Armenian Foreign Ministry, but that there were a number of large gaps which, the Foreign Ministry hoped, could be filled. Therefore, the letter went on, Comrade Aghayan was commissioned to get answers to a number of questions, a list of which followed, filling much of the page: how close was Ambassador McGhee to President Johnson? What were McGhee's personal views of Mayor Willy Brandt? Did McGhee's views coincide with the official policy of the State Department? When Johnson, as Vice President, visited Berlin in August 1961, was there rapport between him and Brandt? What was at the core of French and American differences over Berlin? What were the problems affecting the relationships of Washington, Bonn and Paris? In the next German election, would the United States support the Christian Democratic Union or the Social Democratic Party of Germany? What new directives had RIAS received about East Germany, East Berlin, the socialist countries of East Europe, the Soviet Union? There were also several questions concerning the long-wave capabilities of the VOA transmitter in Munich operating on 173 meters. As I well knew, when in operation, the transmitter drowned out Soviet broadcasts operating on the same frequency and had long been a thorn in Moscow's side.

Aghayan had apparently been watching my eyes, and seeing I had read down through the thicket of questions, he said slowly, in a voice which seemed overcharged, enunciating each word carefully—"Now

---

*Having worked with the machine for eight years I knew the type well and found both irony and amusement in the fact that within the Soviet Union the very same American typewriters were being used as those employed daily by the Armenian staff of VOA.

read the last sentence." It was brief and said simply that the Foreign Ministry was enclosing the honorarium for his last article. The letter was signed "Kevorkian." I looked up. Aghayan was watching me intently, both of us sitting cross-legged Oriental-style on the rug he had spread on the grass. "You saw the reference to the payment, didn't you? Well, you Americans have a phrase—fifty-fifty" (he spoke it in English) "and that is what I would like our arrangement to be." He then reached into his coat pocket and took out a huge wad of money and plunked it down on the rug amidst the remains and offal of our picnic. I looked at the pile of bills in disbelief. The topmost bill was a 50 DM West German note, and the pile was about two inches high.*

When I looked up at Aghayan, I saw he had been staring beyond me, apparently at Ivan who was within sight of us. When he noticed I had looked up, he quickly adjusted his gaze and now looked questioningly at me. "Rafael, what is this all about?" I asked, my voice reflecting the mounting tension within me. "That is your share of the honorarium." "My share—for doing what?" "For the information you have already given me. And there will be more, much much more, when you supply the answers to these new questions." He picked up the wad of money and held it out to me. I shook my head and pushed it back. He shrugged his shoulders—"Listen, don't brood about it. Just put it in your pocket. After all, it belongs to you."

"Damn you, Rafael," I said bitterly, "so this is what our friendship has meant to you. That you, an Armenian, should try and recruit a fellow Armenian into working . . ." I threw down the letter I was still holding . . . "for *them*. How loyal a servant you are to your government!" Unabashed, he replied soberly and firmly—"Of course I am loyal to my government." "Well, so am I to my government which pays me well. I don't need your money." Refusing to be swayed from his purpose, he continued arguing with me with an astonishing persistence until I finally seized his arm and said loudly—"Put the money away." Now he no longer looked me in the eye, but nevertheless tucked the money under my plate. I started to rise, uncrossing my legs—"Get that money out of my sight." "Why are you so stubborn" he cried out in frustration, "all right, if you won't take the money, I'll have to get you something else.

---

*The amount of his payment was not mentioned but even at 4 DM to the dollar, which was the 1964 rate, the money he was offering me could have come to about $1,000.

What would you like?" I shook my head incredulously—"Rafael, you just don't understand. I want no money, no gifts, nothing. I've given you nothing, you owe me nothing." Somehow, this got through to him and dejectedly, he put the money back into his pocket.

Although by now we had finished the vodka and cognac, I shivered from the cold. It was after 4 PM, the sky had become overcast and the abrupt changes in both the weather and our relationship had combined to instill in me a profound sense of apprehension. After all, we were completely out of sight and reach of anyone, and I was alone with one, probably two KGB officers. The only sign of life had been a passing motorboat. Otherwise, silence, but for the rustle of the wind. Checkpoint Charlie might just as well have been 2,000 miles away. I was also not relishing the return ride of one hour.

As we sat in silence, neither of us making a move, I was upset by the crudeness of the situation, and perhaps deep within me a disappointment that things had turned out this way. I had not been playing games but he apparently had. I was not in the intelligence business but he was, and while I was not so naive as to think his intentions were purely social, somehow the confrontation with his true purpose—his mission, as it turned out—and in such dramatic circumstances, affected me. On the long ride out to this lake, I had sensed the possibility of something extraordinary perhaps happening, and while we drank and ate, I did have the feeling that after the meal, a more intense conversation with brisker questioning might take place, but no more. Now, however, I could see the preparation for this climactic day: the early questions on German affairs, the access to classified information, the relations with the senior American staff, the radio propaganda operations at RIAS, appeals to possible ethnic patriotism and the pull of "the homeland," now epitomized in an impressively official letter from the homeland itself. And to cap it off, a direct offer to work for—whom else?—the KGB.

Much as I felt an emptiness within me, as I looked now at Aghayan I realized from the look of extreme dejection on his face that the failure of his mission was of far greater significance, and it gave me heart. Arising I said cheerfully, "Let's go see how Ivan has made out." Unwinding laboriously, Aghayan also stood up grunting morosely. We walked to the bank where Ivan, on seeing us approaching, smiled broadly and held up his hand with five fingers apart. He had indeed caught five small fish—

five more than his colleague, I thought to myself. I felt a sudden warmth toward Ivan in contrast to my current feelings toward Rafael. Ivan had done me no harm, not offended me, seemed like one of those happy-go-lucky Russians always in good spirits, whose infectiousness soon took hold of me. I congratulated him on his catch. He responded, Aghayan interpreting, by saying he hoped we met no East German police because they were severe with drivers who had liquor on their breath. We packed up everything and began the long drive back, first through the small forest and dirt roads, finally reaching the *autobahn*. Throughout this preliminary stretch, Aghayan was broodingly silent, until a curious incident brought him back to life.

Ivan turned his head and said something to Aghayan sitting beside me in the rear of the Mercedes. Aghayan translated into Armenian what I had already grasped, which was that Ivan wanted to ask me some questions, if I agreed. I did, and what ensued transformed the return drive which I had dreaded into a journey full of sparkle, good humor, and a lively exchange of views—in effect an East-West debate between Ivan and me on U.S.-USSR relations, Aghayan now relegated to a tertiary role. Ivan was a formidable opponent, his manner and tone no longer that of a chauffeur but of a commanding presence. Aghayan dutifully translated our back-and-forth like an automaton and by the time we arrived at *Friedrichstrasse,* which I was never happier to see, I was not only impressed with Ivan's intelligence and wit but had second thoughts about the staff structure of this intelligence operation.

As we arrived at the corner where I usually got out, to my astonishment Aghayan said—"If you won't take the money, at least get me the answers to the questions in the letter. You saw where it came from and I hope you remember the questions. Edward, this would be a great service to Armenia. Think of it that way, if nothing else." I glared at him, then turned and for the first time demonstratively shook hands with Ivan and sensed that he had enjoyed our debate as much as I.

Aghayan walked with me to the curb as I prepared to cross the street and asked when we could meet. I said we could never meet again and reminded him that this was to be the last time. Stubbornly, and seemingly reluctant to leave my side, he persisted—"I'll wait for you on May 13. If you can't make it, don't send a telegram, phone the number I gave you. It is much better." I had now reached the other side of *Friedrichstrasse* and turned to look at him. Aghayan was standing across the street, his face a question mark, oblivious of the crowds and traffic which at 5:45 PM made *Friedrichstrasse* and *Unter den Linden* the busiest corner in East Berlin.

As so frequently happens when one has undergone something momentous, the full implications of my lakeside experience, forgotten during the diverting return drive to Berlin, engulfed me now in wave after wave as I entered my car parked in West Berlin and slowly drove home. I had barely reached the *Gedächtniskirche* from the spot at the old *Anhalter Bahnhof* where I had left it—a stretch of ten minutes—when I felt a dread permeate me. It was a feeling comparable to the worst moments I had experienced in World War II, when a V-2 rocket had destroyed a building at dawn in London close to where I was sleeping, or when at Verdun we were threatened with annihilation during the Battle of the Bulge.

As I wormed my way through *Kurfürstendamm* traffic, the full impact hit me. I had been asked to spy for the Soviet Union! This then was what it had been all about. But I had not expected the trappings: the solemn letter, the impressive seal, the ring of authority, the aura of officialdom, the money. These had all been carefully prepared, especially the wording of the letter and its references to matters we had discussed. How many people in East Berlin and in Moscow had worked on these details? For over a year, KGB specialists had focused their attention on me, analyzing and evaluating the reports sent back by Aghayan, debriefing him either in *Karlshorst* or when he visited headquarters. How accurately had he reported on me and what were his true perceptions? Perhaps there had even been factions—those who believed I was ready for recruitment and those who didn't; maybe even some considered defection. But with my pending departure, clearly a decision had been made for immediate action. That it had failed had shaken Aghayan, but that it had been made had shaken me.

I arrived home in *Zehlendorf* where Roseann, aware until then only that I had met once again with Aghayan in the East but now observing my distraught condition, insisted on knowing what had happened. We sat in the kitchen and I related the afternoon's events, following which we both agreed that the time had finally come for a conclusive break.

XXI

I GNORING AGHAYAN'S ADVICE TO PHONE HIM FROM EAST Berlin, on May 11, two days before the date he had proposed, I sent him a telegram from West Berlin, care of the Soviet Embassy. It read—

"Ich komme nicht. Grüsse an die Familie. Auf Wiedersehen. Edward"

I now turned my attention to the business of winding up my affairs and getting our household effects packed. Meanwhile, the superb RIAS Chorus had received an invitation from the Gulbenkian Festival in Lisbon to give a series of concerts in Portugal. The Chorus' Director, Gunther Arndt, insisted that my wife and I go along as official representatives of the City of Berlin. We spent a wonderful week in the north and south of Portugal and flew back ready for the final few weeks of our five years in West Berlin.

On June 16, while I was en route from RIAS, my wife took a phone call from Aghayan at 7 PM. He asked how we were and why we had gone to Lisbon. She in turn asked how he had known. Aghayan said that in our absence he had phoned and spoken with Mark. He had then asked for me, learned I had not arrived home yet and hung up.

Thirty minutes later when the phone rang, I picked it up. Aghayan behaved as though nothing had happened to disrupt our relationship, and after the usual amenities proposed meeting the next day.

"Tomorrow is June 17, which might remind you of our conversation exactly one year ago on the same subject."

"Oh yes, that day I remember," he laughed, "well, how about the 18th?"

I replied that under no circumstances would I meet him in East Berlin. He countered by maintaining that he would not meet me in West Berlin. After a few seconds of silence, he asked if he could phone me. I said he was free to phone me at RIAS but no longer to my home. At that, we said Goodbye, and I had the feeling it was definitive. It proved to be and I enjoyed a sense of relief that all this was now behind me.

Two weeks later my family and I left West Berlin as a gathering of our closest German and American friends saw us off—a Dixieland Jazz Band providing appropriate merriment and atmosphere—from a small airfield in the French sector called *Tegel,* now a major European airport.

PART TWO

Budapest
1965–1969

XXII

IN WASHINGTON, FOLLOWING HOME LEAVE, I ATTENDED the Foreign Service Institute's classes in Hungarian, taking the full ten-month course. My wife joined me in some of those classes becoming remarkably fluent. In August 1965 we left Washington for Budapest and a completely different life in a completely different social system on the banks of the Danube.

We lived in Buda, with its lovely hills and clean air, while the American Legation—raised to Embassy status in 1967—was in the heart of flat, polluted Pest. In addition to the normal complement of official and local employees, the Legation was unique in the world in that it also had another occupant, Joseph Cardinal Mindszenty, who had sought refuge in the Legation on November 4, 1956 when Soviet power had crushed the Hungarian Revolt. His Eminence's residence at the Budapest Legation gave service there a certain piquancy, for at the time there were no Marines to guard the building and the American staff took turns sleeping overnight in the Legation and taking care of the Cardinal's needs. This included his evening half-hour walk in the courtyard—duly observed from neighboring windows by the Hungarian Secret Police—during which those of us who were proficient in Hungarian could converse with him. The Cardinal's vast knowledge of Armenian Church history soon created a warm bond between us which led three years later to his baptizing our two younger sons, Scott and Christian.*

As First Secretary for Press and Cultural Affairs I led a very active and rich life in Budapest in which Roseann participated fully. Among the more

---

*When Cardinal Mindszenty learned one day that I would be visiting Rome with my family, he asked me to deliver a message to his old friend Gregory Cardinal Agajanian, the highest ranking Armenian in the Catholic Church. Cardinal Agajanian received us warmly and gave everyone his blessing and St. Vartan medallions. He also gave me a gold cross to take back to Cardinal Mindszenty which for a time brightened the otherwise sombre recluse of the American Embassy.

exciting things that brightened our existence were art exhibits from other countries, such as Henry Moore's sculpture from Great Britain and Impressionistic paintings from France. It was just such an exhibit sponsored by the Soviet Embassy which was to re-kindle our desire to visit Soviet Armenia and consequently engage us in an experience whose emotional and intellectual impact remains still very much alive.

Among my many diplomatic colleagues was the Soviet Cultural Attache, Valentin Alekseyevich Korolev, a large burly man with an eternally glum expression. Korolev seldom spoke to anyone, much less to me. I once saw him standing with others at a diplomatic function around the great Hungarian author Tibor Dery, who was relating in German the subject matter of the novel he was writing. Korolev did not react to him with even a polite grunt, finally turning away as I broke into the group, anxious to hear what the enormously entertaining writer was saying. (I learned later that Korolev had served in Budapest during the 1956 revolt, which explained his coldness to Dery, one of the intellectual leaders of the revolt.)

It was, therefore, something of a coup when on one occasion at the Bulgarian Embassy Korolev and I found ourselves face-to-face in a corner. It was the first time we communicated. I asked the perennial question diplomats ask each other—where had he served before?

"In Berlin, East of course," he said, and a tingle ran down my spine.

When had that been?

"In the 1960s." This was all in German which he spoke well.

I took a deep breath—"I was in Berlin, West of course, at that time," and in comparing the years discovered we had overlapped by three. In fact, Korolev had departed East Berlin in December 1963. I braced myself wondering if I was asking for trouble but went ahead anyway.

—"While you were in the Soviet Embassy in East Berlin, did you know a diplomat named Rafael Aghayan?"

The impassive expression did not change as he replied that there had not been anyone in the Embassy by that name, asking—"Why do you think someone with that name might have been there?"

Because, I replied, I had known someone by that name at that time.

"No, no, you are mistaken. I knew everyone in our Embassy in East Berlin and I assure you no such person existed." I dropped the subject and never raised it with him again.

In March 1967 Korolev, aware of my ethnic heritage from comments I had made to him, invited us to a Soviet exhibit at the Hungarian National Gallery of paintings by the Armenian artist Mardiros Saryan. Unable to attend because of his advanced years—he was 86—Saryan was represented by a young art critic who delivered a speech in Russian. Roseann and I took one look at him and knew, especially from his eyes, that he was no Russian. During the speech I once caught Korolev's eye and he had tilted his head toward the speaker and nodded with an uncharacteristic smile and I realized he was telling me the same thing.

When the ceremonies were over, I approached Korolev, who was standing beside Soviet Ambassador Titov, and asked for an introduction to the art critic. Korolev leaned over to his Ambassador and must have whispered an explanation for then both laughed and the introduction was made in Russian.

In Armenian I said—"Welcome to Budapest, compatriot." The young man, whose name was Shahen Khatchaturian, let out a cry and began to pump our hands, repeating over and over in Armenian—"But this is unbelievable." We quickly agreed to get together, and noticing the attention our animated conversation was attracting, I broke it off after deciding to talk by phone. I had no wish to create problems for him and in fact it was he who called me at the American Embassy to say he would come that same evening.

He arrived by trolley, his arms laden with gifts of cognac, cigarettes, records, art folios and medallions—all from Armenia. Shades of Rafael! But Shahen was no Rafael. We talked and talked, for six hours, and Roseann and I took to this decent, open, intelligent young representative of that same homeland of which Aghayan spoke so possessively. But how different they were, in so many ways. We learned much about Shahen that evening.

He was born in Syria where his father had worked as a bricklayer. They lived in dire straits, in fact they were very poor, which in the Middle East goes considerably beyond the poverty level we know in the United States. In 1946, during the wave of repatriation inspired by domestic Soviet labor needs, Shahen's father took his twelve-year-old son, wife and three other children to Soviet Armenia to settle in the homeland.

Shahen said his father was desperate and believed that nothing could be worse than their lives in Syria. What awaited them, however, was far from their expectations. All told, more than 100,000 Armenians were repatriated, the Khatchaturians among the very first, for which the Armenian authorities were unprepared. There was no housing, little food, and total confusion, people standing in railroad stations for days, often in the rain awaiting transportation as children cried through the night. But even when some semblance of organization had been achieved, a new phenomenon greeted them—the hostility of the native Armenians, whose speech and ways were so different.

Young Shahen learned bricklaying and worked with his father, later attending a Sports Institute where he became an expert swimmer, winning several championships for Armenia. He soon tired of this, realizing it was not his future, and discovered a talent for art appreciation, which he pursued. He became an art critic and worked his way to his present position—chief art researcher and historian at Yerevan's National Art Gallery. Shahen was very happy with his status and informed us proudly that he had selected all the paintings to be exhibited in the Soviet Pavilion at Expo 67 in Montreal later that year.

Since going to Armenia in 1946, this was the first time he had ever visited any country outside the USSR. At this point he became morose, then excusing himself, explained his sudden shift of mood. He had requested permission at the Soviet Embassy for a trip to Prague to visit its excellent collection of paintings but had been turned down. He then had gone to Korolev and Ambassador Titov, both of whom he found sympathetic and friendly, and asked for their intervention. When nothing happened, Shahen went to the Consular Section where the rejection had originated, and was told flatly he couldn't travel to Prague. (I recalled that back in East Berlin both Shishkin and Aghayan had been in the Consular Section, whose authority seemed to supersede even the Ambassador's.)

—"It's just as well I didn't ask to go to Vienna," Shahen sighed, "but there—oh those Breughels!"

Meanwhile, since his arrival in Budapest, the Soviet Embassy was running him all over town giving lectures on Saryan and Soviet art. He was slightly bitter in describing these activities—"I lecture at the Soviet school teaching their children how to see paintings. I brighten

their lives in the Embassy, but they won't let me go even to Prague."*
This was the first intimation of nationalist friction but not the last, as
we later discovered.

I found Shahen a remarkably well-balanced citizen of Soviet Armenia,
his criticisms of its society and its problems couched in moderate terms.
Shahen said the "Voice of America's" Armenian language broadcasts
had a large audience because since jamming had stopped in 1963 everyone felt this was a green light from Moscow. Through VOA's *Music,
USA* and its moderator Willis Conover, he had developed a love for
American jazz and mentioned Miles Davis, John Coltrane and Dave
Brubeck. *Ameryka* Magazine,** he said, could not be purchased at
newsstands but was read widely in libraries, and that the lucky few who
received it by subscription passed it from hand to hand. "But there are
problems, oh yes, some still exist—not unlike being unable to go to
Prague." That seemed particularly to rankle him.

Shahen said he had spent much time at the *Graphic Arts* American
exhibit in Yerevan, part of the U.S.-USSR cultural exchange program,
which because of its content had especially interested him. Everyone in
Yerevan hoped for more American events.

Then there was Radio Armenia! At the mere mention of this current
phenomenon, we all laughed, as each told a joke from this dubious source.
Shahen said that Armenians were very proud of the fact that Soviet citizens from all over the country were telling Radio Armenia jokes.

"But let me tell you a true story. Not long ago there was an All-Union
Conference of Radio Directors in Moscow at which each director made a
report. After several such reports from different republics, the chairman
said—'And now, we will hear from the Director of the Armenian Radio,'
and the audience which until then had greeted every director with polite
professional applause, let loose with shrieks of laughter and pandemonium followed. Our director came back to Yerevan and told us about it
and said he was so mortified he stood there speechless. The poor man,"
Shahen concluded, laughing still.

---

*In later years he travelled outside the USSR and even visited the United States, lecturing in
New York, Washington and Los Angeles.
**At that time published in 50,000 copies every two months, as called for in the cultural
agreement between the United States and Soviet Union.

He said the last fifteen years had seen vast improvement in Armenia. "After the great slaughter by the Turks in 1915, our next worst period was in 1937 under Stalin, when, as in 1915, the cream of Armenian intellectual life was exiled, this time to Siberia where most died. And yet, despite this suffering, our small nation gave Stalin 300,000 soldiers for the Red Army in the War. You know, Stalin looked after his native Georgia. They say during the war Tbilisi was a good place to be. Mikoyan, on the other hand, is interested in Armenia only at election time. When he makes speeches there, he begins in Armenian but continues in Russian. But Armenians speak of him with pride. He is a great statesman, devoted to the Soviet Union.

"When he was on his way to Cuba, for instance, he learned that his wife had died, yet he continued on to Havana on his mission. That is real devotion to one's country." Roseann and I exchanged knowing looks.

He asked whether we ever intended to visit Armenia. Indeed we did, and perhaps from Budapest. He became exhilarated and said our very first move in Yerevan should be to phone him at the Art Gallery. He promised a full itinerary of side trips and we accepted. Late in the night, after an emotional farewell, he left.

Roseann and I stayed up even later talking about Shahen, about Rafael—how different they were, each in his own way interesting but Shahen stimulating our curiosity about the land of our ancestors to a far greater degree. Meeting Shahen obviously gave impetus to our resolve to make the trip, with no special mission but to see, talk, listen and make up our own minds.

In early May of that same year I was visited by Richard T. Davies, at the time a State Department officer on loan to USIA in charge of the Soviet Union and East Europe, which is to say my superior. (He later became U.S. Ambassador to Poland.) He was also my oldest friend in the Foreign Service, both of us having attended Columbia College before the war.* We discussed the press and cultural programs I was working on in Budapest, the most successful of which was opening an American Library and the regular showing of USIA films to growing audiences.

---

*During his three-day visit we went to the Armenian State Circus which was playing in Budapest, and after the performance went backstage. The Armenian artists turned into disappointments because they apparently lived in Moscow and spoke an almost unrecognizable Armenian. Davies, an old Soviet hand, conversed with ease in Russian with them.

We also discussed plans for U.S. participation in the next annual Budapest Trade Fair, and Davies said he wished to propose an idea. Soon to open in Leningrad under the cultural agreement was an exhibit entitled *Industrial Design,* and he would be attending its opening in June. Knowing that I had never been in the Soviet Union, Davies suggested that I plan a trip to Moscow and Leningrad for the purpose of orientation, discussion with fellow officers at the Embassy, and evaluation of the Leningrad exhibit for its suitability at the Budapest Fair.

I was thrilled at the prospect, concurred immediately, but said I had two special requests: I wished to include Soviet Armenia in the orientation, and I wanted Roseann to go with me, at my expense of course.

"My God!" shouted Davies with explosive joviality, "why didn't I think of that myself. Of course you should go to Armenia. Both of you."

In the days that followed I felt a mounting excitement as our passports were sent to the Soviet Embassy for visas with the proposed itinerary—Moscow, Leningrad, Yerevan, Kiev. But of those four cities, obviously Yerevan shone like a beacon. I would tingle with anticipation when reflecting on the fact that after years of hearsay, speculation and propaganda, I would soon be able to separate fact from fiction and determine for myself—to the extent a few days exposure would allow—the realities of the 'homeland.' Everything I had ever read or heard from my three VOA colleagues would be put to the test.

But what kind of entree would we have since the only person we knew in that entire small country was our newly-made friend from the art world? Correction, I quickly admonished myself. There was one other person, and hardly from the art world. Would he be there at the airport, watching, waiting? In moments such as these, my misgivings would turn to fear. Did I have the right to expose Roseann, or even myself, a Foreign Service Officer, to dangers I could not name? Anxiety and doubt crowded moments such as these.

But then one day, our diplomatic passports were returned stamped with our Soviet visas, and I knew that the seduction was irresistible and that now nothing could keep us from the most fascinating journey we were ever to make.

Yerevan
1967

XXIII

ON JUNE 5 EARLY IN THE MORNING WE BOARDED A Hungarian flight to Moscow, unaware that the Middle East had erupted into the Six-Day War. Although I had a number of friends stationed in our Moscow Embassy, I preferred that we stay at a hotel to get the full flavor of visiting the Soviet Union. We were driven directly to the *Ukraina* where we had our reservation and went to our room on the twenty-second floor. (Years later when tourists told me of their problems with Soviet hotels I could commiserate with them, especially after waiting twenty minutes for the elevator.)

We asked for no favors from the Embassy and refused the offers of colleagues to put us up at their apartments. We genuinely wished to be on our own. The only request I made was for tickets to the Bolshoi. We wandered all over the sprawling city, exploring the Kremlin, St. Basil's Church, Novodevichy Cemetery, the Pushkin and Tretyakov Galleries, walking through GUM, Children's World and many smaller stores where we would make purchases aided by countless friendly Russians, while in asking directions would be ignored by stony-faced policemen. Had Lenin's Tomb not been closed, we would have walked through it as well. Two nights at the Bolshoi were spectacular, the first offering the full-length "Swan Lake," and the second a massive staging of Prokofiev's "War and Peace."

On the third night we boarded the Red Arrow overnight train to Leningrad, sleeping hardly at all, arrived at 8 AM in a driving rain and went to the *Astoria,* a hotel dating back to much earlier times but in its amenities—such as room service—making up for all we had suffered at the *Ukraina* in Moscow. Within two hours we went to the *Industrial Design* exhibit where we learned that in retaliation for our accidental bombing of a Soviet ship in Haiphong Harbor in Vietnam, Soviet 'sailors' were picketing the exhibit, and the day before had even stoned some windows. Nevertheless, hardy Russian visitors examined the exhibit with enormous interest, noting for instance that in the evolution of refrigeration, they were still fifty years behind by pointing to iceboxes and then to themselves as they smiled sadly at us. The rest of the day was spent at the prodigious and exciting *Hermitage* Museum.

The next morning we ordered a taxi to take us to the airport where we had booked two seats on a direct flight to Yerevan. Halfway to the airport the driver wanted to know when our flight was. I indicated in twenty minutes, my heart sinking at the realization that we were already late and to miss the flight might mean loss of hotel rooms and other mixups. To our horror, he drove right past the airport turn-off, accelerating to frightening speed and shouting something in Russian and German, which I made out to mean that no American should visit Leningrad without seeing the Soviet monument commemorating the defeat of fascism. We arrived at the huge monument, took a one second look and I jabbed him in the shoulder to keep on driving.

When we arrived at the airport I ran in frantically and slammed my tickets on the counter. The girl looked at them and pressed both hands to her face and pointed out the window. I saw a turbo-jet plane, doors closed, preparing to taxi out for takeoff. I seized the cab driver and we jumped back into the cab as an Aeroflot official ran over and joined us. As the gates opened up, we drove wildly onto the tarmac right up to and in front of the four-engine plane, its propellors already turning.

The Aeroflot official waved and shouted at the cockpit, the propellors slowed down and stopped. An irate captain opened the door and walked out onto the landing platform now rolled up to the plane. I took one look at him and that was enough—*"Shnoragalutiun, Hayrenagits"* I shouted our thanks. A big smile wiped away the anger as he turned and yelled into the plane—"They're Armenians!"

We entered the plane, packed with passengers, not a seat in sight. The captain told us to keep on moving, murmuring to me that the midsection was not an appropriate place for us. He escorted Roseann and me to a separate compartment in the rear of the plane reserved for his small crew whose cool spacious comfort was a blessing compared to the heat and oppressiveness of the main cabin. There, for the next four hours, we enjoyed not just this luxury but the company of the crew, three of whose five members were Armenians. Whereas in Moscow we had felt like strangers, on this plane we were to enjoy a hospitality which presaged the welcome awaiting us in Armenia.

The three Armenians were the captain, his co-pilot and a steward, and it took but a few minutes of observation to discern that their relations with the two Russian stewardesses were distinctly cool. For instance, I had come aboard with my 8 mm movie camera dangling from my wrist. The captain noticed it and said to me in a low voice—"Don't show that camera too prominently. They" inclining his head toward the two stewardesses "don't approve. Even we can't take pictures, if it were up to them. If you want to take movies over Armenia, wait for a sign from me."

We got to know the co-pilot and the cabin steward best of all. The latter was a youth in his early twenties who told us something about himself: he had been married for only seven months, his wife was expecting shortly, he earned 120 rubles a month, and his ambition was to become a pilot. He saw to our every need, was very helpful and attentive when Roseann became slightly airsick, and tried to keep us company throughout the long trip. The captain took turns with his co-pilot coming back to chat with us, largely about the United States and how Armenians lived there, but he stayed only briefly each time.

It was the co-pilot with whom we talked at greatest length, and from whom we learned something about the captain: he had been a major in the Soviet Air Force, was now earning 500 rubles a month and was the best pilot in Armenia. We enjoyed the co-pilot immensely, especially for his sense of humor. He said he was learning English because of possible new flights now being scheduled, such as Yerevan-Damascus and Yerevan-Beirut.

Roseann asked him to practice some English sentences which could be useful, so he began:

"You are beautiful. I want to kiss you. I have to kiss you. We have to kiss you. I must, you must, he, she, it must kiss you."

We were convulsed with laughter as he rambled on and Roseann told him he would bring a notoriety to Aeroflot that the Soviet airline had not reckoned with. The four-hour trip was thus made entirely delightful and passed quickly.

Periodically the door to our private compartment would open as one or the other of the two Russian stewardesses would enter, at which the conversation and laughter would die as though on signal.

After three and a half hours had passed, the co-pilot left us and in five minutes returned, pointed to my camera on the seat and said—"They are both up front and we are flying over the Caucasus Mountains and entering Armenian air space. The captain says take your pictures now but make it fast!"

I did as he stood guard at the door, capturing on film not only the stunning mountain range but *Lake Sevan* as well, the highest large lake in the world. When I had finished, the co-pilot left to join the captain. We began our descent and in twenty minutes our pilot negotiated a very smooth landing.

We were in Armenia.

XXIV

EREVAN AIRPORT WAS PACKED WITH LOCAL CITIZENS who had come to watch the plane land and to participate in the excitement of travelers disembarking and picking up their luggage. Some were there to greet the Armenians on the plane who were soon whisked away, while an Intourist bus took care of the rest.

Roseann and I, and our four pieces of American luggage, were standing forlornly at the airport gate looking for transportation when out of nowhere an egg-bald stocky bustling figure rushed up to us and asked where we were going. We told him the *Hotel Armenia* whereupon he rammed our luggage into every corner of his tiny battered cab and ordered us to take our seats.

Now he plied us with questions and soon learned that we knew no one in Armenia. In the middle of the dusty road he jammed on his brakes and turned the cab around opposite to the direction of the capital. I shouted at him in alarm, both of us jolted by the lurching motion, and insisted he take us to Yerevan.

"No, no, you cannot go to a hotel. Do you think we are Russians? We are Armenians! I am taking you to my house. My wife and three children will look after you."

I bent forward, seized his shoulders and made him turn around again. At the *Hotel Armenia* on *Lenin Square,* the cab came to a screeching halt. Unsmiling, he carried our four bags only to the steps of the hotel and charged—as I found out later—three times the normal fare. I didn't mind.

In the hotel, new problems awaited us. Although the embassy had made the reservation for us one week earlier, the Reception Clerk denied it had and said there was no space for us. Roseann gave me that time-honored look of the tolerant but impatient wife, so I did the only thing a traveler in the Soviet Union can do—I went to the Intourist office in the lobby of the hotel. There, a business-like but friendly woman named Lina Stepanian heard me out, at first with a studied sympathy developed, no doubt, over many years of listening to similar tales of woe. But then, on hearing all the details, she wrinkled her brow and muttered that this was very different. The problem we posed for her, she said, centered around the fact that while we were traveling as tourists, we possessed diplomatic passports which gave our visit an official aura. Lina scratched her head in puzzlement then suggested we take a walk in *Lenin Square* for an hour or so while she checked it out, noting—"After all, despite your official capacity, you are Armenians here to visit the homeland."

I went out to the lobby where Roseann had been sitting, only to find her on the verge of tears. Several elderly people had approached her asking about relatives all over the United States, and one very old man wanted to know if by chance she knew his sister in Los Angeles. The profoundly sad expression in his eyes had touched her to the core and she said—"You know, if it's going to be like this every day, I'll just go to pieces." I took her hand and led her out into the cool June night.

There were hordes of people in *Lenin Square* just outside the hotel and in the streets leading into it, but the surrounding buildings, which were mostly government offices, were dark. That is, all but one, the post office, even though it was already 8 PM on a Saturday. Standing outside was a throng of people and when we asked the reason for it, several were ready to explain to the two obvious tourists that these people had placed phone calls to other cities of the Soviet Union and were waiting for the connection.

We walked full circle and past the dark hulk of Lenin high on a pedestal back into the hotel, where a smiling Lina said everything had been solved. After thanking her, which I was to do often for she was indeed helpful, I asked about calling Shahen Khatchaturian at the Art Gallery. Lina put the call through and learned that he had gone for the day because of a lecture he was giving exactly at that hour—9 PM—but could be reached on Sunday morning. We were escorted to the fifth floor and to a corner suite, clean and simply furnished, overlooking the square, and to our delight providing a stunning view of a distant but clearly visible *Mt. Ararat.*

This picturesque snow-capped peak with all its Biblical, historical and political—it lies just beyond the border of Turkey—symbolism was to be yet another source of spiritual rejuvenation to both of us each night as we marvelled at its remote serenity while pondering the trying emotional experiences of each day.

Unable to sleep for excitement despite our fatigue, we arose and breakfasted early in the dining room, concentrating less on our eggs and coffee than on the more formidable fare of two male natives nearby— meat, salad and cognac. I tried the Art Gallery again hoping for an early contact with Shahen because we had no plans and our visas allowed us only two and a half days in Armenia, then a flight to Kiev and a con- necting flight back to Budapest.

I reached Shahen and within minutes he ran into the hotel lobby for an enthusiastic reunion. He told us it was an incredible coincidence that on the night before he had given yet another lecture on his travels to Hungary and had again spoken at length about us. (We were to realize shortly that Shahen's visit with us had become the centerpiece of his lectures.) He said there had been some 200 in the audience, among them many prominent intellectuals—"And now, miraculously, here you are. I can't believe it. All the time I was talking about you last night, you were just across the square. Everyone will know who you are when I introduce you."

It also emerged that the following morning, Shahen was scheduled to depart for Rostov to the north for ten days in order to complete work on an art collection being brought for exhibition to Yerevan. That now upset him and, of course, we too were disappointed, but after some silent deliberation he said he would make every effort to postpone the trip and to arrange a fruitful time for us.

I suggested renting an Intourist car and driving to *Etchmiadzin* for a visit to the ancient cathedral, the seat of the Armenian Apostolic Church and its spiritual head, Catholicos Vazgen I, the Supreme Patriarch of all Armenians. Lina arranged for the car and we drove the thirty or so minutes to *Etchmiadzin.* *

It was a very hot Sunday morning but the cathedral and the grounds were packed—testimony to the profound devotion of Armenians, even under Soviet rule, to their church. Young and old walked, lounged, even lay on the old stones of the courtyard and on the adjoining grass, playing, sleeping, picnicking. A few beggars held out their hands and as I looked into their wrinkled wizened faces, Shahen whispered that they were not

---

*In classical Armenian *Etchmiadzin* means "Descent of the Only Begotten" and is the site of a cathedral built in the 5th century following the adoption of Christianity as the state religion of Armenia in the 4th century.

Armenians but Kurds. Again here, elderly Armenians approached us to ask whether we knew a sister in Detroit, a brother in New York, a nephew in Chicago and why they had not visited Armenia to see them. It was getting to Roseann again so we led her quickly away.

Suddenly Shahen shouted for us to jump to one side as a man came running leading a sheep with a bleeding ear. Shahen explained that this was known as *madagh,* meaning sacrifice, and the ritual required leading the sheep around the cathedral three times, after which the animal was to be slaughtered, roasted and eaten. The trench for the fire was already prepared. About twenty yards from the Cathedral was another area where chickens were decapitated and roasted. He pointed out that if we were seen observing the ritual, the custom was to invite us to partake of the chicken. We made certain not to observe any of the rituals.

Inside the cathedral mass was already in progress. The Catholicos Vazgen I, conducted the mass and Shahen said that when it was over he would arrange a private audience. One hour later, however, with another hour-and-a-half to go, we saw the day slipping by rapidly and decided to leave.*

On the road returning to Yerevan we stopped off at *Zvartnotz* to visit the ruins of this once circular, domed church erected in the seventh century and one of the finest examples of Armenian Christian architecture. Beyond, we stopped off again at the lovely little church of *St. Hripsime,* named after a martyred Christian virgin.

Back at the *Hotel Armenia* we washed up, rested briefly and then met Shahen in the lobby to attend the first of two art exhibits that had fortuitously opened that day and which proved to be the beginning of a whirlwind series of encounters with Armenian intellectuals. These encounters, sometimes brief, at other times lengthy, remained for us the most memorable and illuminating experiences of our time in Armenia.

The first exhibit was at the Revolutionary Museum and was a retrospective of the paintings of Arpenik Nalbandian, a very talented woman who, Shahen informed us, had died the previous year of cancer at the age of 48. Her exhibited work of over 100 paintings spanned three dec-

---

*I did meet Catholicos Vazgen I in 1989 when he came to the United States to thank Americans for their generous donations to earthquake relief. At that time,the State Department asked me to escort the Catholicos to the Oval Office where I interpreted the conversation between him and President Bush. Also attending was Catholicos Karekin II of Lebanon.

ades, in a variety of styles but all filled with the rich almost blatant colors of her sunny native land.

We began the slow movement through the exhibit and as I looked at the portraits of children with their mothers, the village life, some nudes, and a few self-portraits, a strange feeling overcame me which Roseann sensed. She asked what was wrong, and I looked around—Shahen had left us momentarily—and whispered in English—"Listen. Remember when I told you Rafael had screened several films for me, that time when you didn't go over with me? Well, the first short film was about this painter, Arpenik Nalbandian. Don't tell Shahen, for Heaven's sake! How could we ever explain that whole thing?" We continued walking but the exhibit flooded me with memories which had nothing to do with it, yet it was truly a remarkable coincidence.

Meanwhile, Shahen was busy collaring others to bring over and introduce to us. The first of the many we met in this way at this exhibit, which was obviously an important cultural event, was the husband of the artist being exhibited, Edward Isabeghian, who was also a painter and director of yet another Gallery of Art. His opening words, which we were to hear often, were—"I know all about you, both of you. Shahen returned from Budapest and told everyone. By now, after his lectures, the entire intellectual world of Yerevan knows how you met."

As we chatted with Isabeghian, Shahen brought over an intriguing looking individual with a goatee. He was the film director Sergei Parajanov who, like some Armenians in the Soviet Union, had Russianized his name (originally Sarkis Parajanian) for easier acceptance outside Armenia. He too referred to Shahen's lectures and asked if we had seen his most recent film entitled "Shadows of Forgotten Ancestors." I explained that in Hungary Soviet films were not popular and therefore not well publicized. Nevertheless, the title was not familiar to me. Parajanov said that in some countries the title had been shortened and changed to "Fiery Horses," but that too rang no bells, though I promised to make every effort to see it.*

Parajanov said, with a pleasing modesty, that the film had won nine gold medals at film festivals. As we spoke, others joined our group,

---

*I eventually saw the film in 1969 at the Circle Theatre in Washington and several more times in 1980 and, thereafter, when it was shown on PBS. I found it a film of visual beauty and cinematic originality, dealing with the love story of an ill-fated couple from a lost tribe in the Ukraine.

filling in gaps in the conversation. In this manner we learned, for instance, that Parajanov had had difficulties with the Ministry of Culture in Moscow after he had begun work on a new film entitled "Kievian Frescoes," employing a surrealistic technique which the Ministry had found beyond its comprehension. (A later source who had seen some of the rushes told us that in his view the film would have been a trail-blazer, but verged on the pathological.) The Ministry, after reviewing that portion of the film which had already been shot, killed the project and Parajanov was crushed.

He then told us of yet another project, a film on Charles Aznavour, the French-Armenian singer-actor, who had visited Armenia just one year before and a great favorite there. To begin the film, Parajanov said, he had requested to go to Paris but was turned down. Thoroughly dejected at getting apparently nowhere, Parajanov said he was now planning another film on the life of Sayat-Nova, the 18th century Armenian lyric troubadour.* I wished him luck and we walked away. When I asked one of the group who had told us about the problems with the Ministry whether Parajanov's problems were in any way traceable to officials in Armenia, the reply came back like a shot—"Definitely not in Armenia."

Meanwhile, as we worked our way through the thicket of people, Shahen kept bringing more and more cultural figures over to us. One of them, Lavinia Pashbeyuk-Melikian, daughter of one of the grand old Armenian painters, was the first to invite us to her studio. Many more did afterwards.

Another painter who stands out in memory because of his innate modesty and pleasant demeanor was Hagop Hagopian. He had repatriated to Armenia from Egypt only four years before. When he, too, invited us to his studio, Shahen said that if we found the time to go, we would have the added honor of visiting a member of Parliament. Hagopian laughed in embarrassment and said he preferred to be known as a painter.

Shahen told us later that in contrast to the severe conditions which the first repatriates of 1946 encountered, such as he and his family, more recent arrivals were being given preferential treatment, such as

---

*Parajanov did complete this film, entitled "The Color of Pomegranates," a remarkably static but visually gripping depiction of a life comparable to his own for its vicissitudes. The film was drastically censored in Moscow before being sent abroad. In 1974 Parajanov was imprisoned in a labor camp, released in 1978, but reports from Armenia in recent years reveal that after another arrest and release, he is now working on new film projects in Soviet Georgia.

nomination to Parliament, for which they received an additional 50 rubles a month.

Another introduction was for me a special surprise, but which turned into disappointment. We accidentally bumped into and stood facing a gentleman whom at first Shahen seemed to want us to ignore. It was not possible, however, so Shahen introduced him—Mher Abeghian. On hearing the name I started and Shahen answered my questioning look with a nod, saying—"Yes, you heard correctly, the son of Manoog Abeghian" (the great literary historian whose name Rafael Aghayan had not recognized.) Mher was the President of the Armenian Union of Painters, a position of power in the Soviet hierarchy, but as I learned, he shared not one bit of the popularity of his revered father. It soon became evident why: overbearing, arrogant, pompous, he delivered a sermon on the virtues of Armenia, as though a button had been pushed on a hidden tape machine. It was a stupid performance, considering the ambiance, and was finally interrupted by an obviously annoyed Shahen. Mher then turned on Shahen and displayed an almost venomous animosity towards our young friend, which seemed like an overkill reaction to being inter-rupted. In fact, as we learned later, Mher Abeghian was incensed at Shahen for some art criticism he had published a few days before which had attacked many of the tenets of Abeghian and his clique.

We broke away from this unpleasant and unplanned—but revealing—confrontation, only to bump into yet another of that ilk. This time it was a sculptor named Ara Sarkisian, a man in his sixties, and judging from the disapproving looks of many as they noticed our conversation, not popular either. Sarkisian, too, like Abeghian, made no mention of having heard of us, which was another indication that both were outside the pale of the group we were becoming a part of.

Sarkisian asked many questions in a manner which sounded more like an interrogation, and I resented him. Shahen noticed this and we pushed on, again learning from others that Sarkisian was viewed as a "remnant of the past," by which they meant a product of the Stalin era. He had done busts of Stalin, Mikoyan (which we later saw) and Khrushchev, and enjoyed considerable influence in party circles. One artist told us he had heard that Sarkisian, whom he described as an opportunist, was seeking to do a bust of Brezhnev and Kosygin.

Painters, graphic artists, critics—they were all paraded past us, and then Shahen brought over the only government official we were to meet

in our entire stay, the Armenian Deputy Minister of Culture Alexander
Tatevosian. He was a very cordial and delightful person, cheerful and
down to earth. He asked very few questions and extended his best
wishes for a rewarding stay. Shahen told us after that Tatevosian was the
official responsible for allowing him to go to Budapest.

"All right, that's enough for this exhibit," he said, "you've met some
important people already. Now, let's go to another one, not the event this
is, but you'll meet some more there." That exhibit in a nearby gallery
displayed the paintings of Hagop Garalian, an artist who had lived most
of his life in Tbilisi. Shahen explained that Garalian had been shunned
by the cultural authorities until this year when, at the age of 70, he was
finally allowed to exhibit. Ten years earlier, on the eve of his first exhibition, he had suffered a tragedy—most of his work had gone up in smoke
when his studio caught fire.

What we were viewing this day were largely recreations from memory,
although as Shahen pointed out, the initial spark of creativity was no
longer there. Garalian was a pathetic figure even if a large bear of a
man. He wanted to know our Christian names and then addressed us by
them. He exuded a warmth to which we responded; he autographed our
catalogue and followed us around his exhibit of what can accurately if
ironically be called "original reproductions."

Shahen said it was now dinner time as we started to leave, but several
young artists spotted him and engaged him in animated conversation as
we walked on. When he joined us finally, looking exasperated, he
explained that this happened to him everywhere, that artists were always
after him to write critiques of their work. We had to hear from others,
however, of the relative level of importance of our friend in the art world,
he being too modest to tell us himself. Shahen Khatchaturian was in fact
the foremost art critic in Armenia whose articles could grant recognition
to unknowns, as well as put down those who were in favor because of old
party ties. It was now quite obvious why Shahen had brought us to this
second and far less important exhibit—he wished to acknowledge not only
Garalian for his work but for the tribulations he had endured.

I looked at our friend with renewed warmth and affection and then
invited him to dine with us and to select a restaurant. His face broke
into a broad and knowing smile as he said the invitation was most kind,
but that his mother would be offended inasmuch as she had prepared a
real Armenian table for us.

XXV

THE KHATCHATURIANS LIVED ON *BROSHYAN* STREET, which is lined with houses built privately by repatriated Armenians. Neither the street nor the houses are particularly attractive, most of them with cinder block exteriors made from the special kind of porous rock peculiar to Armenia, *tufa*—a pink-colored deposit of mineral springs. Shahen's house consisted of four rooms, plus a bathroom and kitchen. Living there were Shahen, his mother and father, his brother, sister-in-law and their two children. It was modestly furnished and seemed roomy enough for them. Shahen said the government granted loans of 3,000 rubles payable within ten to fifteen years at very low rates of interest. The house could have as many rooms as space and materials allowed.

While we waited for dinner, Roseann and I went to Shahen's room lined with art books. He put on an Aznavour record and served us some *Egri Bikaver* (Bull's Blood), the famous Hungarian red wine a bottle of which he had brought back from his trip. He showed us a copy of the brochure from the exhibit *Architecture, USA,* which he had visited in Leningrad when he had to once make a trip to the *Hermitage.*

This seemed the right moment to give him our gifts which we had picked up at the hotel once we knew we would be going to his home. I gave him the brochure from the *Industrial Design* exhibit we had visited in Leningrad and a copy of the current *Ameryka* magazine. Roseann took out some trinkets and a carton of American cigarettes, since we had noticed in Budapest that he was a chain smoker.

Shahen's pleasure and excitement to these small things was evident, and grew even more as I gave him a compact volume on American contemporary painting. But when I unwrapped the major gift—David Douglas Duncan's *Picasso's Picassos*—his jaw dropped, he let out a howl and hugged both of us. His joy was a joy to behold. He picked up the huge book, embraced it, opened it at random, laughed uncontrollably, then said—"This is the only copy in Armenia. Every one of my friends will treasure it. Edward, you must inscribe it," which I did. Shahen raised the heavy book close to his eyes, read the inscription, looked at us and his eyes filled with tears.

Shahen's aged mother's entrance could not have been better timed as she announced that dinner was ready. It was truly an Armenian dinner, and we relished every morsel, knowing that great effort had gone into putting it together and preparing it. We began with *madzoon aboor* (yoghurt soup); then *derevi dolma* (grapeleaves stuffed with rice); *hav* with *pilaf* made from *bulgur* (chicken with cracked wheat); *fasoulya, domates, bamiya* (string beans, tomatoes, okra); *lavash* (Armenian bread); *yeghednadzor* (white local cheese); a variety of fruits, in which Armenia abounds; and finally, coming after a local red wine, the famous Armenian cognac, imbibed where it was made, "in the homeland."

The cognac stirred memories of an outdoor repast on the shores of an East German lake which I quickly squelched, realizing, however, that some of the images called forth were still vivid.

Dinner was served by Shahen's sister-in-law, Serpoohi, a sweet, shy woman who always lowered her eyes when addressed. Just then the doorbell rang and Shahen's father entered, a jovial man who embraced us as his own, and said that from all he knew about our reception of Shahen in Budapest we were more than welcome in his home.

A few moments later, Serpoohi's father arrived, slightly bent, weather-beaten, somehow avoiding our eyes, but with a small smile on his lips. His name was Boghos Varjabedian, and the story I drew out of him held us in thrall for the next two hours. He spoke with deliberation, taking his time to accurately describe the ordeal he and his family had experienced. Occasionally, when he grew silent, as though reliving the past, Shahen would intervene with just the right connecting thought.

Boghos was born in the small village of *Palou* in Central Turkey. This was already an astonishing coincidence because that is precisely where my father was born. In fact, as Boghos went on, I had the impression of hearing my own father's history, especially when Boghos related how at the height of the Turkish massacres of 1895, his father was murdered in front of his eyes, exactly as my father at the age of six had witnessed his own father's murder. When the massacres came to a temporary halt, only a handful of Armenians were left in *Palou,* living in constant fear of assault, robbery and death. Among the survivors were Boghos and the woman he later married in 1929, Serpoohi's mother.

After marriage, Boghos decided to leave *Palou,* where they lived in abject poverty in a village depopulated of Armenians, and moved to Syria.

"In Syria," he explained, "we also lived in poverty, but at least the Turks weren't at our throats."

In 1946, impoverished and desperate, Boghos heard of the announcements by the Soviet Government of its program of repatriation. Serpoohi and her brother had already been born, so this family of four heeded the call of the homeland and joined the tens of thousands who went to Armenia.

What greeted them was totally unexpected. Instead of the welcome they anticipated, they were met with hostility and often open brutality. They received barely enough to eat, no clothing at all, and were not provided shelter. They remained in the railroad station for nineteen days, frequently soaked through by the rain.

"I have taken quite a bit in my life," he said with an ironic smile, "but this was too much. After all, it was Armenians doing it to Armenians."

So Boghos, like some of the others, began to grumble, then openly to complain. One day, he and his family were told to hastily pack their belongings and then were forced onto freight cars and taken to a very distant place.

"It took a very long time, I don't know how many days, they were all like one great nightmare. One thing I was sure of—the homeland was far behind us."

The train finally came to a halt and everyone disembarked, hungry, dirty and in despair. Not informed where they were, they had to learn by asking everyone they saw: they were in the territory of *Altai,* not far from the town of *Barnaul.*

"We were in Siberia," Boghos said gently.

Everyone was put to work, strenuous manual labor for the whole family. They lived a spartan life and while they no longer had to fear Turks, they were still not in their homeland, even though they did not lack for Armenian company.

I ventured my first question—How many Armenians were there all together? The reply came not from Boghos but from the shy Serpoohi, as though to temporarily ease the burden for her father—"Sixty thousand," she replied, looking up quickly and then, her eyes lowered, bending her head down. I addressed the next question to her—What were the conditions like? "Unbearable," she said succinctly. I did not wish this recital of such a gruelling period of their lives to affect them and even caught a fleeting warning glance from Roseann, so I asked only one more question—what was the single worst thing?

Serpoohi took that one as well—"The cold. At times it was more than 40 degrees below zero." She was talking Celsius, of course.

We were all silent, then Boghos, realizing that the story had to be brought up to date, continued in the soft tones he had used from the beginning.

"In 1956, we were told we could return if we wanted to. We had been there for ten years. We decided to return."

I couldn't restrain myself from one final question—In ten years, no matter where one is, somehow he adjusts, develops roots, surely even in Siberia. Together with all those thousands of Armenians they must have made a life for themselves, so why did they return?

Boghos, descendant of a nation persecuted as few others in history, nodded, understanding my question, then with a wise smile said—"We are Armenians, and Armenians belong in Armenia."

I sat transfixed, digesting all that we had heard. Looking at this gentle, modest man who had suffered so much since childhood, I could understand why he found his present life so tolerable, comfortable and secure. Having been born with so little and living in constant fear, finally here in Armenia after the initial hardships, he had found peace and a life with his loved ones.

And I had found courage such as I had never experienced. No rancor, no bitterness, no recriminations. Roseann and I were overcome. Boghos was my father's age and up to a certain date, their fates had been identical. Syria had been the only escape hatch and my father too had gone there, but then westward, working his way to the United States. Had he not, destiny may very well have taken us in the same direction as Boghos and his family.

Shahen broke the silence and began talking about conditions since 1956, when Khrushchev had smashed the idol that was Stalin and revealed him to be a cruel tyrant, murderer and madman, whose policies were responsible for dispatching the Boghoses and Serpoohis to such incredible fates. The status of Armenia and Armenians today must be understood in context, Shahen argued, not in terms of western ideas of freedom and democracy, but in the context of survival with dignity.

I continued looking at Boghos and was overcome with the emotion of the moment—in Soviet Armenia, in an Armenian home, with a survivor of the notorious camps, who, after a life of incomprehensible suffering, could look me in the eyes with a smile of resignation. Roseann and I felt a profound affinity for him and his daughter.

After returning from Siberia, Boghos' family was reunited with Shahen's, and his brother and Serpoohi married and found a home in the present house which Shahen and his father built. There seemed to be no problems of any kind for any of them. Shahen now stood up and announced that the day was not yet over and that a marvelous experience awaited us. I said anything that came after this afternoon would be an anti-climax. We took our leave of these superb human beings, knowing we could never forget them, and outside Shahen said he hoped our afternoon had not been spoiled by these tragic stories. He knew very well that on the contrary, our souls had been enriched by such affirmation of the human spirit.

Shahen hailed a taxi outside the house as he had done from the art exhibit. It was not quite that, however. During our stay in Armenia, we travelled within Yerevan frequently in an odd way. One of our companions would flag a passing car and reach agreement on the fare. Once in the car and our identities clarified, the driver would fire endless questions about the United States and the life of Armenians there. Many taxi drivers did the same, and when on a few occasions I told them of our initial experience at the airport, they became furious and asked for a description of the bald driver and his cab number, which I didn't know.

We arrived at the hotel to freshen up, Shahen still keeping our appointment a secret. Once in the lobby again, we learned what it was—a visit with the painter Mardiros Saryan, whose exhibit in Budapest had been responsible for having brought us together. I knew it to be a rare experience, for the 86-year-old artist had little time for strangers, and the few he saw sometimes were victims of his acerbic wit. Saryan simply did not suffer fools. We caught another passing car and on the way Shahen told us that one of Saryan's two sons, Sarkis, had been killed in a car accident barely two years ago, and it had affected the old artist visibly.

The car stopped at *Moskovian Street* 41 where a large three-story building housed the Saryan dwelling and a soon-to-be-completed museum devoted to his works. The stooped, white-haired artist himself greeted us at the door, embracing both of us with the words—"I know all about you, who you are, where you met our dear Shahen, and I welcome you to our home." We were overwhelmed as the patriarch led us through his neat and orderly home and into his studio. "I have been working on a portrait of our composer Alexander Spendiarian," he said waving towards his easel, explaining that he had known the composer, who died in 1928, but was refreshing his memory from a photograph.

Saryan revealed an agile mind and a winning sense of humor. He poked fun at everyone and everything, seemed to take life lightly. Would we like to go upstairs where he kept his most treasured paintings? We certainly would, and he led the way with no difficulty up the stairs. There, we stood before a series of portraits of Armenian writers, artists, musicians, intellectuals, and above all, paintings of his beloved Armenian countryside, drenched in the golden oils of the brilliant Armenian sunlight.

Saryan began to talk of the Armenian past as we looked at the portraits. "Under the Turks it was bad enough," he said in his aged but firm voice, "but did we have to continue to suffer even after establishing a homeland? Oh, those persecutions! That period in 1936 and 1937. What we lost! Look here."

He picked up a portrait of a mutilated face—"This is Kamsarakan,"* and raising his voice, "look at what those sons of bitches did to him. And to them," he identified portraits of Yeghishe Charentz and Aksel Bakuntz, "our greatest sons of Armenia, tortured or killed by Stalin and Beria. Georgians? Russians? *Who are our friends?*" The studio rang with the echo of his cries; we silent, mesmerized. He began to talk of Stalin, of his personal problems with the dictator—

"He disliked me, even though I brought no dishonor to our country. The answer may be that he disliked me because he disliked all Armenians. I never kept silent about injustice and I never shall. But they, they were all monsters who destroyed people who spoke out."

Saryan was in disfavor from 1937 until 1950 and not fully acknowledged until after Stalin's death in 1953, he said. "How I was saved from the fate of these great men"—pointing to the portraits—"I don't know. I certainly did not speak out less than they. But when Stalin died, the whole Armenian nation could breathe again. That is why Khrushchev will always live for us. He exposed that monster and his evil deeds."

I spoke up for the first time—where was Mikoyan during this time?

*A former art critic and, like Shahen, Director of the National Art Gallery.

Saryan laughed sardonically—"My dear Edward, you must not say *Mik*oyan. You must call him what I call him—*Mook*oyan. (In Armenian, *mook* means mouse.) I went to see him officially in the 1930s to complain of what was happening to our people. He received me in his fancy office in Moscow, listened to what I had to say on behalf of the Armenian people, then suddenly stood up and began shouting at me. I was so taken aback I was speechless. I can't even remember any more what he said, but I knew that I never wanted to talk to him again, and I haven't."

After a few moments, he led us to a window of the studio and pointed to *Mt. Ararat,* graceful and elegant in the distance, and figuring very prominently in many of his paintings. With mock anger he said—"Look at them down there, they now want to deprive me of my beloved mountain. They are building a New York in front of my windows." He explained that a high-rise apartment house was in the process of construction which would obstruct his view of *Mt. Ararat.*

"You know," he continued, a twinkle in his eye, "the Turks want that mountain but it is ours. After I had designed our national emblem, a Turk asked me one day why I had put in *Ararat* since it didn't belong to Armenia. I told him that the Turks had put a crescent in their flag even though they didn't own the moon."

He escorted us downstairs into another room to meet Loosig, his wife. As we went, Shahen whispered that she was dying of cancer, and in fact she was in bed, her face reflecting her pain. Nevertheless, she sat up, said the entire Budapest episode was known to her, welcomed us warmly and ordered Shahen to make some coffee and bring some fruit. Roseann insisted that nothing be done and that we were only staying a few minutes. Mrs. Saryan became agitated at that, so we stayed longer, as she and Roseann conversed.

Saryan continued talking to me about the hostility towards Armenians—

"Those people up north, the way they look down on us! We, who made Christianity our religion in the year 301 before any other people, we who had an alphabet in 406. We should be looking down on them. Every time I hear them refer to us as *armyashka,* I boil." Shahen explained that *armyashka* was a Russian term of contempt for Armenians.

The doorbell rang and two youngish men entered and were greeted by Saryan and Shahen as Roseann and I took leave of Mrs. Saryan. One was Seyran Khatlamajian, a painter who had recently changed his home from Rostov to Yerevan. Seyran, who later tagged along with us all over town, seemed obsessed with the work of Arshile Gorky, the *avant-garde* American-Armenian painter.*

The other new arrival was Wilhelm Matevosian, an intriguing person and personality who described himself as a philosopher, aesthetician and literary critic. He had a lively mind and his language sparkled as he acted out his thoughts, displaying a remarkable range of vocabulary. At one point Saryan referred to him as "a thinker of genius," which amused Matevosian who added, his index finger pointed upwards, eyebrows elevated—"a genius of the highest possible degree," to our general amusement.

I asked Matevosian how an Armenian gets a name like Wilhelm—we later met a Rudolf and a Henrik—and he replied that this was an attempt on the part of Armenian parents to make their children more cosmopolitan, after the centuries of suffering by their progenitors for being Armenian.

"Actually Wilhelm isn't so bad," he said, "what do you think of Hamlet, Macbeth, Desdemona, or Shakespeare. These are Christian names widespread in Armenia."

We chatted briefly of the popularity of Shakespeare's plays and I asked whether Vahram Papzian's much-touted portrayal of Othello was still going strong. Wilhelm looked at me curiously, then replied that Papzian's characterization was known throughout the Soviet Union. I then asked if it might be possible to meet with the poet Khachig Dashdentz—the only request of this nature I made. Wilhelm's curiosity was now fully aroused and he asked how I would know about Papazian and Dashdentz, suggesting neither was a household name in the United States.

I explained that in the late 1950s I had written a series of articles on various aspects of Soviet Armenian life, among them one entitled "Shakespeare's Plays in Armenia" for the *Shakespeare Quarterly,* and knew from my research that Dashdentz had begun the major project of translating every one of the plays into Armenian. Wilhelm said he would look for the article in the archives and if not there would write to the

---

*Gorky's real name was Vosdanig Manoog Adoian. Born in Turkish Armenia, he was one of the pioneers in abstract expressionism of the New York School. Unable to withstand several personal tragedies, he took his own life in 1948, his fame spreading only after his death at the age of 44.

Library in Washington. (He later sent word that Dashdentz was unfortunately out of the country.)

We had, meanwhile, returned to Saryan's studio and Wilhelm went to a pile of paintings stacked against the wall and extracted a portrait of John Steinbeck, who had visited Armenia in 1964. "There is another great writer, a man of steel," he said holding the portrait high for all to see, "it is one of the Master's best." (Saryan was addressed by everyone as Master—*Varbed*—and we too fell into the habit.) It was indeed an excellent likeness. Wilhelm added—"We respect Steinbeck here tremendously."

I asked if the series of articles Steinbeck had written defending the American involvement in Vietnam was known to them. Wilhelm nodded. And did they also know of poet Evgeny Evtushenko's reply to those articles?

Wilhelm paced up and down, his shoulders hunched, then turned to me—

"Steinbeck should never have replied to Evtushenko. It wasn't at all necessary. That Steinbeck! What a fine man. He sat right where you're sitting."

Wilhelm did not seem interested in pursuing the matter of Steinbeck's political judgment, and returning the portrait to the pile, selected another—William Saroyan. "And here is *our* William," he said proudly.

"At present, he is the rage with our youth. His play 'My Heart's In The Highlands' just opened and every performance is sold out. William is a true artist, and he made a tremendous hit with all of us when he visited. We took him everywhere.

"Once we held an open meeting with some of our leading figures, and he offered to answer any and all questions. Several were asked of a more or less regular nature to which he gave almost predictable answers. Then, one man stood up and cried out—'Mr. Saroyan, *what* do you like?'"

Wilhelm here imitated the questioner, both arms extended outward, face lifted in anticipation, noting—"We understood the question only one way—in this whole wide world, what very special thing pleases you more than anything?"

"'I like watermelon!' Saroyan replied and the audience roared its appreciation."

So did we in Saryan's studio, laughing hard at mention of this most indigenously Armenian of fruits by the most famous Armenian writer in the western world. Wilhelm said Saroyan could say and do nothing wrong after that.

"Think of all the things he might have said," Wilhelm still laughing, suggested, "chess, jazz, Shakespeare, football, girls, but no, like the true son of Armenia he is, William said watermelon (*tsumeroog*). We'll never forget him," all present as well as the Master nodding in agreement.

By now it was clear that Wilhelm held some kind of senior status in the intellectual community, and we noted that both the Master and Shahen seemed to defer to him. Wilhelm asked if most Armenians in the United States had retained their cultural heritage as Saroyan had, and whether they had any serious problems.

I said that both questions could be answered in the affirmative, the second not for any other reason than that they were Armenians and, therefore, created their own problems. All smiled in recognition of the familiar phenomenon, especially in the diaspora, as I listed the problems, headed by opposing political parties, dissension in the Church, in some instances even feuds the origins of which had been long since forgotten. Nevertheless, I continued, there is a younger generation which is making heroic attempts to overcome past divisive rivalries and to achieve *collective strength.*

"Many do not know who Yeghishe Charentz was, but they are heeding his message," I said, looking straight at Wilhelm. It was a risk I thought worth taking especially since the martyred poet had been fully rehabilitated. Wilhelm's piercing glance seemed radiant and in that brief moment I knew that across the gulf of geography, history and perhaps ideology which separated us, we were joined then and there in Mardiros Saryan's studio.

We remained silent, but Armenians have an expression, "blood talks," which obviated the need for words. It was a fleeting moment but one of burning intensity and communication. The silence was finally broken by Wilhelm who complimented Roseann and me on the quality of our Armenian which he thought proved my point about retention of the heritage. "Oh that old enemy of the Armenian people, assimilation," he said shaking his head.*

---

*In the Middle East Armenians refer to assimilation as "the white massacre," as opposed to the Turkish decimation known simply as "the massacres."

It was now 10 PM and we had been on the go since early morning
and feeling it. The farewells took yet another half hour as though none
of us wanted to part, most of all the Master. He padded around after us,
holding us tightly by the arm, calling us repeatedly by our Christian
names for the sake of hearing them, his halo-like white hair giving him
the appearance of a Biblical ancient. He walked out to the sidewalk with
us and spun around as though struck by a new idea, which he was—
"But you haven't met my son and his wife. Come with me, they are only
next door."

We all went to the adjoining house, almost as large as the Master's,
occupied by his surviving son, Lazaros, a composer, and his wife. both
were home and insisted we stay, but we were exhausted. I asked what
he was working on and Lazaros said a violin concerto. Wilhelm saw a
book that he had written about the Master lying on a table and suggested he and the Master inscribe it to us, which they did. We then took
our leave a second time and though Wilhelm said he would catch up
with us later in our stay, we unfortunately did not again see this fascinating individual. As for Mardiros Saryan, this, too, was to be our only
meeting, the sadness of our parting tempered by the hope that we might
see him again.*

Once outside now and joined by Seyran, the indefatigable Shahen said
we must be hungry and that on the way to the restaurant we could make
a fast visit to the *Matenadaran*—the famed and fabled museum reposi-
tory of ancient manuscripts. Roseann and I looked at each other hope-
lessly, resigned to no sleep at all that night. At that hour, the museum
was of course not open, but Shahen's authority became clear when after
speaking privately to the two guards at the main entrance, the doors
were opened and we entered the imposing building which looks down on
the Armenian capital.

I know of no other manuscript museum anywhere to equal what we
saw. The *Matenadaran* contains 10,000 manuscripts and 4,000 frag-
ments, essentially dealing with Armenian philosophy, history, mathemat-
ics, the sciences and countless works of literature. One can find
palimpsests, miniatures and one rarity—an Indian manuscript consisting

---

*Showered with honors in the Soviet Union and Western Europe, Saryan lived to see the
opening of his museum in Yerevan and died in 1972 at the age of 92.

of palm leaves. While the bulk of its contents is of Armenian origin dating back to the 5th century, the *Matenadaran* includes some 1,000 manuscripts in Persian, Arabic, Syriac, Latin and many other languages. If any one feature of this remarkable place struck me as having universal value, it was the existence in Armenian translations of works in other languages whose originals were lost. In this category are works by the Greek philosophers Zeno, Hermes, Trismegistus and Aristides, as well as Theon, Philo Judaeus and Dionysius—the last three from Alexandria. In fact, Greek philosophy was a major preoccupation of 5th and 6th century Armenian scholars who translated the major works of Aristotle, all of which are available in the museum in three hundred separate manuscripts. Our heads were buzzing when we finally emerged from this incredible treasure house, only to hear the guards recommend that we return to the *Matenadaran* during daylight hours.

We walked up still higher, onto the cliff above the museum and now stood looking down on a stunning view of Yerevan at night. Shahen and Seyran showed us a pedestal on which had stood the largest statue of Stalin in the Soviet Union, knocked down in 1956, they said, with great jubilation after Khrushchev's revelations of the dictator's crimes. I had at that instant a fleeting recollection of Rafael Aghayan pointing to a screen in East Berlin to inform me that in the film we were viewing, the 60-foot bronze statue was still standing.

We ended the long day with a fast meal at a restaurant which was on the verge of closing. Although we were just about talked out, Seyran continued to ply me with questions about the life and art of Arshile Gorky, about whom I think I learned more from his questions than he from me.

Returning to the hotel after agreeing to an early morning pickup, Roseann and I fell into our beds but could not sleep as we reviewed this first full day in Armenia—the visit to *Etchmiadzin*, the art exhibits, the intellectuals, the dinner at Shahen's home, Boghos' harrowing story of survival in Siberian labor camps, the hours with Mardiros Saryan, the *Matenadaran*—and all the fascinating things between.

We wondered how anything could surpass that first day.

XXVI

S HAHEN CALLED FOR US EARLY ON MONDAY MORNING
with the news that he had been able to postpone his departure for
Rostov. It was a stunning June day and he suggested we make an outing to *Keghart,* the 13th century church hewn out of solid rock.

On the road to *Keghart,* Shahen proposed making a brief stop which,
as he put it, "will be of special interest to you." We left the car and
approached a nearby hill on which was a slight structure.

"I have observed your awareness of Charentz, especially in his more
esoteric aspects," he said, obviously alluding to my comments in
Saryan's studio. "I think it appropriate that you see this small tribute
erected after his rehabilitation. It is called the Arch of Charentz."

I was moved, both by Shahen's consideration and by this modest
memorial to the great poet who in his living and dying personified so
much the tragedy of Armenia, and whose legacy to his people was the
injunction to simply stick together. Roseann and I stood under the Arch
as though on hallowed ground.

I have never been much for memorizing poetry, in any language, outside of remembering famous phrases from classical poets. But there is
one poem by Charentz which epitomizes his love of native land and
which is ingrained in the mind of anyone who is familiar with him and
his fate. The opening words now surfaced as I mumbled—*"Yes im anush
hayastan."* This paean to Armenia had just been published twelve years
after Charentz's rehabilitation in 1955, in a booklet I found in Yerevan
which contains this famous poem in thirteen languages. This is the
English version:

> I love the sun-savoring word of my sweet Armenia,
> The sad, plaintive chord of our ancient lute, I love;
> The blood-red flowers and the burning scent of roses,
> And the soft supple dance of our maids, I love.
>
> I love our sombre sky, the clear waters, the lighted lake,
> The summer sun and the howling winter sublime,

The black uninviting walls of shacks lost in darkness
And the thousand-year-old stones of ancient cities, I love.

Wherever I may be—I shall never forget our mournful songs,
I shall not forget our iron-lettered books, turned prayer;
However deeply our blood-drenching wounds pierce my heart—
Orphaned and bleeding—I still love my beloved Armenia.

For my homesick heart there is no other tale,
No hallowed brow like Narek's and Kouchak's;
Tour the world: there is no summit as white as Ararat's,
As an unreachable peak of glory I love my Mount Massis.

Lost in translation are Charentz's imagery, alliteration and the many intriguing devices of superb poetry. But the thought is there.

Shahen snapped some pictures of us with my camera, after which we resumed our drive to *Keghart,* some thirty minutes away, with only one delay when a large flock of sheep blocked the road.

The church stands in the middle of a desolate part of the country and is surrounded by cliffs on which are sculpted artifacts unique to Armenia—stone crosses. Known as *khatchkars,* the crosses date back to the 9th century and were thought to protect the people from external enemies.

Because we were getting hungry Shahen went into the home of the priest and emerged with native cheese and *lavash* bread. As we devoured this delicacy, a group of teen-age girls on a school outing discovered us and soon they were devouring Roseann—the first female American they had ever met who, as they noted, even spoke Armenian. The questions about America and teen-age life there filled another hour before we finally got back into our car and returned to Yerevan.

At the hotel I told Lina Stepanian that Intourist of Armenia was missing out in not publicizing the ancient attractions which easily paralleled some of the better-known antiquities of Rome and Greece. Lina inclined her head sadly and rubbed her thumb and forefinger together in the age-old gesture connoting money.

In Yerevan, Shahen took us to the Literary Museum and introduced us to the curator with the words—"When I tell you her name you will know whose daughter she is." The attractive woman's father was the famed philologist Hrachia Adjarian, whom I had mentioned earlier to Rafael

Aghayan. As we left the museum I said to Shahen that while museums and ruins were worth seeing, nothing compared to meeting people which Roseann and I found most enjoyable. He replied that he had already set up a series of visits with various artists whose work he valued and who were apparently anxious to meet us. One artist in particular, he said, was presently out of Yerevan but would return before our departure and with whom a meeting was absolutely imperative. He identified the painter as Minas Avetisian, about whom we were to hear often, always mentioned by his first name only.

The first of the meetings took place that same Monday—with Rudolf Khatchaturian, no relation to Shahen or the composer Aram. We went to Rudolf's apartment where he lived with his wife and little daughter. Rudolf's parents had come from Turkey in the 1920s to Yerevan, where he was born. For almost forty years, they all lived in one room, four persons after another son was born.

"We resented those who were repatriated after the war," Rudolf said in front of his close friend Shahen, from whom we had already heard this, "at a time when we didn't have enough to eat and the housing situation was absolutely dreadful."

Then came new construction, such as the building in which we found ourselves, for which his family had to wait eight years. The apartment, which was immaculately clean, was 75 square meters in area, for which Rudolf would normally have had to pay only seven rubles a month. But because the state had also given him an artist's studio of almost equal size one floor above, the top floor, he had to pay thirty rubles.

We later visited the studio and found it wonderfully light and airy. Rudolf said that in Armenia, families up to four persons received apartments of two rooms, plus kitchen and bath, such as he enjoyed. Five or more persons received three-room apartments. (All told, we visited four such apartments, but in each one, family activity seemed to center around the kitchen table since there was no other place to lounge or relax.)

Rudolf had been eyeing both of us very closely and though I could understand his attraction to Roseann, I found myself receiving equal attention. This became clear when Shahen, having noticed his friend's preoccupation, said with a laugh—"All right, Rudolf, which one for the portrait." Fortunately for posterity Rudolf selected Roseann, but we decided that there wasn't enough time and agreed he could execute it the next day. As we were leaving, Rudolf turned to Shahen—"Is Minas back yet? They've got to meet him." Shahen shook his head but said it was high on the agenda. Then Rudolf said to me—"Even if you have to delay your departure, wait for Minas." It certainly aroused our curiosity. We were beginning to think of Minas as a cult figure.

In the afternoon we met another of Shahen's friends, an apparently gifted young violinist named Jean der Mergerian. Jean's family had been repatriated from Marseilles, and in Armenia his talents had developed to the degree that during a concert in Moscow, he had been praised by visiting American violinist Isaac Stern. Jean idolized Stern—

"Isaac Stern came to Yerevan not long ago and gave a recital, and after the concert I went backstage and congratulated him on his performance. And do you know what this great artist said to me? 'That's very nice of you but perhaps only you know that I played badly in the first part.' Can you imagine such honesty?"

Stopping off at a sidewalk cafe for refreshment and a rest between visits, Shahen, Rudolf, Seyran and we were talking animatedly, when I noticed an uncommonly well-dressed elderly gentleman with a broad-brimmed black felt hat worn at a rakish angle sitting a few tables away. Shahen saw my curious glance and asked if I recognized him, and when I shook my head he said—"That is Gostan Zarian."

I was astonished to hear the name of perhaps the foremost Armenian writer in the western world, and one never associated with left-wing politics.

"But he lives in Italy," I said, and Shahen corrected me—"He did but now he lives in Armenia. On turning 80, he decided that he wished to spend the last years of his life in the homeland. He came on his own terms, lives as he pleases, travels back and forth, visits his daughter, a sculptress in Italy. He also speaks his mind, but the authorities leave him alone. Let's go over and meet him."

Shahen went first and spoke briefly with the distinguished writer who arose as we approached and invited us to sit at his table. The paper he was reading was *L'Unita,* the organ of the Italian Communist Party. We talked for about thirty minutes with Zarian, revered in the Armenian world of letters but little known beyond.* It was from Zarian that we learned the

---

*Except for appreciative colleagues such as Lawrence Durrell, Marc Chagall and Picasso. The letter and spirit of his works have been captured in splendid English translations by Ara Baliozian.

Soviet Government had broken diplomatic relations with Israel, t. gary was expected to also, and that Israel had won what was to ....ic known as the Six-Day War. I realized then how removed we had been from world events, and that the portable radio we had brought was seldom turned on primarily because I was hardly ever at the hotel.

Zarian said he was concerned that the Middle East would turn into a second Vietnam. I noted that Israel was a good example to Armenians of a small nation, persecuted over the centuries, now independent and fighting for survival. Zarian did not disagree but said the Turks made all the difference in Armenian history. In stating this he at one point used the Armenian word for minority. I asked if that was a commonly used word in the Soviet Union. Zarian said it was on occasion, why did that interest me?

I related an experience with a Soviet diplomat in Budapest wherein he had spoken proudly of the great role Russians played in the Soviet Union where they were the majority and every other nationality a minority. I had replied that that was all highly relative because in Armenia, it was the Russians who were the minority.

Zarian liked that and burst into hearty laughter, even applauding. We arose, bade him good health and farewell, and as we walked away I turned for a final look at the elegant figure with the wide-brimmed black hat, the heavy-rimmed tortoise shell glasses, the bow tie and the vested grey suit— an incongruity, this western-oriented gentleman-artist living out his final years in a communist society. I waved from a distance and he, still standing, waved back, affectionately, it seemed to me.

We were already vastly impressed by the level and variety of Shahen's circle of friends and deeply aware of our good fortune in having met him in Budapest. The enlightened conversations with all of them would fill far more pages than the essential story to be told here allows. But one more on this day must be repeated for its impact.

Henrik Igitian was a colleague of Shahen's at the Art Gallery and like Shahen an art critic and the author of several books. He insisted we visit him in his apartment, very similar to Rudolf's and for which he, too, had waited eight years. Henrik wanted us to see his art collection which consisted primarily of Soviet and French-Armenian painters, such as Garzou.* Again we sat at the table in the kitchen and discussed art and

---

*Shortened from his full name Garnik Zouloumian. The artist had visited Armenia just eight months before about which his wife wrote a book in France.

criticism. But within minutes Henrik had switched to the Vietnam war and said that America was admired everywhere in Armenia, but Vietnam was something else—

"It is not worthy of America that you are destroying women and children. A small nation . . ." his voice trailed off as he looked pointedly at me.

I could not reply with what was truly in my heart: that the war was not only unpopular in the United States but with me as well; that a Budapest mob had burned President Johnson's effigy and the American flag on the sidewalk in front of us; that ironically I had just missed injury by a jagged rock thrown at me in protest against a war I too opposed. Instead, I took cover in the rejoinder that while a side of the war not reported by the Soviet media might give him better perspective, why didn't we let history decide, and he accepted the stand-off.

That same evening we strolled through the streets of Yerevan, eight of us: Shahen, Seyran, Rudolf and his wife, Henrik and his wife and the two of us, everyone hailing friends and announcing our visit to one and all. It was during this lengthy period of walking when we would sometimes pair off that I found myself with Henrik. He asked if I was impressed with what I had seen of Armenia. I confessed that it was the people with whom I felt most engaged, the people and of course the antiquities, but that to go beyond would get us into politics.

Henrik replied that he had only one purpose in asking me that—

"Edward, this is your native land. Why do you waste your time in a foreign country. You are a native son. We desperately need help. Come here and work for the fatherland."

He was so gentle that I was not taken aback. Unlike the offer made to me in East Germany, Henrik's appeal was genuine and sincere and on quite another level.

"You don't even know me, Henrik,"

"But I do, I do, better than you think."

I took his arm as we walked ahead of the others and quietly and calmly reviewed my early life, my family, my education, the environment I grew up in, my career, and finally my loyalty to my country and my government, concluding—"One can be a good Armenian and a good American at the same time, and that is the way I have served and shall continue to serve Armenia."

Henrik said no more.

XXVII

A T 10:30 PM SOMEONE SUGGESTED WE VISIT ARTZVIN
Grigorian, one of the best-known architects in Yerevan. Shahen
said the architect owned an excellent private collection, Rudolf noting
proudly that it included three of his paintings. As we approached the
apartment building, one of our company asked if I knew what the Russian letters KGB meant!

I froze, Roseann and I exchanged startled looks and before either of
us could respond, several arms were extended and fingers pointed to a
dark building across the street.

"That is KGB headquarters for Armenia," someone said rather
loudly, to the accompaniment of laughter and several wisecracks. At
that moment, we were directed into an apartment hallway, but
Roseann and I both had the same thoughts—we were in the native
habitat of our friend from East Berlin, in the country he had offered
so many times to bring us. Was he here now? Would he show himself?
If he did, what would we do?

Shahen knocked on a door and our thoughts abruptly returned to the
matter at hand. I looked at my watch, saw it was 11:10 PM, and
expected an irate and reluctant host to open the door. Instead, Artzvin
took one look at the throng on his threshold and welcomed us all in with
a big grin.

Poor Mrs. Grigorian, Roseann murmured to me. The woman was
nursing a baby in the kitchen. She quickly arose and disappeared as her
husband, apologizing for the delay, said it would take a few minutes to
prepare a snack. He promptly did so and everyone began pouring drinks
and gorging on food.

The kitchen walls were covered with paintings, including the three by
Rudolf, which I liked very much. Here and there we saw some ceramics,
which Artzvin said were by his mother, Hripsime Simonian, whose
name I had already heard earlier. She was a distinguished artist about
whom her son presented us with a book. I couldn't suppress the obser-

vation that almost every intellectual in Armenia seemed to be the son or daughter of a famous Armenian. It was very late when we left the Grigorians—and their now well-fed and sleeping baby—and it was decided we should eat again. This turned out catastrophically for Roseann.

In a simple restaurant we all had generous portions of a pizza-like food very popular with Armenians called *lamajoon,* a mixture of beef and lamb, green peppers, tomatoes, parsley and all-spice, all chopped together and spread on Armenian bread rounds. The beverage accompanying it was another Armenian standby called *tahn,* which is yogurt diluted with water.

We were escorted back to our hotel by the entourage in the early hours and soon after retiring, the consequences of our incaution kept us ambulatory until dawn. I recovered enough to rise and dress but Roseann remained in dire straits; nevertheless, she encouraged me to go alone, take advantage of the short time at hand, and not to worry about her. Though I could not help but do so, I was in fact more worried about another problem from which I wanted to spare her.

This day, June 12, was to have been our date of departure for Kiev, where a new connecting flight to Budapest had been announced. Far more urgent, however, was the all-important fact that this was the day our visas ran out. As of midnight, we would be illegally in the Soviet Union, far from the protection of our Embassy in Moscow. The truth of the matter is that my concern also extended to the reaction of the Embassy, which would begin to visualize every kind of intrigue and the burden eventually of a diplomatic incident. I left our room and went down to the lobby.

Lina Stepanian greeted me warmly as I entered her Intourist office.

"Lina, I've got a serious problem," I began and explained my wife's sudden indisposition and the impossibility of making the Kiev connection. Lina's first reaction was to call for a doctor but I said it was not that serious. She then looked up her schedules and informed me that the Kiev-Budapest flights had not yet become operational.

"You would be going to Kiev for nothing, and you're not even Ukrainian," she said light-heartedly, "why not stay here in the homeland and enjoy yourselves and leave the rest to me."

"You don't understand, Lina," I responded realizing that there was no way I could avoid the truth, "our damned visas run out tonight. Can you get me an extension through Intourist?"

At that instant, an idea crossed my mind and I was pleased with myself for having thought of it—"Look, this is supposed to be a sovereign republic with a Ministry for Foreign Affairs.* Can't you get your own Armenian Foreign Ministry to extend my visa?"

Lina looked at me non-committally for some time, finally murmuring—"I'll try, I'll try," in an unconvincing way. Poor Lina, I thought, surely it was the first time anyone visiting Armenia had made such a request. I left her to her devices and went into the lobby filled with no more hope than before. I decided to wait there for Shahen and confront him with my problem.

As I stood facing the elevator doors, they opened revealing two familiar American faces, whose astonishing appearance momentarily dispelled my gloom. They were Ambassador and Mrs. James Penfield, he the senior member of a State Department Inspection Team, currently inspecting our Embassy in Moscow, both of whom we knew because he had performed the same function only three weeks before in Budapest. My loud joyful greeting was reciprocated as I helped them with their baggage.

The Penfields, as inspectors frequently do to familiarize themselves with parts of the country under inspection, had made a trip to the Caucasus for orientation and had spent a few days in Armenia. Because of the highly irregular hours we had been keeping, our paths had not crossed. We sat down now in the lobby as I explained Roseann's illness, and went on to describe some of our adventures, the Penfields incredulous at the depth and intimacy of our encounters.

Finally, I pointed out that Roseann was simply unable to travel, and, in any case, our visas would expire at midnight.

Jim Penfield stared at me, then said with the practiced coolness of the excellent diplomat he was—"Ed, you realize of course that as of midnight, both of you will be in danger and there is nothing the Embassy can do for you until things are sorted out, if they are."

"But there is something *you* can do for us, Jim," I said, another idea having flashed through my mind, as I wondered whether *lamajoon* and

---

*Article 53 of the Constitution of the Armenian Soviet Socialist Republic as amended through July 11, 1947.

tahn—in contrast to the emetic effect on Roseann—had driven me to new heights of ingenuity. "Would you be willing to take our two diplomatic passports back to Moscow where our visas could be extended?"

"Let me understand you, Ed. You are prepared to remain here, deep in the Soviet Union, you and Roseann, *without diplomatic passports?*"

"Yes, I am, because somehow, I don't feel us to be in any danger here. I shall accept full responsibility if something does happen. I know the Embassy will go through the roof, but I have weighed the two possibilities: either holding on to our passports with expired visas, or sending them back with you for extensions. The latter at least legalizes our presence in the Soviet Union, even if we do not have the passports in hand."

A concerned Mrs. Penfield asked whether Roseann was in full agreement with my solution, and I had to admit she didn't even know of the problem—yet. The Penfields had still another fifteen minutes before departing for the airport so after giving them my passport, I went upstairs for Roseann's.

I explained the situation to her and felt a profound sense of love and pride as she said—

"Whatever you think is wise is all right with me. By the way, last night wasn't really that bad. Every time I got up, I could see the twin peaks of *Mt. Ararat* gleaming in the moonlight." Armenia was working its spell on her too.

Downstairs, the Penfields shook hands with me with what seemed extra cordiality and as they boarded the bus and looked back, I had a romantic flash-forward vision of Jim Penfield saying to an archivist of diplomatic disappearances—

"God, I'll never forget that moment. Ed was standing in the lobby looking perfectly content and happy. That's the last time anybody from our side ever saw him—and that was over ten years ago!"

I was jolted back to the present by Shahen who embraced me and asked when Roseann would be joining us. We spent that day without her, Shahen sad because he could no longer postpone his trip to Rostov and was leaving that night.

We decided to confine our activities to the city so that I could periodically look in on Roseann. Two experiences that day stand out.

The first was on a trolley car with Shahen, Rudolf and Seyran, all of whom seemed to know at least one person on the crowded vehicle, especially Shahen. For instance, there was a young man he identified as a champion swimmer with whom he had been teamed earlier, but who had since become a literary critic. "Meet Vache Sarafian," Shahen said as he led me through the crowd to a smiling individual who said—

"Of course, the American diplomat from Budapest who speaks Armenian."

This comment, made loudly above the din of the trolley, was greeted—as Soviet reports often note—with animation. Everyone now strained to hear our conversation. Vache's questions focussed on Armenian life in the United States and frequently touched on dissensions in the Armenian community. He was also interested in the views of American-Armenians towards Soviet Armenia and spoke without inhibition, which I found striking considering the audience.

I sought to avoid any provocative matters, such as Armenian political parties, always an explosive issue, but at one point used the word 'freedom.' Vache repeated the word twice in a declamatory way as though reciting to the audience—

"Freedom, freedom, it means so much to us. I wanted to go to Jerusalem to do some research. No, they told me, that is out of the question, you must stay here. They . . ." he half-shouted over the noise, "they won't let the young ones out. We'll see too much. You know who I mean when I say they? Not *here.*"

Vache turned to Shahen and said something. I overheard Minas's name, at which Shahen turned his palms upwards, indicating emptiness. Vache now said to me—

"Have you heard about Gostan Zarian returning home? Isn't that wonderful! It is an inspiration to us all." At mention of Zarian's name, I saw smiles all around us.

Later that day Shahen led us to an outlying part of Yerevan for a visit with one of Armenia's most revered and gifted sculptors, Yervand Kochar, in his workshop. Kochar was a small man of 68 with blue eyes and curly hair, peppery in spirit, a pipe firmly clenched between his teeth. He was an affectionate man and soon his warmth and exuberance had transferred as much gypsum to my suit as was on his hands.

Kochar was working on a massive figure of the famed Armenian hero Vartan Mamigonian, who had defended Christianity in the fifth century against the Persians. Unlike Ara Sarkisian, the other sculptor we had met, Kochar was adored by the younger intellectuals for his courage and outspokenness during the Stalinist era. His questions to me concerned Armenians in the United States and how they lived.

Then suddenly, in an abrupt switch, he revealed that same dichotomy in the Russian-Armenian relationship I had already witnessed in others—on the one hand, the anger and humiliation of being looked down upon, while on the other, a deep longing for acceptance and respect.

"Shahen," he called out, "did you hear that last week when they showed some Armenian films in Moscow (at an Armenian film festival), the Politburo attended and even Brezhnev applauded. Imagine that, Brezhnev actually applauded an Armenian film. High time they appreciated us instead of calling us *armyashkas*. Let them see what our small nation can do."

Kochar turned to me—"Go back and tell them in America that we are small, we are where we are, but we have spirit and we are not afraid."

Our final embrace covered me with even more gypsum as we left the short bubbling figure of an otherwise very tall man.

I returned to the hotel and found Roseann feeling better, but not quite up to going out. It was close to 5 PM and I suggested we telephone the children in Budapest to brighten her up. We placed the call and relaxed in the foolish expectation it would come through, as the operator said, within the hour.

Meanwhile, Roseann told me amusing stories of the parade of elderly cleaning women who, knowing she was ill, took turns entering and consoling her. Roseann quoted one—"My daughter, don't worry about it. This happens to everyone who comes here. We have a good cure for it," which was to bring endless bottles of soda water, now everywhere in our suite.

I told Roseann that the absent Minas had come up again, to which she responded that this was turning into a one-acter with the title "Waiting for Minas." I agreed but reminded her that neither Godot nor Lefty ever showed up. After two hours I checked on our phone call and learned it would take more time, so I decided to go out again, having arranged to meet Shahen by 8 PM but disappointed I would probably not be talking to the children.

In the lobby I saw Lina waving to me—

"I'm very sorry but our Foreign Ministry cannot help with your visas. However, I have changed your reservations to a Moscow flight tomorrow at noon."

While I was thanking her, a call came through for me from Moscow. I took the call in Lina's office. The opening words sent a cold shiver down my spine—

"Mis-ter Al-ex-an-der, what have you done?"

It was Nancy Dean, our Embassy secretary. Nancy was so conscientious in her job that to hear the admonition and reprimand in her voice was more chilling than if it had come from the Ambassador himself. Lina understood some English but discreetly displayed unawareness of the conversation, though I had nothing to hide from her—or the eavesdroppers on the Embassy lines.

I explained everything to Nancy and that Roseann's illness had precluded our departure for Kiev which, through Lina's good offices, we had learned was pointless since there were no flights as yet to Budapest. To take some of the edge off of Nancy's ire, I added that the Embassy's travel section might have informed us of that non-existent schedule when it first received my travel plans by cable three weeks earlier. That mellowed Nancy who explained that the Embassy was in a dither ever since Ambassador Penfield had brought in our passports. Meanwhile, Nancy said she would arrange for the visa extension, sleeping arrangements in Moscow and departure June 15 for Budapest.

"Are you sure you'll be all right way down there?"

"Nancy, we've never felt more at home." I saw Lina's broad smile as she fussed with papers on her desk. I hung up after thanking Nancy and Lina said—"Your friend Shahen is waiting in the lobby."

I joined him and knowing of my professional interest in music, he suggested we visit the concert hall and opera house. On the way he said that most of the intellectuals we had met, plus some others from the art world, had gathered at his house the previous night—after dropping us off—to examine *Picasso's Picassos.* They had spent most of the night discussing the problems of form, aesthetics and expression, unable to sleep because of their excitement. Shahen said he wished to convey their thanks for the gift, quoting one of them as saying that no artist but Picasso could stir their imagination and no book bring them such inspiration.

We entered the *Spendiarian State Opera and Ballet Theatre,* named after the composer whose portrait was being painted by Mardiros Saryan. In the lobby I heard the Prelude to "Pagliacci," and looked forward to hearing my first opera in Armenian. At the first Russian words I turned to Shahen who, understanding my stern look, apologized and said that only a handful of foreign operas had been translated into Armenian. We walked out. On leaving, I saw on a poster that two nights before, Menotti's "The Consul" had been performed.

Next door a concert by the Armenian State Symphony Orchestra was in progress with a variety of young soloists who had just won first places in the Conservatory competition. While the young artists were worth listening to, the orchestra was not, the musicians seeming to play against rather than with each other. After twenty minutes we left that also, Shahen again apologizing that the orchestra did not rehearse or perform often enough.

Both of us were conscious of the finality of this meeting—Shahen having to leave for Rostov within hours, we for Moscow the next day. We walked in silence for many minutes. I was intoxicated by the ambiance of this place, and especially by these people, studying, working, creating. Within the confines of loosely defined boundaries, their activity was ceaseless, buzzing and swarming in every direction.

Unconsciously, I mumbled "collective strength," and Shahen asked what I had said. I looked at my young friend and overwhelmed at that moment by a deep affection for him, I put my arm around his shoulder as we walked.

Even in the privacy we now enjoyed, totally alone and walking up and down avenues named after Armenian cultural figures of the past—Abovian, Nalbandian, Spendiarian—Shahen was admirable for his reasoned acceptance of all that surrounded us with all its shortcomings. He had escaped abject poverty and a bleak future as a bricklayer in Syria and come to an assured subsistence and an illustrious career in Armenia. In the twenty years since his family's repatriation, he had built a home and established himself as a critic, art historian and a fully recognized and respected member of the cream of progressive Armenian intellectual life.

As we resumed talking, Shahen, somewhat hesitantly, stopped and held my arm. We were standing in the center of the city by a large pond known as Swan Lake, and indeed the graceful white birds were gliding back and forth.

"I know about your conversation with Henrik the other night and what you answered, and I understand," he said to my surprise.

"Do you really understand, Shahen?"

"Yes, I really do and I hope that *you* understand."

"I do and I also appreciate the spirit in which it was said. I will not explain the details to you but a few years ago I was asked to serve Armenia in a context that was totally repugnant to me. But these days here will remain with me for the rest of my life. My wife and I are deeply rooted in the Armenian psyche and these few days have sunk the roots even deeper. But we can serve the Armenian cause in only one way, as Americans."

Shahen murmured his gratitude which I interpreted to be for not taking umbrage that he had raised the issue. We returned to the hotel and as we entered he said—

"By the way I have good news. Minas just returned and tomorrow the boys will take you to him. I am really sorry not to be there with you but you will be in good hands. Minas will be an experience you will not forget. He is the most talented of them all."

At the hotel, we went upstairs and I entered our rooms to inform Roseann that Shahen was waiting to say goodbye. It was an emotional ten minutes for all three of us, and we wondered if we would ever meet again. We both stood in the doorway and watched Shahen disappear down the long corridor. We did not see him again.*

As Roseann and I sat on the bed talking and I reviewed the evening's activity for her, the phone rang. It was Budapest—after seven hours—but we both needed the lift in spirits which talking with the children gave us. They were overjoyed to learn we would be home in two days, and with the customary exchange of mutual affection, shouted because of the poor connection, we ended the call. Our hearts now less heavy, we retired.

I was almost asleep when the phone rang again. I went to the outer room and picked up the receiver.

"Hello, this is Anahid," said a soft feminine voice in Armenian, "how are you?"

Taken aback for a moment, I replied—"Hello, Anahid, I'm fine, thank you. Do we know each other?"

"You are from America, aren't you?" and when I confirmed that, she continued—"But of course you know me. We met two days ago,

---

*During his trip to the United States in the mid-seventies when I was in Greece, Shahen lectured in New York where he met my parents on whom he showered affection and recalled in great detail our visit to Armenia. In 1984, he visited the U.S. again and spent several hours with us in our home.

don't you remember? I am your girl friend. Now, let's speak English," which she began to do very poorly, finally asking that I meet her. I said first I would have to have my wife's approval, upon which she abruptly hung up.

That incident left us even more light-hearted than before and just as we were getting over our amusement and even wondering what Anahid looked like, I suddenly remembered what awaited us the next morning.

"I almost forgot to tell you that Minas is finally here. We get to see him tomorrow morning, just before leaving for the airport."

At that precise moment, the phone rang a third time.

XXVIII

ANNOYED THAT I HAD TO ONCE AGAIN GET OUT OF bed and walk the twenty feet to the telephone, I lifted the receiver and whispered a curt "Yes?" The male Armenian voice which responded, slightly hoarse but devoid of any regional accent, was unhurried and apologetic in tone—

"I am sorry to disturb you at such a late hour, but your phone has been busy for some time." His pause was meant, I suppose, to get a reaction from me, but all I could say was—again—"Yes?"

The fact is that my throat had become so constricted that one word was about all I could speak. His single opening sentence had already worked its effect on me: someone somewhere, at this late hour, had been making a deliberate attempt to contact me, had not provided his identity nor even sought to confirm mine because he already knew very well with whom he was speaking.

In those few seconds, I was already aware of a rising sense of foreboding. From the bedroom I heard a sleepy—"Now what?"

"I realize it may be awkward," the voice continued, "but I am asking that you meet me in fifteen minutes."

Foreboding now turned into apprehension. A total stranger, and nameless at that, wanted me to leave my wife and my hotel room near midnight for a talk. Fleeting images of Rafael Aghayan raced through my mind, but this was most definitely not his voice.

"It would be in our mutual interest." Another pause, then, "It is important."

The emphasis he placed on that last word had such an urgency that almost involuntarily and without fully realizing that I was committing myself, I asked—"Where?"

"Behind Lenin's statue on the square," he replied, his voice now edged with a certain satisfaction as though having gotten over an initial hurdle.

Was I about to encounter my moment of truth, I asked myself? Would there be an element of danger to Roseann if I refused to go through with this? Would there be for me if I did? Just as I began to think about the ramifications either way—both of them blind paths—his raspy voice inquired with what sounded now like slight concern—

"You are coming, of course?"

"Yes," I said in a half whisper, even then not fully aware of the nature of my commitment, and hung up.

Roseann had snapped on the lamp and was sitting up in bed. She looked at me as I returned to the bedroom, her face filled with curiosity—

"That was a strange conversation. Do you realize that all you ever said were four words, three of which were 'Yes' and the fourth 'Where'?"

I had resolved as I walked back that my wife must not know, for two reasons: she would certainly try and talk me out of the meeting, and if she did—and I knew she could—it might be considered a provocation, with consequences I could not begin to imagine.

"Do you remember that writer I've been trying to see who's been out of town? You know, Dashdentz. Apparently he's been trying to get hold of me; said our phone's been busy. I just agreed to meet him briefly in the lobby."

"Oh, him, the translator of Shakespeare. Well, don't be long. Remember, we've got a strenuous day tomorrow, and there's also Minas."

She lay down and turned her back to me, but I knew she was not convinced. Something in her eyes had told me she would be waiting—anxiously.

I dressed quickly and stole out of our suite. On the way down, I considered the various possibilities for mischief that lay ahead, for there was no doubt whatsoever in my mind that I was about to confront my past with the KGB. It had been three years since that fateful afternoon in East Germany when the true nature of Rafael Aghayan's mission had been so elaborately revealed. My rejection of his blandishments had been categorical. But for the last two years, when most assuredly they knew that I was in the Hungarian People's Republic, there had not been a peep or a sign from anyone.

And now, I thought as I reached the lobby, contact was being re-established and surely they had something in mind other than merely letting me know that they knew I was in Armenia. Aghayan had been thrown out of the game and a relief pitcher was being sent in, I said to myself wryly. I also said something else to myself which made me wince: I was deep in the Soviet Union without my diplomatic passport and beyond the protective reach of our Embassy in Moscow.

When I reached the main floor I thought of that flashforward when the Penfields had looked back at me standing in this very same lobby, and I wondered if there hadn't been a stroke of precognition in that fiction.

The lobby contained very few people and Lina's Intourist Office was dark. I walked out of the *Armenia Hotel* into the cool night and turned right. During the day the heat in the mile-high Yerevan often went to 100 degrees and higher, but at night the city cooled rapidly and some people were still strolling about for a breath of the invigorating air.

Lenin loomed large in the reflected light just ahead, towering over the square, and because there was no traffic I crossed over with ease to the statue. At one particular point, a curious visual juxtaposition took place: Lenin was silhouetted against the deep blue sky and beyond were the snowy glittering twin crests of Mt. Ararat. It was a poetic sight—the Armenia of old and the Armenia of today caught in one and the same image. I took some small comfort in the thought that those ancient peaks, which may have once provided anchorage to Noah and his family of animals, were indestructible, while Lenin . . . .

But now I stood directly in front of him, that is to say, at the huge foot of the statue which has on its four sides pyramids of seven steps each leading up to a large base, to the rear of which is a high granite pedestal on which stands the full figure of the founder of the Soviet state. My instruction had been to meet him at the rear so I walked to my left and around the base, the tension within me growing rapidly. Despite the gentle breeze, I felt uncommonly warm.

The pungent aroma of native Armenian tobacco reached me just as I saw him. He was as much an outline as the giant figure which loomed above us. His face was in shadow, partly because of the dark, but also because he wore a kind of hat whose brim kept even reflected light away from his visage. I stopped about five feet away from him, charged with the clandestine nature of the occasion and its aura of mystery.

"Pari yerego, Bahron Alexanian."

His use of the Armenian form of my name was a master stroke, for it disarmed me with its painfully personal tone, just as it said in so many words that I was no mystery to him and, separating me from my American-ness, identified me with the soil on which I stood. At the same time, the Mister before my name was courteously spoken, in sharp contrast to the easy informality with which "Edward" was used by everyone else.

"Good evening to you too, Mr. . . .uh . . . ."

I saw an impatient wave of his hand—"Names are not important, except that we . . .I . . .know you."

Obviously a slip, I thought, was he nervous too? But that "we" had an unnerving effect on me. Perhaps it was calculated to do just that.

"I know you want to return to your hotel, so let's not lose time. You have seemed to enjoy these four days."

Harmless on the surface but oddly phrased. I peered at him but the dark of his face was impenetrable, and he had stamped out his cigarette.

"Yes we have. But why do you think it has only *seemed* so?"

I no sooner said this than the answer became obvious to me: for the last four days every move we had made had been under close surveillance. As the thought flashed through my mind, he said—

"Because you should know that we have watched your every move."

How could there have been any doubt in my mind. After all, we were in the very lair of the beast. The opportunities had been legion—the crowds at the art exhibits, in the streets, on the trolley, in *Etchmiadzin,* maybe even at the very outset with that mad cab-driver who wanted us to stay with him. But I could not in my heart implicate any of that small exciting group of artists and intellectuals with whom we had become so intimate.

So now, this . . .what could I call him, he was a mere shadow . . .this shadow would also know that on the next morning we were meeting Minas, were flying out of Soviet Armenia at noon, and that we were without our passports. Feeling very defensive, I said—

"Then you also know that we have behaved properly," thinking that if he were truly astute, he should interpret that as acknowledgment of his organizational identity.

A husky but mirthless laugh greeted my remark—

"Everyone who comes here from the United States has some private mission, proper or not. Yours has not been clear."

"What is not clear about an American-Armenian's curiosity about the country of his ancestors? That is why we are visiting your country—if it is *your* country."

"It is most certainly my country," he replied quietly and solemnly, "and you should feel that it is also *your* country."

"We have been made to feel very much at home. I imagine you know what and whom I am talking about."

Deep down I was earnestly hoping that nothing would emerge from this encounter on the eve of our departure which would mar the excitement, gratification and elevation of spirit we had experienced. I was also getting impatient—

"But this cannot be why you have asked me to meet you at this hour."

As I said this I realized that while I wished to avoid unpleasantness, I was actually inviting him to get to the point.

"It is not, but it has bearing on it. Do you not feel something special here in the fatherland?"

"If this is my fatherland, what do you think America is?"

"You yourself just said this was the land of your ancestors. America is where you live, Armenia is where your heritage is." He waited for a reply and when none came, continued—

"Armenia's sons are scattered far and wide and do Armenia no good. Armenia needs their help, even from afar."

My throat was now dry and taut and although I wanted to ask the key question—"How?"—I couldn't get the word out. But he read my mind—

"There are many ways, many many ways. Honorable ways. Just remember this—here, we are Armenians first, and loyal to our Armenian traditions. Think about that."

I tried to grasp the implications of what he was saying: if he were truly KGB, and I understood him correctly, he was drawing a line between the all-powerful apparatus operating out of Moscow and the local branch in Yerevan; he was saying perhaps that while the Russians up north use one set of criteria, the Armenians in the south employ quite another. Nationality and blood made all the difference. There could be no doubt as to where this conversation was leading and I was sure I didn't want to hear any more.

The midnight air sent a chill through me and I shivered as though coming out of a trance. I said to myself: I am standing in the main square of Yerevan in Soviet Armenia, behind the statue of Lenin, talking to an officer of Soviet Intelligence and he is about to make another pitch like the one his colleague did three years ago. I cannot let that happen.

"I must go. My wife will be concerned. I would like to forget this meeting ever took place."

"Even so, I am glad you agreed to come. We shall be in touch. But think about it. *Tsedesutiun, Bahron Alexanian.*"

He was not only repeating that evocative form of address, but now adding the Armenian equivalent of—Til we meet again. I did not reply, turned sharply and walked briskly back to the hotel. If he had intended to disrupt my equilibrium, he had succeeded eminently.

This midnight tryst had had some very strange aspects. Although he had declined to give his name, neither had he evoked that of Rafael Aghayan nor made any mention of that entire episode. This was obviously a wholly new chapter, independent of the Aghayan phase. But weren't the goals the same? He had tried to inject some morality and patriotism into his aborted pitch with phrases like 'honorable ways,' 'Armenian traditions,' 'Armenians first.' While the implications of all this were astonishing, especially that this tentacle of the octopus in Moscow had a life all its own, in the final analysis, the shadow's pitch was really no different than Aghayan's, nor presumably were the objectives.

It was all very complicated, confusing, and yet quite clear. I decided not to tell Roseann about any of this until we returned to Budapest. When I slipped back into our rooms, she had fallen fast asleep which mercifully precluded an explanation—on this disquieting night, anyway.

XXVIII

W E AWOKE ON OUR LAST DAY IN SOVIET ARMENIA, aware that we had only a few hours left, that Shahen was no longer with us, that Rudolf wished to do a portrait of Roseann, that we were finally to meet Minas, and that our plane was taking off at noon.

We completed our packing and went down to meet Rudolf, who took us and our luggage to his studio. Roseann had recovered enough to travel, the soda water cure, however, having been politely ignored. We arrived at the studio and Rudolf immediately set himself to his task.

As I sat near him chatting and watching Roseann's image gradually take shape, the door slowly opened and I turned to see a tall figure with an ascetic face and a black drooping mustache framed in long black hair, a figure which commanded attention. I extended my hand—"Minas, at last."

He barely changed his doleful expression, said he was sorry to have missed our company the previous four days about which he had been hearing since his return last night, and suggested he and I go to his studio in the adjoining building, like Rudolf's on the top floor.

As we entered his studio I was dazzled by the quality and quantity of his output. I saw the early influences of Matisse and then Saryan, progressing to the more subdued earthy colors of his recent work. I seated myself and Minas began to exhibit his work, asking for no comment and making none himself.

I saw him in many of his portraits and once when I commented on one which I found excellent, Minas said reflectively—"I spoiled that one by doing too much." I said that that seemed to be one of the secrets of art—knowing when to stop. For the first time, he smiled, but even his smile was melancholy, and said—

"How curious you should say that. Last week I wrote an article on that very subject in which I pointed out that a work of art is finished only when between the artist and his work there existed a complete harmony. But how they butchered my words! What finally will appear is hardly what I wrote. You understand the problem."

I asked if he felt restraints in the practice of his art. Minas replied— "The tough ones are still among us, in the Painters Union and in the Central Committee of the Party. They still think in the old way. Did Shahen introduce you to a sculptor named Ara Sarkisian? There is a dangerous man. But we are forging ahead. A very good thing is happening. They have begun to make distinctions among us. Now they are examining artists very carefully to find out who is genuine, who merely imitates, and who is an outright fraud. This speaks well for the future."

And what about the status of the artist in terms of economic security?

"It has improved a great deal. For an exhibit devoted entirely or partly to one artist, we get good money, as much as 2,500 rubles. We can also sell privately and keep it all. If we have the luck to sell abroad, the State keeps 30% and we keep the rest. Some of my colleagues work on salary as graphic artists, some decorating walls in factories. That may be necessary for survival, but for the true artist it is death."

Conversing further with Minas I was able to draw out of him—he was far too modest to volunteer it—that he also worked in the theatre and had done sets for operatic and ballet productions.*

We continued looking at the canvasses he placed on an easel: scenes in his studio, self-portraits, with his mother, his father, his wife, and a number reacting to the horror of the Turkish massacres of 1915 which Minas himself never experienced but, as with most of our generation, with which he was all too familiar from survivors, mothers, fathers, and the abundance of historical material in the Yerevan museums.

As Minas placed these canvasses before me, I found my attention turning as much to him as to them. I was experiencing what Shahen had suggested—the mystique which surrounded Minas, an aura of saintliness. He had so much presence that I was convinced had I been alone

---

*This was 1967 and Minas was 39 years old. Ten years later in East Berlin, I found a monograph published in 1975 by Henrik Igitian, from which I learned of exhibits abroad and honors heaped on Minas in the Soviet Union and that his stage productions included sets for Gershwin's *Rhapsody in Blue,* Ravel's *Bolero* and Khatchaturian's *Gayane.* In January 1972, Minas suffered a tragedy when his studio burned down destroying a large number of his best paintings he had selected for a solo exhibit. But the greater tragedy occurred in 1975 when a speeding car struck and killed Minas as he was crossing the street in front of the opera house, plunging the intellectuals, as Shahen told us, into inconsolable mourning.

in a room which he had entered and my eyes were closed, I would have known he was there.

Minas placed each new canvas on the easel for inspection in silence, absorbed, as though reliving its creation. In every one there was the soil, the people, the landscape of Armenia; even in the portraits, there seemed to be a holy communion with his native land. Minas would be an orphan anywhere else but in Armenia, I thought, and to abandon it would be for him spiritual death.

More than in anyone else's presence or work, whether old Master Saryan's or the brilliant young Rudolf's, I felt an electricity surge through me as artist and work fused in my consciousness. Minas became for me the embodiment of our ancestral past, the struggling present, and the hopeful future. Perhaps it was the accumulation of five days highly charged with the impact of time, place and personalities, but I experienced emotions which were inchoate and amorphous. I do know, however, that with less than one hour left in Armenia, in that studio and with Minas, I was under a very special spell.

That spell was broken by a stranger who entered the studio. He was a young man and Minas did not seem at all surprised to see him.

"Edward, this is Telman Zourabian, the Armenian Radio correspondent in Moscow."

Telman was very friendly and when I asked how an Armenian came by a name such as Telman, he shrugged his shoulders and said simply, "It is German," and laughed. He took a seat and we continued examining Minas's canvasses, except that now Minas spoke—

"Telman is one of the most fearless journalists, especially of the art scene. Those conservatives I mentioned earlier, you know, the tough ones, well, Telman stands up to them. He is a great help to all of us, a great ally."

Despite his reputation, Telman seemed not at all interested in discussing art, preferring national political issues. He asked, for instance, what was being done by the Armenians in the United States about the territorial question? I replied that if he meant restoring Kars and Ardahan, now part of Turkey, to Soviet Armenia, nothing was being done because the Soviet Union had renounced any claims since 1953.

Both of them now made cynical references to the role played by "the Russians" in all the territorial claims of the Armenians, and in other matters as well. I was startled to hear the bitterness which now filled the studio and I said that the Armenians in their small republic seemed to have nothing but enemies—Russians, Georgians, Turks.

"Why do you leave out the Azerbaijanis?" Minas asked, "they are perhaps the worst right now. Look at that map on the wall. Do you see Nakhichevan and Karabagh? Stalin gave them to Azerbaijan even though they are primarily Armenian. Don't overlook the fact that the Azerbaijanis are Turks too, only with a different name and location."

At his mention of the Turks, Minas began a colloquy, wanting to know how much I knew, how much Americans knew, about the Turkish-Armenian past. In the short time remaining, Minas asked what figure was accepted as the number massacred; whether the word genocide was associated with the Turkish action; whether Turkey was so valuable and reliable a NATO member that the West wished to forget what had happened; whether the West and particularly the United States intended to right this great historic wrong?

Minas and Telman looked at me with searing eyes. I tried to answer their questions, knowing very well that if the truth were known to them, it would be shattering. But I explained that certain figures seemed unassailable, such as the twenty million Soviet and six million Jewish dead of World War II, while the generally accepted figure for the Armenians was one-and-one-half million, contested only by the Turks and their collaborators. I explained that many historians agreed that the events of 1915 in Turkey were tantamount to a genocide, but because Europe was embroiled in a major war followed by the post-war economic and political turbulence throughout the continent, the extensive press coverage, especially in *The New York Times,* of harrowing eye-witness accounts by American diplomats, missionaries and travelers of Turkish brutality somehow did not arouse the public.

I concluded by stressing that the tragic events of 1915 and thereafter were the universal agony of all Armenians everywhere in the world and had the considerable virtue of uniting Young and Old, Left and Right, overshadowing political and religious schisms arising from the existence of a Soviet Armenia.

From the somber expressions on their faces I sensed that they had understood the underlying message of my response: the world was too preoccupied with other matters and the super-powers with their own national interest to be concerned about or even show interest in the

plight of a small people victimized by history and the murderous policies
of mad despots.

Looking at my watch, I said we had to fetch Roseann and get to the
airport, but didn't want to lose this rare opportunity of hearing Telman
in these final moments in Armenia tell me the latest Radio Armenia
joke. Telman rose to the occasion:

"Question—Why is there no Radio Armenia any more?

"Answer—Because the Jew who wrote all the jokes died."

Meanwhile, Minas had selected two prints and inscribed them, one for
me and one for Roseann. Together we raced back to Rudolf's studio
where Roseann was holding her pen-and-ink portrait, still glistening, for
me to see. We scrambled down the flights of steps to the street and
hailed a cab, everyone holding one of four pieces of luggage.

We caught a taxi and tumbled in, the conversation wild and disjointed
and hysterical. The cab driver was all ears, hardly attending to his driving, so great was his curiosity about us and what we were saying. I was
grateful that the traffic was so light in Yerevan.

Once at the airport, everyone jumped out and I reached for my wallet.
The driver seized my arms and holding them tightly, said—

"I can't take money from you, but if you really want to pay me, just
never forget us and come back."

Then he, a total stranger, was the first to embrace us, after which
each did in turn several times, reluctant to let us go, we reluctant to
leave. We finally swam out of this sea of affection and staggered into the
waiting aircraft, totally spent and drained of all emotion and energy.

Buried in our own separate thoughts, Roseann and I hardly spoke
throughout the three-hour flight to Moscow, on her lap the still wet
portrait, mute testimony that we had in fact been in Armenia.

XXX

W E ARRIVED BACK IN MOSCOW LATE IN THE AFTER-
noon and were met at the airport by a much-relieved Nancy
Dean who gave us our passports, visas extended, and directed us to
overnight sleeping quarters—the vacant apartment in the Embassy compound of an officer on home leave. Trying to sleep was difficult, our
thoughts still far away to the south, deep in the Caucasus.

The next morning at the Embassy I encountered a variety of reactions
from Foreign Service Officers: those who couldn't have cared less about
passports, our experiences or that we were even there; those who considered it unthinkable to be in the Soviet Union without passports,
rejecting our mitigating circumstances; and those of substance and intelligence who couldn't hear enough about our adventures which they considered unique—officers such as Jack Armitage, Chris Squire, Bill
Shinn, Dabney Chapman and Yale Richmond.

I was disappointed not to have seen our able and understanding
Ambassador, Foy Kohler, who was back in the United States on consultation. Kohler had been my very first chief in the government as director
of the "Voice of America" in 1950. That afternoon, our passports
securely clutched in our hands, we boarded a Hungarian flight to Budapest and to our children.

A week later at a diplomatic reception, I spotted my Soviet counter-
part across the room. Korolev saw me and walked over, his expression
as dour as ever.

"How was your trip to Moscow and Leningrad? Did you also go somewhere else? Oh yes, Armenia, of course," and without further ado, simply walked away.

I shook my head, ready to agree with my new-found friends in Armenia about the condescending attitude of the Russians. I wished at that
moment that Mardiros Saryan could have been present to tell Korolev

off—Saryan, and Kochar and Minas and the hosts of other artists whose creative work was exploited by the Soviet state abroad, but who at home remained mere *armyashkas*.

I remained disturbed until spotted by a group of Hungarian intellectuals—writers, poets, artists—whose company I always enjoyed. Now, they couldn't ask enough questions, not about Moscow, not about Leningrad, but about Yerevan: What was it like to be among one's own people; to speak one's native language; to see the monuments of one's ancestors?

Several had been to Soviet Armenia and knew it well and their questions were highly informed: What about the limits of ideological control over the arts; the vestiges of Stalinism; and, looking meaningfully at me, these Hungarians asked about the relationship of the small subject nation to the domineering Russians? Pointed questions, knowing questions.*

As I drove home, Korolev's manner once again returned to trouble me, but in a leap which the mind on occasion makes and by so doing illuminates a dark corner, the thought occurred to me that Korolev was no more a representative of the good in Russia than Rafael Aghayan was of the good we had witnessed in Armenia. Nor the mysterious stranger.

Once home, I asked Roseann to take a walk with me in the Buda hills, for I reminded myself that she still did not know the details of that midnight meeting in Yerevan.

As we entered a footpath, she anticipated the occasion by remarking that she had been waiting for this moment—

"I knew all along that something odd happened that night. When you returned, you know, I was still awake, because it was the only time I was really anxious in Armenia. To tell you the truth, it was the worst half hour I can ever remember. What did happen?"

By now, the mysterious stranger had assumed the identity of The Shadow in my mind and I described him as such. I repeated everything that had been said, especially his admonition to "think about it." I suddenly realized that I had not told her of the earlier conversation with Henrik Igitian, and when I did, we compared notes on the two proposals and reached the same conclusions: Igitian's was genuine, heartfelt,

---

*Among the few in Budapest least interested in our experiences in Armenia was Cardinal Mindszenty for whom anything said about the Soviet Union which was not totally derogatory was, in one of his favorite expressions, "Bolshevik propaganda."

uplifting, untainted, while The Shadow's was none of these; in a nut-
shell, Igitian's was an appeal to the nobler and The Shadow's to the
baser instincts. Even if made independently of Aghayan and for all its
"honorable ways," the stranger's offer was part and parcel of the KGB's
attempts to ensnare me one way or the other. There was really nothing
to "think about."

But that phrase and the accompanying *Tsedesutiun* enjoyed an omi-
nous persistence in my mind in the remaining two years of my tour in
the American Embassy in Budapest.

Washington and Moscow
1969–1972

XXXI

MY ASSIGNMENT IN HUNGARY CAME TO A CLOSE IN July 1969. We had begun our farewells after four years in that fascinating, melancholy country, with Roseann looking forward to putting the boys back in American schools and setting up house while I, having been assigned to the Senior Seminar, was eager to begin this high-level year of study at the State Department's Foreign Service Institute, which was considered the threshhold to senior advancement.

Two developments affected these plans. The first was President Nixon's decision to visit Romania in August, an historic event since it would be the first visit by an American President to East Europe. Presidential visits, as I well knew from Berlin, entailed endless planning and massive support, for which Foreign Service Officers throughout the area were pulled in. Sure enough, a cable arrived directing me to spend one week in Bucharest for the Nixon visit, with the specific task of preparing the Overnight Book—an all-night duty of compiling the day's most significant news events for the President and his staff to be read by them at 7:30 every morning.

Inasmuch as we had never been to Bucharest, I told Roseann to join me in a few days (which she did) and prior to driving to the airport, I checked in for last-minute messages at the Embassy. I had no sooner entered the old building on *Szabadsag ter* than everyone I met informed me with a big smile that there indeed was a message for me. It was a cable from USIA Director Frank Shakespeare explaining that because of top-level changes he was instituting, he was cancelling my Senior Seminar nomination and appointing me Deputy Assistant Director for the Soviet Union and East Europe—actually the No. 2 position and one which would have logically followed after the Senior Seminar. With one

cable I had gained a year of career advancement with the strong likeli-
hood that I would move into the No. 1 position in about three years.*

When I arrived at our Embassy in Bucharest, the congratulations
fresh in my ears from Budapest were repeated. As it was, most of my
colleagues assigned to support the visit from surrounding countries were
officers over whom I would have supervision on reaching my new post
in Washington, and this brief temporary duty gave me the opportunity to
know them better. Even though I worked all night, the occasion was so
extraordinary that I simply did with but two and three hours sleep during the day so as to enjoy the festivities—the always exciting arrival of
Air Force One, the motorcade into the capital, the many receptions.**

I was most anxious to talk with my immediate supervisor in Washington, Kempton Jenkins, a State Department officer on loan to USIA
whom I had known in West Berlin. I asked one of the White House staff
at the Embassy how long it would take to place a call. He drily handed
me a phone through which I heard a clear voice say "White House."
The switchboard simply 'travelled' with the President. Within seconds I
was talking with Jenkins, who urged me to return directly after the duty
in Bucharest because of major changes we would make together in our
programs and policies towards the communist half of Europe. Even as
he said that, "Jenks," as he was known, could not have fully realized
how far-reaching those changes were to be. That became evident only
after I returned to Washington and assumed my new post as his deputy.

With the incoming Nixon administration was a new crew of 'specialists' on how to deal with the Soviet threat. To the best of my knowledge,
none of them had ever served in positions comparable or related to the
ones they now assumed in USIA, which was perceived by them as an
ideological Pentagon.

The approach Jenks and I employed in dealing with the Soviet Union
and the Eastern European countries was of a pragmatic character, that

---

*I dwell on this career advancement because of its obvious interest to the KGB, elevating me
to a much higher position, with greater access to classified information, closer to the highest
levels of government, and with a voice in the process of deciding policy towards the Soviet
Union and its allies.

**At the main reception hosted by President Ceausescu, standing three feet in front of Nixon,
I was astonished to observe that during the playing of the national anthems, when most look
ahead with an unseeing stare, our president kept shifting his eyes left and right, an image of
nervous suspicion.

is, exercising flexibility, maintaining continuous contact, indulging in give-and-take, feeling out views, testing, bargaining. In contrast, our agency's new approach seemed to call for bluntness and inflexibility, retaliation in kind, dealing in absolutes. There was also the re-emergence in the agency's vocabulary—from an era whose eponym had blemished our nation's image—of the term 'anti-communism,' which better described a posture than a policy, and was in any case inadequate and superficial as a label for the foreign policy of a great world power with such diverse and complex interests. Our work was cut out for us.

USIA had been founded in 1953 by President Eisenhower as an agency separate from the State Department, under which until that year it had administratively fallen. The new agency's directors were all political appointees selected by the White House several of whom had stood out, such as George Allen who had integrated the agency's work more closely with that of State, and Leonard Marks who had engineered our conversion into the career foreign service.

Then there was Edward R. Murrow. If USIA has had one continuing staple, it is ideas, and with Murrow at the helm, we generated and advocated ideas of freedom and democracy and engaged emissaries of the Soviet Union wherever we encountered them to prove the superiority of our ideas over theirs. But now, we began to wonder if ideas were to become suspect.

Frank Shakespeare, who became the seventh director of USIA, had been one of Nixon's campaign advisors and a vice-president of CBS. An intense, dynamic conservative, Shakespeare was fervent and impassioned when addressing the subject of the Soviet Union, its government, system, leaders and policies, and in this initial period of our association tending to view matters in black-and-white terms. Shakespeare found in USIA the ideological weapons with which to wage combat against the Soviet behemoth and looked to Jenks and me as his lieutenants to lead the struggle.

Shakespeare lost no time in acquainting himself first-hand with the target of his interest which, until then, had been only an abstraction. He made a quick trip to the Soviet Union soon after taking charge to inspect the USIA exhibit *Education USA,* and finding it "lacking in political freight," a phrase we were to hear often from him, he promptly relieved two senior career officers whom he held at fault: one the Deputy Director for the Soviet Union and East Europe, and the other our

Moscow Embassy's Counselor for Cultural Affairs. These precipitous 'firings' took place while I was still in Budapest and explained my new appointment.

Jenks had served in the West Berlin Mission's Eastern Affairs Section—where I had first known him in 1959—which dealt with the problems of East Germany prior to our establishment of an embassy in East Berlin in 1974. He had also served in Moscow which, together with my service and familiarity with that part of Europe, added up to considerable experience for Shakespeare to draw on.

While Jenks and I recognized that Shakespeare's and our evaluation of Soviet aims and objectives coincided, we encountered problems with him and his in-coming aides not in the ends but the means. Jenks proved to be a formidable match for the new director, counter-acting the many proposals which bombarded us daily from the sixth floor of USIA with equal dexterity; my style was more deliberate and circumspect in trying to persuade the director of our manner of dealing with our adversaries in the eastern half of Europe. Both methods took some time to be effective, but they eventually produced a useful amalgam that could be properly identified as policy.

Shakespeare eventually developed a receptivity to some of our ideas, and we to some of his. Although occasionally old prejudices would surface, we worked out a *modus operandi* which in time effected the expansion of our informational and cultural programs and staffs in the Soviet Union and throughout Eastern Europe. Jenks and I took pride in this achievement, which provided vital branches of the United States Government and the academic community with fresh insights into Soviet and East European society and institutions. The evolutionary impact of radio broadcasts, cultural centers, libraries, films, exhibits, lectures and seminars over these last two decades played a palpable role in the revolutionary explosions of 1989 which shook and transformed those societies.

Shakespeare's deputy was Henry Loomis, an affluent civil servant who had worked in various government agencies, eventually winning appointment as Director of the "Voice of America" in the Eisenhower administration. After the Republican victory of 1968, Loomis had served on a Republican Task Force and been appointed USIA's Deputy Director, but he did not have the same set of USIA priorities as the Director. What set the two officials philosophically apart was Loomis's disagreement with Shakespeare concerning policies and programs in the Soviet area, Loomis not finding it feasible to expand resources there in view of the limiting nature of the political environment.

Shakespeare's obsession with communist affairs frequently required that Jenks or I accompany him on his many travels. In fact, we spent a major part of our three years as Shakespeare's deputies for the USSR and East Europe informing and educating him before, during and after such travels. The most enjoyable trip I made with him was to Bulgaria to attend the opening of a USIA exhibit at the Plovdiv Trade Fair, where we made the surprising discovery that the mayor of the city was an Armenian.*

Jenks decided that because of Loomis's view, and to make our future relations with him more productive, we should arrange a trip through the Soviet bloc and that I should accompany him. This was done three months after I had assumed my new duties and took us in the dead of winter—and blinding snow storms—to Moscow, Warsaw, Prague and Budapest. But Moscow was to have more than one surprise for me.

Visiting our new Ambassador, Jacob Beam, was his predecessor, Foy Kohler, whom I had missed two years earlier, and our reunion—the first since Kohler's time as Director of the "Voice of America"—was warm and nostalgic. Ambassador Beam hosted a lunch for us at his residence, Spaso House, to which he invited some of the senior working-level officials whose names were familiar to all of us who had to negotiate American-Soviet issues. The informal chit-chat during and after lunch was what always made these functions enjoyable and rewarding because the Soviet officials were usually relaxed and somewhat off-guard, saying things they would never dare in public.**

The next day, Deputy Chief of Mission Boris Klosson held a lunch for us to which he also invited Soviet officials, one of whom, hitherto unknown to me, was especially on my behalf. He was Pavel Gevorkyan, chief of the American Desk at the *Novosti Press Agency*—and an Arme-

---

*Mayor Diran Parikian displayed true Armenian hospitality and drove us around the city in his Mercedes for three hours, delighted to be host to such a senior American official as Shakespeare "and his Armenian interpreter."
**Example: after finishing his coffee and brandy, Alexander Zinchuk of the Foreign Ministry who had been talking with Beam, Kohler and me, slapped his thighs as he arose exclaiming—"Well, back to the jamming!" Jamming of VOA had resumed after the invasion of Czechoslovakia in 1968 but was never admitted either privately or publicly by Soviet officials.

nian.* We paired off directly after the introductions and although two of his superiors were among the other guests (and another two being Georgy Arbatov of the USA Institute and Valentin Berezhkov, Editor in Chief of "USA" and recently stationed in Washington), Gevorkyan and I jabbered away in Armenian to Klosson's visible pleasure as we virtually ignored everyone else and had a grand time.

Gevorkyan was short, chunky and outgoing and anxious to communicate. I told him of having dined two nights before at the *Ararat,* Moscow's Armenian Restaurant, and of having ordered in Armenian as our Counselor for Press and Culture McKinney Russell, an excellent linguist, had seen it produce Armenian delicacies not often served to foreign patrons. Gevorkyan also enjoyed my description of how two years earlier my wife and I had tried in vain to get seated at the *Ararat* until I spoke to its Director in Armenian which immediately conjured up a free table in the jam-packed restaurant. Gevorkyan was delighted with these stories which he said only confirmed the solidarity of Armenians in the Soviet Union and the strong bonds of Armenians throughout the world. Concluding our conversations he said there were plans for a further get-together before our departure and that we would be informed in time.

This materialized on our next to last evening in Moscow. Gevorkyan, his chief Vladimir Larin, the Deputy Director of *Novosti,* and various Foreign Ministry officials hosted a supper at the Press Club for Loomis and me which was a riot of laughter, shouted jokes by everyone, and toast after toast to the accompaniment of a mountain of clanking bottles. Among the toasts were several to Armenia and her sons everywhere. At one point, Gevorkyan raised his glass and above the din saluted me with the words—"We are proud to see our compatriots in high places, no matter where."

When the party finally broke up and I began to say farewell to Gevorkyan, he stopped me saying one never knew when we would meet again unexpectedly, and to always look ahead. *"Tsedesutiun,"* was all he said, the Armenian for *Auf Wiedersehen.*

---

*While *Novosti* appears on the surface to be similar to USIA, it is not: it is a propaganda agency operating also inside the USSR, guiding journalists and selling them films, magazines, radio and television programs. But the greatest difference is the use of *Novosti* for KGB cover, whose presence in the press agency is as ubiquitous as in Aeroflot, Amtorg, TASS, Intourist and other Soviet agencies operating abroad. After defecting to the USSR, Kim Philby worked for some time in *Novosti.*

On our final day in Moscow, we attended a reception at Spaso House hosted by Ambassador and Mrs. Beam for the visiting Illinois Jazz Band which was touring the Soviet Union under the cultural agreement. Loomis and I figured we could only spend an hour at the reception before catching our night train to Poland.

I was standing chatting with the Beams when through the doorway there entered Aram Khatchaturian. He came right up to us and greeted his hosts in Russian. My *"Parev, Hayrenagits"* stopped him cold. He looked at me with surprise and when I continued in Armenian—"We met in Berlin a few years ago," he broke into a big smile and said—"Of course, I remember very well."

He asked me to translate for him from Armenian into English, and said a number of pleasant things to the Ambassador about cultural exchanges as a medium for bringing the Soviet and American peoples closer together. He then seized my arm and we went into a corner where he wanted to know all about me.

It was a long and wonderful conversation in which I told him about our trip to Armenia and the lasting impressions it had made on us. Khatchaturian was very enjoyable and relaxed, with no pressures on him and no 'escorts' watching over his shoulder, always holding on to me as though the physical contact made communication more intimate.

I told him of my four years in Hungary and mentioned the dates. For a moment he looked like he was trying to recall something, then said—

"You know, I visited Budapest only last year. Were you still there?"

We were, and I knew why he had gone there—for the Hungarian premiere of his ballet *Spartacus.* I said we had watched him sitting in his box and thought he looked displeased.

"Displeased? I was furious. They butchered my music. They cut out whole sections. They turned it into something else."

I defended the Hungarians and asked if he didn't think the choreography and the production were good.

"Yes, yes, I had no problem with anything but the music."

I got him off that track and we talked about Armenians in Moscow. Khatchaturian said there wasn't an important body within the Soviet system that didn't have one or more Armenians in senior positions. I told him that a prominent journalist in New York (it was actually Harry Schwartz) always maintained that without the Jews and the Armenians, the Soviet system would collapse. Khatchaturian roared with laughter and said there was much truth in that.

I caught Loomis's eye across the reception room and knew it was time to go. Khatchaturian shook hands, then stopped and impetuously embraced me. I was very touched by the gesture.

Embassy cars rushed us to the Belorussian Train Station where we found our separate sleeping compartments. Just as I was getting settled and wondering who would be occupying the upper berth, I heard my name through the window. Standing on the platform was Pavel Gevorkyan with a big smile. I rushed out to him with only minutes to spare and we chatted hastily about nothing in particular, just for the joy of talking in Armenian on this freezing December evening in Moscow.

It was time to go. He pressed two bottles of *Stolichnaya* vodka on me which I did not refuse, thinking ahead of the long overnight trip. I thanked him with a handshake, but like Khatchaturian he threw his arms around me affectionately and said several times—"Come back soon." When I returned to my compartment and the train began slowly to pull out, he was still standing there, waving to me.

I sat down feeling quite emotional and took a fast nip from one of the bottles. Just then the door opened and an Asian buried in furs entered, nodding and smiling, and threw his suitcase on the upper berth. It emerged that he was a Mongolian automobile salesman working in East Europe, as I was able to establish later when we discovered the only common language in which we could discourse—Hungarian.

The remainder of the trip to Warsaw, Prague and Budapest was taken up with routine briefings for Loomis and lengthy discussions with our ambassadors. When we returned to Washington, I was not convinced that Henry Loomis had changed his fundamental views on USIA potential in this area of the world or that he was willing to allocate more resources for the somber totalitarian states we had just visited.

XXXII

A S THE TWO SENIOR USIA OFFICIALS IN CHARGE OF programs and policies for the Soviet Union and East Europe, Jenks and I were on the invitation lists of every embassy representing those countries. Since I had most recently served in Hungary, it was natural that invitations to its embassy functions were frequent, and the fact that the Hungarian Ambassador was Janos Nagy, whom I had known in Budapest and who was often a guest in our home in Bethesda, only added to the cordiality with which we were welcomed.*

In mid-February of 1970, one such function found us in the company of the usual collection of diplomats and Washington officials, but also members of ancillary organs from East Europe with a large group from the press corps. Among them was the experienced journalist Csaba Kis, who was the representative in Washington of MTI, the Hungarian News Agency. A very personable Magyar, Kis had also served in Moscow and we would often talk about the role of Armenians in the Soviet world.

After greeting me, Kis pointed to a stranger across the room and asked if I knew him. When I shook my head, Kis identified him as the Washington Bureau chief for TASS, the Soviet News Agency, adding— "He will be of special interest to you, I'm sure." He then walked me over and introduced me to Artem Melikyan.

As things turned out, it was of special interest to both of us. Melikyan spoke Armenian as well as Gevorkyan, neither of them burdened with

*Nagy left Washington in 1972 and in Budapest assumed the position of Deputy Foreign Minister in charge of North American affairs, primarily the United States, on which he is now Hungary's foremost expert. In late 1980 he was elevated to State Secretary and First Deputy Foreign Minister.

the guttural accent of Aghayan. We chatted about my recent trip to Moscow and when I mentioned having met Gevorkyan, Melikyan said that he of course knew him. After touching on my earlier trip to Armenia as well, we agreed to meet for lunch the following week.

When we joined forces at his TASS office on the second floor of the National Press Building, I had to ring because the doors were locked. Melikyan opened the door himself with a hearty welcome.

There were three relatively small offices to take care of the five TASS correspondents. During our preliminary conversation, we were interrupted by one of them who asked if I could give him the name of a bookstore selling right-wing literature "in addition to the outlet of the American Nazi Party in Arlington." I looked at Melikyan in bewilderment and replied that I could better name outlets for left-wing literature which might make a more informative story for his readers about American liberty. He left with a grunt.

Melikyan opened a small closet and took out a bottle of Armenian cognac, even as he complained that TASS was paying $343 a month rent and not getting its money's worth, especially in char services. Then, as he poured out two glasses, he gave a brief lecture on Armenian cognac, explaining that there were five kinds ranging from the Five Star which was the weakest, to the *Dvin* which was the strongest and which we were about to drink. He said a new brand called *Nairi*—an ancient name for Armenia—had been produced for the 50th anniversary of the Bolshevik Revolution and was the smoothest.

Seated in his office we chatted mostly about Soviet Armenia and his own early life and experiences. Melikyan was born in Baku, where his parents and brother still lived and whom he always visited when on leave. The previous summer he had spent some ten days with them, then a month in Armenia resting in a sanatorium in *Dilijan,* known for its recuperative springs and air. After his early schooling in Azerbaijan, Melikyan went to Moscow to complete his education, following which in 1951 he joined TASS in Moscow.

He married a Russian woman, whom I never met, and in 1960 had the double good fortune of becoming a father and being assigned to London where he remained for five years, which explained his excellent English. Two more years thereafter in Moscow prepared him for his major overseas assignment in 1967—Washington. Tall, mustached, elegantly dressed and extremely congenial, Melikyan seemed to have absorbed the most attractive elements of the British and the Americans in his manner, style and personality. He bore no resemblance to the public image of most Soviet officials.

Melikyan expressed admiration for Anastas Mikoyan but admitted never having met him, though he did know one son, Sergei, a fellow journalist. Melikyan was better informed than Aghayan on intellectuals, both Armenian and Russian, which led into a discussion of Russian-Armenian relations. Melikyan claimed that a close friendship had been forced on the Armenians by the genocidal policies of Turkey. I asked Melikyan where the Russians were in the 1930s when thousands of Armenian intellectuals were arrested, tortured and killed by the NKVD, as the KGB was known then.

Melikyan responded immediately—"But those persecutions were carried out by Stalin and Beria, his secret police chief, and as you know, both were Georgians. Do I have to tell you how Georgians hate Armenians? Even today in Tbilisi, where there are almost half a million Armenians, the Georgians make life difficult for them."

He suggested we lunch in Gadsby's Tavern beneath the Press Building. In the restaurant he began in Armenian but when we became the subject of stares from nearby tables, he switched to English. Melikyan spoke continuously, was always courteous, never offensive or provocative even when critical. He was exceptionally well-informed about American politics and policies.

Melikyan wanted to know how well I knew USIA Director Shakespeare and his Deputy Loomis, and when I told him that contact with them was daily, he probed for information on their familiarity with Soviet affairs; for instance, how well did they know the Soviet Union? I said both had visited there in the first year of their tenure and that I had accompanied Loomis only two months before, describing some of our meetings with Foreign Ministry and media officials and a session at the Institute for the Study of the USA with ten of their specialists. Throughout our meetings and conversations, I told Melikyan, Loomis and I had become aware of an escalation of Soviet propaganda against USIA, even if the atmosphere of the contacts was not uncordial.

Melikyan confirmed the existence of a stepped-up campaign against USIA in the Soviet media and attributed it directly to what he termed "slander against the Soviet Union." He placed the blame on VOA and said its broadcasts had poisoned the atmosphere between the two countries at a time when closer relations were not only necessary but had already begun.

"But look," I interrupted, "when the Red Army invaded Czechoslovakia a year and a half ago . . ." but could go no further as Melikyan didn't allow me to finish, waving his arms and saying he didn't want to hear anything on that subject. I persisted, wishing to make my point that Soviet jamming of VOA had resumed on the very day the Red Army entered Czechoslovakia, but again he stopped me, insisting that any discussion of Czechoslovakia was irrelevant. He asked for more details of the Loomis trip. I had no objection to that because it gave me an even better opportunity to return to the jamming issue.

I described a meeting in Moscow between Loomis and Melikyan's own boss, TASS Director-General Lapin, which was taken up completely with Soviet complaints about VOA and reporting by American correspondents stationed in Moscow. The virtually symbiotic relationship of both was rooted in a fruitful process whereby what the correspondents reported to their newspapers was broadcast back by VOA, listened to in the USSR where new stories were generated and picked up by the journalists in a seemingly never-ending and productive cycle. Lapin had focussed vehemently on the attention VOA had accorded to the defection of Stalin's daughter Svetlana, and protested with equal vigor to the reporting on dissident Soviet author Anatoli Kuznetsov. But he had become almost apoplectic about a series written for *The Washington Post* by its Moscow correspondent Anatole Shub after his expulsion in May 1969, a series exposing Soviet life and society.

At my mention of Shub's name, Melikyan almost leaped from his chair and denounced Shub as a "disgrace to American journalism" because the series had done "irreparable damage" to U.S.-USSR relations. I rejected that, asserting that on the contrary the series had told the American people what it was really like in the Soviet Union, a country about which Americans had an enormous curiosity. "I assume that your people also have an equal curiosity about the United States," I continued, "but by resuming jamming, you cut them off from their main source of information. Isn't that irreparable damage to our relations?"

Melikyan muttered that slander was slander. I said that in my eight years at VOA, I had never considered what we did as slander, even though jamming at that time was intense and relations poor. I reminded him that much of what we broadcast about the Soviet Union had been confirmed by Khrushchev in his seven-hour speech exposing Stalin's crimes at the Twentieth Party Congress in 1956.

He softened his tone and said that Stalin had been responsible for many injustices, as Armenians knew so well. I conceded that perhaps the Cold War had generated some propaganda excesses which seemed out of tune now, Melikyan nodded and admitted that he had written much in the 1950s of which he was now ashamed.

Melikyan dropped the subject and switched to our relations with China and to a foreign policy speech by President Nixon, whose attention to China Melikyan found irritating—"Such warm words for a country we have scorned for years is a deliberate provocation intended to give you leverage against the Soviet Union. In this critical time in Soviet-Chinese relations, you are employing psychological warfare."

He attacked Nixon and said the president was not honest, "even in his war planning," and that because of the overtures to China, the Pentagon would no longer contemplate war with that large Asian country. Noticing my puzzled expression, for I clearly had no idea what he was talking about, Melikyan explained that from his extensive readings—the sources of which he was not willing to reveal—Pentagon plans until now had allowed for two-and-a-half wars—one against the Soviet Union, one against China, and a half, small-scale war somewhere else. But now, he said, the new Pentagon estimate was for one-and-a-half wars, with the China war no longer a probability.

Because of my own ignorance about all of this I was unwilling to discuss it further and noted, in a change of subject, that the first round of SALT had appeared to go well. This too got a rise out of Melikyan, who charged former President Johnson with duplicity—"It was known in Soviet quarters that Johnson had intended to initiate the talks much earlier but had used an irrelevant event to postpone them."

What was that irrelevant event, I asked him?

"August 20, 1968," Melikyan said sharply, which was astonishing to hear. His unwillingness to recognize and identify the invasion of Czechoslovakia except by the euphemism of the date of that event—an event apparently anathema to him—verged on the paranoid.

We ate in silence until he raised some personal problems he was having of a professional nature. Five TASS correspondents to cover the American political scene were simply not enough, he maintained; four of them were so busy that he, the bureau chief, had to cover both the State

Department and the White House by himself. He said that most of the journalists from the East European news agencies—MTI, Agerpress, PAP and Ceteka—often phoned him asking for leads or news breaks, but that he had no close relations with them except for two Hungarians, Csaba Kis, who had introduced us, and Peter Vajda of *Nepszabadsag,* whom I had known in Budapest and was seeing regularly in Washington. Melikyan had known both of them when all three were in Moscow.

The lunch ended and we agreed to arrange another in the near future.

XXXIII

I RETURNED TO MY OFFICE AT USIA AND WAS SUB-merged the rest of the afternoon in staff meetings chaired by Jenks on press and cultural problems in the communist countries: our embassy in Poland wanted more space films to lend out; the Romanian Embassy in Washington was again complaining about our seeming reluctance to give them a library in New York; Hungary would not allow us to use Hungarian-speaking American guides in our annual exhibit in Budapest, and so on.

This was routine stuff which we encountered almost every day, and hearing the beginning of most sentences by our various desk officers, I could construct the ending even in my contemplative state. My mind was troubled as though a computer had been fed conflicting questions and couldn't provide an accurate printout. Jenks continued with the agenda—"And, surprising none of us, more problems with our guides in the Soviet Union working at the *Education USA* exhibit. God-damned KGB, won't let them alone!"

I snapped out of my reverie and looked at him quickly, not because such problems were startling or new; guides were forever being sexually compromised, male and female, in the very same classical ways year after year, despite our warnings and briefings. It was mention of the KGB that had triggered the reaction within me.

My thoughts now turned to the lunch I had just come from, how it had come about, its substance and the questions, so reminiscent of those put to me by Rafael Aghayan in Berlin, and their relevance to my work and experience. Employing journalistic cover was standard intelligence procedure with the countries of the Soviet bloc, and while the many communist journalists I knew went through the motions of normal journalistic work, I did not necessarily think of them as straight intelligence officers.

Aghayan, on the other hand, was a KGB officer, pure and simple. But was Melikyan? Could it be that Aghayan, having failed in his mission and now vanished from the scene, was being replaced by Melikyan, extending the reach of the KGB from Berlin to Washington? These and other questions stayed with me that afternoon and in fact in the weeks and months that followed as Melikyan and I came into contact at Soviet Embassy functions on a variety of occasions—the annual celebration of the Bolshevik Revolution, a visit by Minister of Culture Furtseva, or the 100th anniversary of the birth of Lenin.

It was at the Lenin anniversary that Melikyan introduced me to the long-time ambassador of the Soviet Union, Anatoly Dobrynin, who on learning of my ethnic origin was effusive in his praise of Armenians, for whom he seemed to have a special feeling, the reason for which I was to learn later.

When I commented on the excellent buffet, Dobrynin beamed and said the Soviet Embassy chef was an Armenian. He asked me what my precise title was at USIA and when I told him he became very serious— "That means you have control over 'Voice of America' policies, so let me tell you something. If the 'Voice' slanders the memory of Vladimir Ilyich Lenin, the George Washington of the Soviet Union, the damage to Soviet-American relations will be profound," and continued his lecture with frequent poking of his forefinger hard against my chest.*

Melikyan covered an enormous spectrum of political activities in his conversations with me, some connected to USIA, some to State and other government agencies, but differed from Aghayan in that he was never reluctant to discuss Soviet matters, up to a point, of course. I often turned to the Soviet domestic scene when he would begin to complain about the reporting of Moscow-based American correspondents. Expulsion of correspondents by both sides had become frequent and Melikyan referred to the "game of retaliation" when for instance the Soviet Government expelled *Newsweek's* John Dornberg and the State Department expelled one of Melikyan's TASS staff.

"The problem of dissidence is serious enough for us," he argued, "without American journalists like Dornberg making it worse and

---

*When I passed this message to Richard Davies at State, who had now become Deputy Assistant Secretary responsible for the USSR and East Europe, he sent it on to Secretary of State Rogers because, as he put it, of its source and forcefulness. In fact, VOA paid oblique attention to the Lenin observance.

embarrasing the Soviet Union. Dornberg violated the principle of non-intervention in the domestic affairs of the Soviet Union."

"Oh, come off it, Artem," I said with irritation, "you've served in London for five years and you've been here three, and by now you should have a broader view of press freedom and what is news."

Giving no ground, Melikyan complained that the problem of controlling the dissidents was very difficult. He referred to a CBS program in May entitled "Voices from the Russian Underground" in which correspondent Bill Cole had interviewed a number of prominent dissidents— "We confiscated the first interview Cole did with Amalryk, but then he did a second one and got not only that one out but all the others too. Our controls are not what they used to be."*

He complained about the current *Washington Post* correspondent, Anthony Astrachan, suggesting he too was heading for trouble and facing expulsion. But Melikyan saved the most vitriol for Anatole Shub, whom he had mentioned at our first lunch. Shub seemed to be a *bete noire,* apparently even more after his expulsion in May 1969 with his series of articles illuminating the darkest corners of Soviet society.

"Shub is a very cynical journalist. You know, he was already aware in the spring of 1969 that he would be expelled any day. He had been warned by the Foreign Ministry months before, but he said he was not worried because if he were expelled, it would raise his lecture fee in the West to $1,000."**

Nevertheless, Melikyan continued, the Foreign Ministry should have waited for Shub's visa to have expired. "He had only two months to go. It was the same story with my TASS colleague. You had to retaliate, I understand that, but he too had only two months left. My government is sometimes too impetuous. I really don't think we should be so nervous."

We talked frequently about the major dissidents in the Soviet Union, especially Alexander Solzhenitsyn and Andre Sakharov. Melikyan took the standard Soviet position that Solzhenitsyn was an opportunist who exploited the foreign thirst for anti-Soviet literature, and labelled "The

---

*Andrei Amalryk, author of "Will The Soviet Union Survive Until 1984?" was tried and sentenced after CBS aired this program to three years in a labor camp, his second exile to Siberia. In 1976 he was allowed to leave the USSR and came to the U.S. for a series of lectures. On November 12, 1980, the eve of the Madrid follow-up human rights conference where he hoped to join other former Soviet human rights activists, he was killed in a car accident near Guadalajara.

**Shub denies having been warned or having made this statement.

First Circle"—which I had said was a great novel in the grand old Russian tradition—trash. He also repeated the charge that the Nobel Committee had been politically motivated, as in the case of Boris Pasternak,
in having awarded the Literature Prize to Solzhenitsyn.

As for Sakharov, Melikyan said he had only read the much-publicized
letters in their American versions and agreed that in nobility of concept
he could not argue with the dissident scientist, but that "it is unhealthy
to nourish such anti-Soviet ideas."

When I asked his opinion of the recently published Khruschchev
"Memoirs," he charged that it was not genuine because "retired Soviet
politicians just do not write their memoirs, only retired generals. But my
candidate for the most fascinating memoirs of all is Vyacheslav Molotov.
He knew everybody from the beginning and unlike Khruschchev was in
on everything." He said he often ran into the old Bolshevik on the street
because Molotov took strolls near his apartment which was close to
TASS headquarters.

We of course also talked about the most prominent Soviet Armenian,
Anastas Mikoyan. Would Mikoyan emerge from retirement and go to
Armenia to celebrate the 50th anniversary of the Soviet 'liberation' in
November? Melikyan smiled at my irony but replied it was doubtful
since Mikoyan had not done that for the Azerbaijan anniversary—"As
you know, he played an important role in the Soviet victory in Baku."

I was delighted that he had brought that up because Mikoyan's true
role in Baku and the establishment of communism in the Caucasus
has been the subject of scholarly dispute, and asked—"Are you aware
of one aspect of that important role which American scholars have
investigated?"

"Yes, I am. You mean the death of the 26 commissars, one of whom
was the great Armenian communist Stepan Shaumyan."

"Exactly," I responded, welcoming his willingness to explore this subject so sensitive to Soviet historians, "especially since there is the view
by those who have delved deeply that Shaumyan was a much greater
figure than Mikoyan."

Melikyan ignored that and went on to describe his version of what
Western historians speculate was a massive double-cross in the 1918
attempts by the Bolsheviks to seize power in the Caucasus—

"Mikoyan and his comrades were struggling against the anti-com-
munist Mussavatists in Baku. He was wounded and together with the

other 26 commissars was captured and imprisoned. He escaped, however, and conspired successfully in the underground to facilitate the
release of all 26, including Shaumyan. Everyone went on a ship and
set sail in the Caspian Sea for Astrakhan. The real culprit is the
captain of the ship, who betrayed them, not Mikoyan. In mid-journey,
the captain changed course and arrived in Krasnodar which, at that
time, was still held by the British. On landing, all 26 were shot by the
British. That's the true story."

I looked at Melikyan for a long moment—"All but Mikoyan. How do
you explain that? Maybe that is why he didn't help celebrate the Baku
take-over." He shrugged his shoulders as though to say—take it or leave
it, but that is our official version.

Melikyan did not hesitate to talk about Stalin, maintaining that the
Soviet dictator's deeds were not fully known to the public.

"When Stalin died, I was 28 years old. We had heard all kinds of
rumors about some of those things but only the inner circle, the Politburo, knew of the evils he had inflicted on us. You must understand,
however, that in a country as backward as the Soviet Union, a strong
man is required at the top."

We would then discuss, often argue, the essential differences between
a strong man and a criminal, which sometimes took us far afield of the
Soviet Union and into exploration of dictatorial regimes friendly to the
Soviet Union or the United States. Sometimes, it seemed to me, these
differences were blurred, but not in the case of Stalin.

In the year we were meeting, 1970, Melikyan's new boss, Leonid
Zamyatin, just appointed as TASS Director-General, and Mikhail
Zimyanin, Editor-in-Chief of *Pravda,* visited Washington. Shortly after
they left, Melikyan and I talked about the visit and I found his views on
both officials remarkably candid.

He played down Zamyatin, both as a personality and as a figure in the
Soviet hierarchy, almost as though there were a personal animosity figuring in their relationship—"Zamyatin is not even a member of the Central Committee, as all his predecessors were, although at the next party
congress he will certainly become one."

I told Melikyan that I had met Zamyatin only a few months before
when Ambassador Beam had hosted a lunch for Henry Loomis and I
had sat next to Zamyatin. At that time I had repeated to Zamyatin a
rumor in Washington that he might succeed Dobrynin as Soviet Ambas-

sador. Zamyatin had smiled and denied it in his soft voice, saying merely that he was satisfied with his position as Foreign Ministry Press Chief, that is, Soviet spokesman.

Melikyan said that Zamyatin had no choice but to deny the rumor, but that in fact Zamyatin had been a candidate for the plum post—"He had already been in the Foreign Ministry for eight years, which for that job is a very long time. So, he was instead transferred to TASS."

For Zimyanin, however, Melikyan had nothing but praise—"Being *Pravda's* chief editor carries tremendous prestige and authority in our country, and besides, Zimyanin is a dynamic person with the temperament of an Armenian. He enjoyed hearing me say that to him. Why didn't Washington appreciate his importance? So little was done."*

It was not true that we had underestimated the importance of either visiting official, I countered, neither at USIA nor at State. I reminded Melikyan that the visit had coincided with that of President Ceausescu and almost the entire Romanian Government, and that most of our Washington official forces had been deployed for them. I teased him by asking why the Soviet Government hadn't checked with Bucharest about schedules in order to avoid conflict, to which Melikyan responded with a sardonic laugh.

And of course there was always USIA, as well as Frank Shakespeare, and VOA, and jamming. Melikyan's most reiterated questions centered around why Shakespeare made USIA and VOA so anti-Soviet, so cold-warrish. I pointed out that most of the news he considered anti-Soviet was of Soviet making and largely events taking place inside the Soviet Union, which VOA merely reported, objectively and without polemics, as all news organizations did. "You should be flattered we pay so much attention to you," I told him, but which he didn't appreciate. He retaliated by drawing a line between news and interference in internal affairs, a subject on which we could never have a meeting of minds.

Shakespeare, who was often himself the maker of news because of his strong views on the Soviet Union, was of particular interest to Melikyan,

*On the contrary, both Soviet visitors were considered important enough that the White House Press Office hosted a lunch, attended by Melikyan too. Soon after the visit, Zamyatin was transferred again, to the post of Central Committee Chief of International Information, and with equal bureaucratic logic, Zimyanin was elevated to Secretary of the Central Committee in charge of ideology. But when Mikhail Gorbachev came to power, the fortunes of both changed dramatically: in 1986 Zamyatin was appointed Soviet Ambassador to the United Kingdom and in early 1987 Zimyanin was ousted from the Central Committee.

especially at this time because of an increasingly publicized policy difference between Shakespeare and Secretary of State William Rogers concerning approaches towards the Soviet Union—a professional difference
apparently colored their personal relationship as well. Seeing my reluctance to discuss such a sensitive matter, Melikyan did not pursue it.

There was never an occasion when he couldn't find a private corner at
some reception for a few minutes to continue his relentless probing.
Throughout the summer, his and my duties brought us together at official functions for chats of varying length, but by the fall, I had no
illusions anymore that in conversing with Melikyan I was dealing with
only a journalist. In my dealings with Soviet and East European representatives, my manner was always relaxed and natural, no matter what
my instincts dictated, and that is how I behaved with Melikyan.

But the nature of his questions, often taking on the atmosphere of an
interrogation, soon put me on guard and my growing concern began to
brake my responses. I dreaded the thought of having to repeat the experience by that lake in *Königswusterhausen,* even if on the home territory
of Washington. Consequently, because I wished to avoid conditions
which might invite such a repetition, I declined several invitations from
Melikyan, especially one for dinner at his apartment, and decided to put
him on ice for awhile.

Meanwhile, I had become aware of a gradual new phenomenon
taking place at the Soviet Embassy on Sixteenth Street. Over the
months as I had attended receptions there, Melikyan would introduce
me to yet another member of the embassy of Armenian origin. In this
way I soon became acquainted with three—Third Secretary Vladimir
Adamyants, Third Secretary Georgy Assaturov, and Second Secretary Ashot Nanagyulian.

While I had always been aware of Armenians serving in Soviet embassies in the Middle East where there were large Armenian colonies, such
had not been the case in the Washington embassy. Perhaps it had to do
with detente, I thought, or with the closer ties of American-Armenians
to the Mother Church in *Etchmiadzin,* and the fact that packaged tours
to "visit the homeland" had sharpened the need for more Armenian-
speaking personnel at the embassy. Perhaps.

Since returning from Soviet Armenia, I had not thought too much
about that midnight meeting at Lenin's statue. That may have been
Freudian—suppressing unpleasant experiences—but I cannot say the

encounter was unforgotten. Once on a nostalgic radio program of mystery story favorites of past years when we heard an episode of "The Shadow," Roseann and I burst into laughter, maybe a bit nervously, but we did have more serious moments without such artificial reminders when we speculated on that curious incident. In my meetings with Melikyan, occasionally my thoughts would revert to the mysterious stranger and his identity would trouble me.

As I reduced the frequency of meetings with Melikyan finally down to absolute zero, I did wonder if he was going to pass me on to one of his newly-arrived colleagues, all three of whom I had casually met. Their voices—the only thing I might recognize in The Shadow—were totally unlike his. But the matter of succession hung in the air: would it be Adamyants, Assaturov or Nanagyulian?

The answer, when it came, stunned me.

XXXIV

IN MID-OCTOBER I ARRIVED HOME LATE ONE EVENING to find Roseann in a mood of curious amusement. "I think you'll want a drink before I tell you about a phone call I just received." Mystified, I did as she said but detected in her manner that it had been no office call, as often happened while I was en route. "Come on, let's have it," I said impatiently.

"You'll never guess who's in town. About an hour ago I got a call from none other than your old Berlin buddy, Rafael Aghayan."

I stared at her—"Here in Washington? You're kidding!"

"I'm not kidding at all. He was very friendly, asked about the boys, spoke of our close friendship in Berlin and asked for you and when I said you hadn't come home yet, he said he would phone again."

We looked at each other in silence. I felt a weight pressing down on me which must have been reflected in my expression for Roseann's amusement now changed to somberness—

"Some nerve, wouldn't you say? After what happened!"

"Some coincidence, is more like it. You know, he had told me he had never been to the United States. He chose the time for his maiden visit carefully. Let's eat and see what he wants, if he calls."

It was well after our dinner that the phone rang. I jumped, even though I knew it would ring at any moment. I was tense when I picked up the receiver; after all, I was about to be talking once again with a Soviet intelligence officer whom I hadn't seen in six years.

At his first words, I smiled disbelievingly, as Roseann later told me. He was the same old Rafael with his guttural Armenian, his overdone joviality, the very epitome of warmth and camaraderie—

"Edward, how are you, man, where have you been. You disappeared, and I've missed you."

He said he was in Washington for only a brief time and had looked me up in the phone book. He wanted to meet because he had to leave soon. I said he could visit me at my office.

"Your office is for business, and my seeing you is personal."

I then proposed he meet me in front of USIA headquarters on Pennsylvania Avenue, but he rejected that as well, reminding me of our very first attempt to meet in Berlin. We finally agreed to meet in front of the hotel he was staying at, the Alban Towers, two days later at 3 PM.*

Arriving at the corner of Wisconsin and Massachusetts Avenues on time, I saw him standing in front of the hotel entrance looking nervously here and there. As I alighted from the cab, he spotted me and his gold teeth flashing through his smile, came running to greet me, wrapping his arms around me. When I didn't respond he seemed disappointed and asked if I were in a hurry. I nodded and said there was time only for a quick cup of coffee. We walked up Wisconsin to a small grill, he shifted a paper bag he carried from hand to hand, all the time asking about my wife and family. He seemed nervous, but so was I. We entered and sat in a booth.

Aghayan began by noting that my hair had turned gray and attributed it to heavier responsibilities (which is why you're here—I said to myself).

"What are you doing in Washington?" he asked.

"What am *I* doing in Washington, Rafael? What kind of a question is that? I should be asking what *you* are doing here? You really don't know what I do? Come on, Rafael, I can't believe you haven't discussed me with your friends in the Soviet Embassy who know me—Dobrynin, Chernyakov, Kamenev, Yevstafyev, Isatchenko, plus the Armenians."

He nodded at all the names, the second being Dobrynin's deputy and the other three all in the press section, with which I had a great deal to do.

"But I didn't know they knew you," he said, looking very innocent.

"How about Artem Melikyan at TASS?"

"Yes, I know Melikyan, but your name did not come up. No, Edward, really," he added quickly when he saw my smile of derision. So I laid it

---

*'My people' as Aghayan had referred to them in Berlin, were greatly intrigued by his emergence in Washington which represented a revival of interest by the KGB and encouraged me to keep the appointment.

on, with my title and my responsibilities, and he acted as though it were all new to him.

"So, you are still making propaganda against the Soviet Union," he laughed, trying to minimize the harshness of his comment.

"We all have our professions. So let me ask you again—what are you doing in the United States?"

The juxtapostion brought a frown to his face—"I am doing the work I always do, Edward. Just as I did in Berlin."

"I remember that work very well."

"Yes, it was consular work, very boring, stamping visas all day. I am now here to do the same. I arrived in the United States on September 23 to assist in consular affairs at our United Nations Mission in New York and made an official request to visit Washington. I stopped off in Philadelphia—what a terrible city, with such narrow streets—and arrived here a week ago. I leave for the Soviet Union at the end of the month."

He took out a picture of his son Edward, now attending the university studying to be a diplomat, and said one of his two daughters was also at the university.

"Will you ever be visiting Moscow where you have never been?"

I couldn't believe my ears—"Still playing games with me, are you? You mean to tell me you don't know that in June 1967, my wife and I went to the Soviet Union and visited Moscow, Leningrad and Yerevan? And you also don't know that in December of last year, just nine months ago, I spent four days in Moscow with the Deputy Director of USIA?"

For the first time that I could remember, Aghayan lost his self control. His eyes and features were filled with dismay as, abandoning his normally operatic style of drama, he sat in front of me paralyzed and speechless. It was so enjoyable that I pursued it, telling him that after Berlin, I had spent four years in Budapest. Now his face registered consternation.

"You were in a socialist country for four years, and I didn't know it," he said listlessly, as though talking to himself. He shook his head and looked down into his cup of coffee.

There was now a long pause but I looked at my watch and made an impatient gesture. Aghayan leaned across the table and held my arm—

"You will surely be going to Moscow again in your present senior capacity. It will be unforgivable if you don't phone. We have no telephone book, as you do here, but you can get me through the Foreign

Ministry. Or else, in other countries, I can meet you anywhere in East or West Europe. Incredible that you were in Hungary all that time. And in the homeland!"

He took out a small date book and said—"I want to invite you to dinner, to a nice restaurant near here called *The Three Thieves*. What is the best night for you?" Pen poised in mid-air, he looked at me expectantly.

I smiled at him, shaking my head, and thinking—Maybe this is the time to call a spade a spade—

"Rafael, how can you sit there so blithely and talk about meetings and dinners, as though what happened back in East Germany never took place?"

He put his pencil down and seemed taken aback by this evocation of the past and asked gravely—"What troubles you about our friendship in Berlin?"

"You are incredible, man, simply incredible. Is your memory so weak? How about that letter from somebody in the Soviet Armenian Republic asking for information; how about all that money you were pushing on me; how about what I told you then and what I'll repeat for your benefit now—I am a loyal official of my government. My work is open and public. I want no part of the kind of dirty work you asked me to perform. That is your kind of work, Rafael, not mine. I will not betray my government. Is that clear?"

The conversation had clearly taken a turn he had not anticipated for he showed growing alarm, even looking around although we were, as always, talking in Armenian. He toyed pointlessly with his pencil. The ball was clearly in his court and he knew it. He cleared his throat and in a thick, tense voice he spoke—

"Dear friend Edward, I knew you were deeply offended then, because you left Berlin with your family, whom we liked so much, without even telephoning me. I'd like to say something about that incident in Germany. It was not my idea to ask you to do what was in the letter. Not my idea. It came from others. I would never have asked you to do such a thing. But they insisted I talk to you about helping us."

I leaped at the opening—"Did you say 'they'? Tell me who 'they' are, Rafael? Who do you mean?"

He shook his head indicating he was not at liberty to say, and when I scowled in disappointment at him, he seized my arm—"Please believe me, Edward, please. I had nothing to do with it. Except, maybe, for the money."

The man was full of surprises!

"Did you say—except for the money? Rafael, that was quite a bit of money you were forcing on me."

"Yes, I know. It was all mine—my own money and my own idea."

"You have that much money to give away? Really, Rafael, why would you give me money out of your own pocket, and so much?"

"Because I thought it might help you make up your mind. I was wrong."

"Not only you but 'they' too were wrong. Listen to me, if 'they' still have any ideas, tell them to forget me. I repeat that for you—*tell them to forget me.*"

We both now sat in silence as though the air had been cleared. My watch showed that one whole hour had gone by. Then, he spoke again—

"Would you forget what has happened and have dinner with me, please. I beg you."

I had the strange feeling that before my eyes, Aghayan was becoming almost a genuine human being.

"Listen, although it is difficult for me to forgive you, which I have not, I did agree to meet you today because this is your first time in the United States. All right, if you insist, we can meet again, but not for dinner, for lunch. I do have one condition, however—any ideas which sound like plans you had in the past will mean the end of our relationship. Agreed?"

He was crestfallen, and I was amazed. My God, I thought, after all that I have just said, how could he still entertain any thought of recruiting me. Don't 'they' ever give up?

"Agreed," he said finally and proposed the following Friday. He now opened his paper bag and took out gifts: for me a bottle of Armenian cognac, for Roseann some jars of caviar, and for the boys three plaques from Armenia.

"Something for everyone," he stressed and asked about them again.

Aghayan was fishing for an invitation which he was not going to get.

But he had given me much to think about. His reaction on learning of my having been in Budapest, Moscow and Yerevan was far too startling to have been anything but real. My own reaction to his could only be one of astonishment, for it told me something about the adversary's coordination and sense of networking.

After almost one-and-a-half years of continuous contact in Berlin, how could there be no awareness of my assignment in Hungary, especially after Aghayan's persistent efforts to draw it out of me? And if they knew, why the silence? But something must have happened during our visit to the Soviet Union, and the only thing that occurred to me was that The Shadow was not a follow-up to Aghayan's project but a totally independent effort by the KGB once it had learned of my trip, before or after arriving in Soviet Armenia. Even so, weren't there cross-files so that they could connect me with the Berlin meetings? And even if they had made the connection, why had they not informed Aghayan?

Beyond that, what was Aghayan now doing in Washington, and why was he making these strange confessions to me? Since Armenia, no one had made any allusion to that visit and I certainly did not expect Aghayan to do so, especially now that it was obvious he had been unaware of it. Why had he been kept in the dark? Because he had once failed? Was he now re-instated and back on the case?

There were many questions and two few answers, but then, I told myself, since when did the KGB tell you anything.

XXXV

M Y AGREEMENT TO MEET AGHAYAN A SECOND TIME
for lunch was met with some astonishment at home. But when
I described the substance of our conversation, my wife was
impressed by Aghayan's admissions and concurred that it just wasn't
every day one sat down with a KGB officer and discussed the whys
and wherefores of recruitment.

"You know, I'm getting the impression that perhaps you might like
Rafael a little."

I thought that was going a bit too far, but had to admit I did not
hate him. In turning over what had happened, I had concluded that
he had been sent on a mission to Berlin and it had failed; the job had
been bungled because someone had misjudged the quarry—whether
he, Aghayan himself, or Shishkin, or a faceless case officer in Moscow. I certainly did not feel sorry for Aghayan, and somehow he must
have enjoyed some equity, else he would not now be in Washington
and so heavy in pursuit. I could not help being curious about Aghayan's interests, which always told us so much, and in fact this was the
widely held view of interested parties—'my people'—at whose urging
I kept the appointment.

We met at *The Three Thieves* for lunch. I gave Aghayan a picture
book of Washington for his family which he said they would enjoy. I
ordered for both of us, following which he wasted no time.

"Edward, I ask permission to inquire about public matters, not secrets."

I gave permission but noted that what constituted public and secret matters
depended on who was doing the defining. What did he have in mind?

His first item concerned two air incidents which had just taken place:
two Soviet hijackers had forced an Aeroflot plane down in Turkey, killing
the stewardess and wounding one of the pilots; meanwhile, a U.S. Air

Force plane with two American generals had been forced down in Soviet Armenia.* Aghayan's comments linking the two incidents strongly implied that his government was considering an exchange and whether the Turkish Government would return the two hijackers. Naturally, I couldn't tell him anything, but he said I might want to make a try for the sake of a countryman—

"You perhaps don't know that the injured Soviet pilot, now in a hospital in Trebizond, is an Armenian. Armenians are really everywhere, aren't they?" he laughed.

"They certainly are, even in the Soviet Embassy. You now have three, and counting you, four. What's going on?"

I named them, whereupon Aghayan informed me that Adamyants and Assaturov were Third Secretaries assigned to the Consular Section, while Nanagyulian "is working in the embassy." He said that on the previous Sunday all three had spent the day with him on a fishing picnic. I was tempted to say "like Ivan enjoyed doing" but realized it would have broken the pledge I had demanded of him not to mention the past.

"Rafael, it just isn't clear to me what you are doing here."

He began a complicated description of his function, apparently not in the Consular Section as he had said before, and as he spoke it became clear he was defining the duties of an Inspector—like Ambassador Penfield—a function which every embassy in the world undergoes periodically, an independent examination by professional peers. When I mentioned this, he quickly seized on it—

"Yes, yes, that is it, and that is why I travel so much in Europe. I requested this assignment because I had never been in the United States."

Despite his inconsistency, I asked if he intended to inspect the new Soviet Consulate General in San Francisco. He said there was inadequate time for that but claimed to know the Consul General, Alexander Zinchuk—the same Zinchuk who had joked to me in Moscow about jamming. I asked if any of the three Armenians would be assigned to San Francisco. Aghayan thought not, although he said it would be a good idea because of the large concentration of Armenians in California.

He said he had asked the Soviet Embassy to send me an invitation to its reception on November 27 commemorating the 50th anniversary of the

*This was at least the third time that U.S. reconaissance planes were either forced or shot down over Soviet Armenia since 1958.

Soviet Armenian Republic. I thanked him but pointed out Melikyan was doing the same.

But all of this was merely the curtain-raiser for what really interested him—the policy differences between USIA and the State Department, especially as they involved the Soviet Union. I thought to myself—surely that is top priority KGB business.

I could not tell him that at USIA and State we were concerned about the leakages to the media of fundamental differences between the heads of the two agencies, Frank Shakespeare and William Rogers, who were labelled respectively as being a hawk and a dove on foreign policy towards the Soviet Union. This was the time when Egypt was under Soviet influence and 10,000 Soviet 'advisors' enjoyed Egyptian hospitality (until July 1972 when Anwar Sadat expelled them). Only four days before *The Washington Post* had described one of those differences as centering around whether Egypt was responsible for a specific violation, as Rogers wanted it known, or the Soviet Union, as Shakespeare wanted it attributed.

Aghayan obviously had been given the task of probing for some information through his USIA contact who worked so closely with Shakespeare on Soviet affairs, except that I was proving to be sphinx-like on that one.

Giving up, Aghayan asked—"Isn't it true that American propaganda is going to become even more hostile?"

"Listen, if you people do things which break the rules of international conduct, and we say so, is that hostile propaganda? What about all the nasty things you say about us all the time in your press, on the radio?"

"Only about Mr. Shakespeare, but not about the rest of you."

It was strikingly evident that Frank Shakespeare was very much a thorn in the Soviets' side. Aghayan said the Soviet Embassy was following the debate with great interest "and believing what it reads in the newspapers."

"As far as personal relations go between them, are they good friends?"

I was amused to hear the question because it reminded me of the time in Berlin when he asked the same about Ambassador McGhee and President Johnson. I said simply that they were on a first-name basis.

He didn't know what to make of that, although he said—"I see," so I decided to confuse him more.

"Would you agree that Secretary Rogers and Ambassador Dobrynin have policy differences?"

"Oh, of course, very basic ones."

"Well, Dobrynin calls Rogers 'Bill' and Rogers calls Dobrynin 'Toly.'"

I enjoyed watching him sink into utter confusion, and it took him some time to break his silence, which he did by ostentatiously putting down his knife and fork and leaning forward—

"Let me tell you why this story interests us so much. I am speaking not only of our embassy but our Mission at the United Nations in New York as well. We think Shakespeare and USIA are preparing a personal campaign against our foreign minister, Comrade Gromyko, and that you want to embarrass him. The article in the *Post* says that a memorandum exists mentioning both Ambassador Dobrynin and Comrade Gromyko and compares the present situation with the Cuban problem. You can understand our concern and why it is so important to know how accurate that newspaper report is."*

"If I were to ask you about internal discussions among officials in the Soviet Foreign Ministry or even at the Soviet Embassy here in Washington, would you reveal them to me?" My question produced an awkward smile, and Aghayan picked up his knife and fork and resumed eating.

We finished our lunch. He said there was still a week left before his departure and that perhaps we could meet one more time. I made no commitment on the spot, but later consultations recommended one final meeting so it was arranged that we have one last lunch at the end of the month. It proved to be highly substantive.

---

*The *Post* had equated the situation of Soviet bases in Egypt with Soviet missiles in Cuba, the existence of which Gromyko had denied to President Kennedy in 1962.

XXXVI

WE MET INSIDE THE *ROMA* RESTAURANT, TOOK seats at a table, and Aghayan zeroed in forthwith. I was taken aback at the immediacy of his attack, without even a transparent attempt to camouflage the focus of his interest.

"Let's talk about USIA, Shakespeare and the State Department. You saw that article by that fellow in *The Washington Post?*"

He was referring to Chalmers Roberts, veteran writer for the paper, whose point of departure for the article was the dispute between USIA and State as articulated by Shakespeare and Rogers. Aghayan continued—

"Your Mr. Shakespeare wants to stop the SALT talks and sever relations with my country," wagging his finger at me, his tone grave and accusatory, "we know this Roberts fellow and he always has a red line of truth in his reports."

I laughed—"Your embassy truly believes that after all these years, we would simply cut our relations with you, just like that? What nonsense."

"No, not nonsense, Edward, and I have to know the truth from you."

The waiter came and we ordered, my mind meanwhile buzzing with one specific aspect of Aghayan's preoccupation of which he was probably not aware—that neither Shakespeare nor USIA made policy, that was State's function. That's what I told myself anyway. I also reminded myself of something Frank Shakespeare had once told me when we had travelled together to East Europe. The important thing in Washington, he had said, is not your title but access to the president. None of us ever had any doubt that he had access, not only to Nixon, but to his close aides Alexander Haig and Leonard Garment, yet not very much to Henry Kissinger, at the time still National Security Advisor and himself at some odds with Secretary Rogers, until he succeeded him. I could understand Soviet suspicions even if they struck me as unfounded.

Aghayan interrupted my reverie—

"Why has Mr. Shakespeare surrounded himself with so many tough anti-communists? Aren't we supposed to be getting friendlier? My embassy sees American policy toward the Soviet Union hardening. Why so much belligerence towards us? Your newspapers scream against us all the time. Who is this man Buckley? Tell me what is happening."

William F. Buckley, Jr. was at the time a member of the U.S. Advisory Commission on Information, a non-paid, five-man group of distinguished Americans, which also included novelist James Michener and CBS President Frank Stanton, its chairman. Members of the Commission, whose role it was to advise on the operations of USIA, frequently travelled abroad to acquire first-hand knowledge of the work of our missions.

Buckley had just made such a trip to the Soviet Union and after returning had testified before a Congressional committee about strengthening the broadcasts of the "Voice of America." This testimony interested Aghayan and he asked if I could give him details because, he said, he did not think they had been fully reported.

He looked tentative in making the request and seemed relieved when I burst into laughter—"Then you are not offended that I asked?"

"For God's sake, Rafael, I'm not offended at all, only amused at the workings of your embassy."

"You'll tell me then!"

"I will like hell, primarily because I don't have to. Don't you know that within your own embassy you have an excellent source. Your Press Counselor Yevstafyev was there the whole time. Don't you guys talk to each other?"

He was irritated at the revelation and dropped the subject, only to surface another—

"Why did Ceausescu come to Washington? Did he want trade preferences? What promises were made? Did Nixon and Ceausescu discuss China?"

I raised both hands palms out, as though in defense against this onslaught—"Calm down, Rafael, you'll get indigestion. Now, tell me, is all that really of such importance to you—and your friends?"

"Yes, very. Romania and China are . . well, you understand, of course. Please tell me, why did Ceausescu come?"

"Because he was invited when Nixon went to Bucharest."

"If we invite Mr. Nixon to the Soviet Union, would he accept?"

"Extend an invitation and you'll find out," I replied, unwilling to second-guess the White House.

He now focussed on the talks between the two presidents and repeated the question on the role of China in the discussions. I said that only a very small handful of people were ever privy to the content of high-level talks between chiefs of state. He bent towards me over the table and in a low voice asked—

"Edward, if you were, however, would you tell me?"

"My God," I said, staring in disbelief at him and continuing to stare as the full implication of his request began to engulf me—*they had not given up.* I of course knew what I was dealing with and who it was sitting opposite me. But what amazed me was that after all that had been said and done, the KGB would venture again to subvert me through these overtures on my own home territory.

"Listen to me, Rafael, carefully. If I did know what they talked about, and thought it was in our interest for you to know, I still wouldn't tell you, because I should not deprive Ambassador Dobrynin of the opportunity of finding it out for himself—from the Secretary of State."

My total lack of cordiality hastened the frigid climate which descended on our lunch. As though seeking to repair the damage, Aghayan babbled on now about his days in Washington, sneaking fast looks at me and how he had spent many hours in his hotel room watching television, not seeing much on his first visit to America, never getting an invitation to an American home. He wanted to return and bring his wife. He deplored Washington, said it was not comparable to Paris, London and Moscow, because it was a "Negro capital," and that his colleagues in the Soviet Embassy complained always of "Negro hooligans."

I had no desire any more to engage in debate with him and had no interest in how he felt about anything. I was also perturbed at the outcome of this particular lunch and that a confrontation had been forced on me. As I finished my coffee and decided to end the occasion, I became aware that he had asked a question—

"Who did you see when you were in the homeland? What did they tell you?"

I turned on him now with a vengeance—

"I'm delighted to answer your question—I met artists, writers, musicians, film-makers, critics and many, many wonderful people I shall never forget. They are for me, Rafael, real Armenians. They are Armenians I can be proud of."

He seemed stung, but only momentarily, shrugged his shoulders, and asked when I intended to visit Armenia again. I didn't know.

"When you do, I will take you around myself and introduce you to the right people. Not those so-called intellectuals. Good people, such as the Armenian Foreign Minister, Balabag Mardirossian, a close friend of mine. He will lay on a program for you you'll never forget."

I looked at him reproachfully and shook my head. He frowned—

"Since Berlin, I see your views have not changed. I can understand why Shakespeare appointed you to the Soviet Department of USIA. Anyway, the next time you visit Moscow, call me and give me one day's notice. I'll show you the Soviet Union you don't know."

Outside of *Roma* it was raining and when I hailed a cab, he got in with me and asked if I could drop him at the Soviet Embassy.

During the ride, he continued his attempts at cordiality and spoke again of bringing his wife on his next visit and taking her to San Francisco. But when we entered the short curved driveway of the embassy where several Soviet staffers were standing and looking with curiosity into the cab, Aghayan leaped out without a word and disappeared through the entrance.

I breathed a sigh of relief at having seen the last of this emissary from the KGB—for the second time.

Riding back to my office through the slow Washington traffic, the image of the Soviet Embassy still vivid, I found myself contemplating once again the monstrosity of what was expected of me. This had happened more than once. At a dinner party one evening, I found myself the object of inquiring glances because, as I quickly realized, I had been shaking my head vehemently at a moment when no one was speaking to me. Another time, as I paced up and down at a bus stop, a well-groomed woman irately inquired—"I *beg* your pardon?" and I knew immediately I had been talking to myself, probably angrily if my mood was any barometer.

Now in the miasmic atmosphere of the cab, I succumbed to another kind of reverie, a 'what-if' fantasy prompted by the flippant comment of a senior colleague in Berlin which had stuck in my mind. Fully informed of the details of the climactic incident by the lake, he had given me a mock punch in the jaw and said—"You know? You should have taken the money. No one would have known."

At the time and ever since I had found that both cynical and naive. Take the money and do what—*nothing? They* would never have tolerated that. And it was not true that no one would have known; no one on our side, if I had kept silent, but *they* would have known.

But the fantasy went on: I had taken the money and agreed to cooperate. For awhile, and until departing Berlin, I fed them innocuous bits of information, but as time went on, the demands grew—for copies of cables and memoranda, reports of private conversations, details of personal lives of colleagues. What if I turned into a double agent, where would that have led? Meanwhile, with my bank account getting fatter, how would I keep all this from my wife? Or would I eventually have to bring her in on it?

How would it all end? How had it begun with Alger Hiss and Julius Rosenberg? When had *their* wives been drawn into it? What kind of people were they, and so many other Americans, so weak-willed and motivated by a bankrupt ideology to have acquiesced to treason? Had they witnessed the East German and Hungarian revolts and the several Polish uprisings, would it have affected their commitment? On the other hand, there was Kim Philby, who *had* lived through several East European rebellions, impervious to their messages, and now safely living in Moscow.* Would I also, if uncaught, be safely living in Yerevan? Doing what, staring endlessly at *Mt. Ararat?* The KGB could hardly be expected to trust anyone already guilty of betraying his own country.

My fantasy now built up to dramatic confrontations before Congressional committees, in court rooms, evidence from wire-taps, secret films of secret meetings and pick-ups at dead drops, and the horror grew and grew and almost engulfed me as the cab's squealing brakes and jarring stop brought me back to my senses. We were in front of the USIA building on Pennsylvania Avenue.

Seduction, indeed! In the deepest recesses of my heart I knew it could never have come to any of that.

*He died in 1988.

XXXVII

ARLY IN NOVEMBER, BECAUSE OF PROBLEMS WHICH had arisen in our programs in Bulgaria, Hungary and Czechoslovakia, Jenks decided I had to visit those countries and try to work things out with the host governments.

Meanwhile, Ambassador Dobrynin had scheduled his reception commemorating the 50th anniversary of the founding of the Armenian Soviet Socialist Republic for November 27, which happened to be the very day I was to depart. Regrets were phoned in officially to the embassy, but then I phoned Melikyan privately, with whom I had not spoken for some time, especially while Aghayan had been in town.

Melikyan was extremely disappointed, insisted on knowing why I couldn't attend, and tried to sway me by stressing that over 100 prominent Armenians from various parts of the United States would be present but that I, as the highest U.S. Government official of Armenian heritage, would lend prestige to the occasion.* He concluded with a laugh that "chauvinism will prevail when Russian vodka will be banned and Armenian cognac the only drink in sight."

He was very persuasive but there was no changing my plans, which consisted not just of plane schedules but of carefully worked-out appointments at East European foreign ministries, cultural institutes and working lunches. Despite Melikyan's persistence, therefore, I declined the invitation, but after hanging up, my thoughts turned to the sudden appearance of Aghayan and how it might be connected with Melikyan.

It was clear that Melikyan had tried to cultivate me and despite his manner, personality and technique, so different from Aghayan's, had come up with the same lack of success. It was certainly more pleasant

---

*It was for that very reason that Richard Davies at State viewed the coincidence of my departure for Europe on the same day as the reception as fortuitous.

ing with him: his functional title was excellent cover for him to openly approach me; he always phoned me at the office; and at no time did he caution against telling my superiors about him, as Aghayan always had. For all I knew, perhaps his ploy had been merely to size me up anew, and then have Aghayan re-appear in order to assess its impact. No matter which way it went, fishing in troubled waters was the every-day business of the KGB, and in the intervening years, the quarry had gotten bigger.

Two days before the reception, Melikyan phoned yet another time to ask whether I would reconsider postponing my trip to attend the embassy observance of the Armenian anniversary.

"You surely have more important things to think about these days, Artem," I noted, referring to the bombing a few days earlier of the TASS bureau which had caused great damage to the offices where he and I had shared Armenian cognac, and also the bombing that very morning of the Aeroflot offices in New York.

"Oh, you mean those sons of bitches," he retorted, referring to the militant Jewish Defense League, whose violent protests against the Soviet Union had proliferated all over the country where there was a Soviet presence in the form of concerts, ballet, exhibits and the like.

"Like everything else in life, it's all relative," he said with resignation, and again deplored my inability to attend Dobrynin's reception "for our homeland."*

---

*In May 1985 I attended the Human Rights Experts Meeting in Ottawa as a member of the United States Delegation and its Press Spokesman, and discovered that the Chief of the TASS Bureau was none other than Artem Melikyan. I sent him several messages through other journalists and the Soviet Delegation, but to no avail. I had to assume that as far as he was concerned, the case was closed.

XXXVIII

I T SEEMED TO ME THAT I HAD HARDLY RETURNED SOME three weeks later, just in time for Christmas, when the makings of another trip began inexorably to take shape, this time to Moscow.

Our Counselor for Press and Culture was McKinney Russell, the best Russian speaker in the embassy whose talents—outside of the amusing incident at the *Ararat* Restaurant when I had ordered for everyone in Armenian—had been an enormous asset in the many meetings which Loomis and I had had in Moscow. But there was one aspect of Russell's background which was of special interest to his Soviet colleagues, namely that he had once worked as a news editor at "Radio Liberty" in Munich, a station which during his employment was funded—if secretly—by the CIA.* Had this been a particularly critical problem for them, they could have theoretically protested his assignment at the outset in 1969, or even made known their displeasure through forms of harassment. They did neither, however, that is, until the spring of 1971, and for quite transparent reasons.

The information and cultural policies advocated and implemented by USIA Director Frank Shakespeare towards the Soviet Union had obviously struck home. Convinced that the USSR had been getting away with murder in the propaganda war all these years, Shakespeare geared all our programs and activities in radio broadcasts, films, magazines, books, exhibits to a hard-hitting campaign—the Soviets called it a crusade—against communism in all its forms, often letting the chips fall where they might. This sometimes had unfortunate results, so that ardent and intelligent opponents of totalitarianism such as Willy Brandt

---

*In late 1971, this source of funding ended and, as noted earlier, was transferred to the Board for International Broadcasting, set up by Congress to oversee the operations of "Radio Liberty" and "Radio Free Europe."

and Bruno Kreisky fell into the director's disfavor simply because they were socialists.

Shakespeare instructed Jenks and me to review every program to make certain it carried political freight, and if it did not or could not, to cancel it. Sometimes such cancellations would attract wide attention if the program was one of high visibility, such as when the United States pulled out of the Moscow Film Festival in 1971.*

But there were many other factors which incurred the deep displeasure of the Soviet Government: the growing thaw in American-Chinese relations, of which the Soviet Union was enormously suspicious; the much-increased harassment of Soviet elements abroad by the Jewish Defense League, which Moscow labelled "a bunch of Zionist hooligans"; the increased penetration by American scholars of Soviet society—a price the Soviets had to pay if they wished to enjoy the same access; and not to be overlooked, the huge popularity throughout the Soviet Union of American cultural attractions, to which the Soviet masses flocked in the millions, learning about the United States from extraordinarily attractive artifacts and from Russian-speaking guides who were youthful and bright, reflecting the dynamic American society from which they came.

The Soviets were angry at this confluence of manifestations and showed their ill temper in a long series of newspaper articles. The Soviet propaganda apparatus went into high gear and the organs of the Communist Party and the Soviet Government pulled out all stops.

One of the major attacks was by *Pravda* commentator Viktor Mayevsky, who threw the book at Shakespeare and linked the cultural policies of the United States to his anti-Sovietism, blaming him for creating in the American media an atmosphere which was destroying US-Soviet relations. As an example, Mayevsky singled out columnist Joseph Kraft for having written a series of articles attacking Soviet foreign policy and Soviet cultural programs in the United States.

The atmosphere in Moscow had become so tense that we in Washington decided it was time to move Russell out. In early April, Shakespeare announced a shift of key Public Affairs Officers in Europe wherein

---

*Without USIA's knowledge, Hollywood had submitted the film "Soldier Blue," which concluded with a grisly massacre of an Indian tribe by the U.S. Cavalry—a recurrent theme in Soviet propaganda.

Russell would be transferred to Bonn in July. In Moscow, Russell continued calmly to go about his duties, conducting business as usual and
biding his time. So did we—until the first week in May when it became
quite obvious that I had to get to Moscow as quickly as possible.

For in that week, *Liternaturnaya Gazeta,* the organ of the Union of
Soviet Writers which with time seemed to be less and less devoted to
literary matters, unleashed a vicious personal attack on McKinney
Russell, charging him with subversion of Soviet intellectuals and espionage. Shakespeare, Jenks and I now concluded that Russell had to
leave Moscow even sooner and that I should fly to Moscow and discuss the orderly transfer of Russell and his successor, Andrew
Falkiewicz, with Ambassador Jacob Beam. Because Beam's previous
post had been Prague, where Falkiewicz had worked for him, we
anticipated no problems.

It was a grim Russell who met me at *Sheremetyevo Airport* on the
evening of May 4. During the long ride into Moscow, he pointed out
the large caricatures and slogans lining the road, accusing the United
States of every form of trickery and deceit. "That's what we're up
against these days," he said but left the details for private chats later,
looking pointedly at me as he inclined his head in the direction of the
Soviet chauffeur.

At the Embassy Russell gave me a translation of the *Liternaturnaya
Gazeta* article, written jointly by Andrey Grachow and Yiri Bobrov, com-
menting that it had apparently taken two authors to dream up the elaborate charges concocted against him, charges of the purest fiction.
Naturally, they did include the one detail that he had once worked as a
radio journalist at "Radio Liberty."

I retired early, going home with Assistant Cultural Affairs Officer
Harry Gilmore, a close friend with whom I had served in Budapest. It
was refreshing, after the events of the evening, to enter the happy atmosphere of the Gilmores, whose high spirits did not seem affected by the
gloom outside or the labyrinthine oppressiveness inside their apartment
on *Leninskiy Prospekt.*

The following morning I met with Ambassador Beam who agreed that
Russell should leave early for his own and the embassy's sake and that
Falkiewicz was welcome as his successor. In early afternoon, Russell
and I went to the apartment in the embassy compound of the Deputy
Chief of Mission, Boris Klosson, who had again arranged a stag lunch in

my honor. One of the most knowledgeable Foreign Service Officers on Soviet affairs, Klosson greeted me warmly and announced this time he had invited not one but two Armenians.

The first to arrive was again Pavel Gevorkyan, head of the American Desk at the *Novosti Press Agency,* who on entering embraced me like a long-lost brother, and I reciprocated the pleasure.

The second Armenian was Mikhail Sagatelyan, Deputy Foreign Editor of *Izvestiya,* who spoke no Armenian, not a word. "I have my Russian mother to thank for that," he said grinning, "as well as for my beautiful un-Armenian nose."

Russell's presence turned the conversation very quickly to the press attacks on him, and Russell, Klosson and I tried to ascertain more about them. But both guests, while deploring the need for such public denunciations of diplomats, did not come to his defense, and in fact Sagatelyan, clearly the senior of the two, made the point that there were obviously many aspects of the case with which he was not familiar and, therefore, preferred not to discuss it. The remainder of the lunch was otherwise very pleasant and even filled with political jokes from 'Radio Armenia.'

When we withdrew to the library for coffee, Gevorkyan guided me to a corner and said—

"A few months ago, I received a phone call from a Soviet diplomat I had not known before. He said his name was Rafael Aghayan and that he was bringing me regards from you."

He watched me carefully as he spoke and must have observed my sudden change of expression, for he touched my arm and asked—"You do know someone by that name, don't you?"

"Yes," I said wearily, "I certainly do, and I did ask him to give you my regards."

"Well, I'm glad it was no mistake. You see, we've been in touch since then and right now I know that he is in Baku, vacationing. He'll be very upset when he hears that you've been in Moscow while he was away."

I drank my coffee in silence, aware of Gevorkyan's eyes on me. Then I asked if he could confirm that Aghayan was indeed a Foreign Service Inspector, a function Gevorkyan would be aware of from his own service abroad. He replied that it was true, but I detected little conviction in his reply. No more was said about it at lunch.

Before departing Klosson's lunch, both Gevorkyan and Sagatelyan invited me to their respective offices the next day. I accepted and said that Russell would take care of the arrangements. Sagatelyan's smile disappeared—

"It would be in everyone's interest if Russell did not accompany you."

I replied that we would inform him of our decision, whereupon Sagatelyan added that he hoped I would be free for lunch after the *Izvestiya* visit—alone.

We decided later that afternoon not to be hard-nosed about the visit and that Russell should not accompany me. He in turn made the generous point that he did not wish me to miss the opportunity of visiting the two Soviet institutions. Instead, it was agreed, Press Officer Roger Lydon would go along, and when this information was passed to both Soviet hosts by Lydon, he reported their spirited approval.

The next day, Lydon and I went to *Novosti* on Pushkin Square and were met by Gevorkyan and an assistant named Rukhadze, a Georgian who also spoke Armenian and English. I had alerted Lydon to the possibility that Gevorkyan and I might lapse into Armenian and that he should find someone else to talk to. The participation of Rukhadze now made that possible. After some refreshments and reminiscences of Gevorkyan's tour of duty at the Soviet Embassy in Ethiopia where he had been active in the Armenian community, he suddenly lowered his voice and switching to Armenian said—"You and I have a few things to discuss privately," upon which, as though by pre-arranged signal, Rukhadze arose and led Lydon out of the office.

Now alone and continuing in Armenian, we had an exchange which I had a foreboding would eventually take place. Gevorkyan began—

"First of all, I have news for you. Your friend Aghayan is back from Baku and anxious to see you. In fact, I am now to extend a lunch or dinner invitation to you from him."

This was my last day, I reminded Gevorkyan, and I was to have lunch with Sagatelyan as he knew, and that evening was to be spent with the Russells and Gilmores.

Gevorkyan pursued it by suggesting a late afternoon or early evening meeting, but I declined that too, arguing a busy schedule. He then said that Aghayan might phone me at my hotel, but I reminded him again that I was not at a hotel but staying with the Gilmores. He nodded thoughtfully, obviously searching for some other opening, but gave up, noting that Aghayan would be very disappointed to have missed me but that I would certainly be returning to Moscow and another time might be more opportune.

The other matter he wished to discuss with me, Gevorkyan said, was the press attack against Russell, from which he wished to dissociate himself. He praised Russell as an excellent American representative, then looking soberly at me, said—"You know, Edward, sometimes it is not advisable to be too successful."

His meaning was very clear to me: Russell had more contacts in Soviet society than anyone in the embassy and was seeing people at many levels on a constant basis.

"Russell is one of our best officers and for that you wish to squeeze him out," I commented, referring to the fact that since the press attack, Russell's many contacts had refused to see him. Gevorkyan let that pass without comment, we sipped our drinks, then he opened up a new avenue—

"On a more general subject, let me make an observation which might be helpful in our relations. The director of your agency, Mr. Shakespeare, is too outspoken about the Soviet Union. His recent statements and policies are far too aggressive for us."

We argued back and forth for almost an hour, each of us citing instances and incidents in our bilateral relations which appeared to our respective selves to have contaminated the atmosphere and rooted the mutual suspicion and distrust even deeper. Finally, having purged ourselves, we called it a draw. We joined Lydon and Rukhadze.

Gevorkyan phoned Sagatelyan to announce our departure from *Novosti* for *Izvestiya* and as we walked to the door he said—

"You have not seen the last of me, I think. There is a good chance I will accompany the *Soviet Arts and Crafts Exhibit* to the United States soon. I shall certainly look for you in Washington."

I said finding me was easy because USIA was the responsible agency for such cultural attractions. After a warm farewell, our embassy car took Lydon and me to *Izvestiya* and to yet another Armenian. But I assured Lydon that this time he would not feel excluded because Sagatelyan spoke no Armenian. As for lunch, however, I couldn't be sure.

XXXIX

SAGATELYAN GREETED US WARMLY IN HIS EDITORIAL office. He first gave a long talk about *Izvestiya* in which he told us that it enjoyed a circulation of eight million—"the largest in the world"; that it had thirty foreign correspondents; and that when evaluating their reports, he, as Deputy Foreign Editor, had to tackle some very knotty problems, especially on the reports from the United States. Having served in Washington in the 1960s, Sagatelyan was considered an American expert, about which I was to learn much more at a later date.

He then took us on a tour of the newspaper, in the course of which I ran into its former Budapest correspondent Rodionov, whom I had known. He was surprised and chatted with me in Hungarian, seeming to enjoy himself. Some moments later as we stood waiting for the elevator, a dour-faced gentleman stood alongside us, whereupon Sagatelyan said—"Ed, meet another of our countrymen, Mr. Melikyantz."

"I hope you speak Armenian," I said in the native language.

"Of course I speak our mother language, because unlike others, I am a *true* Armenian. Call me Gevork."

We beamed at each other, both aware of the dig that no one else could understand, and as we descended and he got out, we shook hands and I said—"Gevork, keep the Armenian faith," and he replied—"Both of us."

The tour soon over, Sagatelyan instructed Lydon to have our embassy driver take us to the Soviet Press Club, where we got out. Sagatelyan then turned abruptly to Lydon and said "Goodbye" in what can only be described as a curt dismissal.

Once inside, we were seated in a corner which was quiet until within minutes a large North Vietnamese delegation took over a long nearby table and endless toasts between them and their Soviet hosts rang through the dimly-lit room.

Sagatelyan at first frowned at the interruptions but finally shrugged them off, and when I commented that we were getting a first-hand dose of jamming, he laughed and wagged a finger at me. After ordering a special Georgian wine called *Akhasheni* which he claimed had been Stalin's favorite and now quite rare, we settled down to a marathon debate which covered the horizon of American-Soviet issues.

As though announcing our agenda he said—

"Well, Ed, this is quite an organization you work for, and quite a man this Mr. Shakespeare. Your 'Voice of America' beats us over the head every day; Shakespeare brings in people like Mr. Buckley for advice; you make Solzhenitsyn a hero; you play games with our Chinese friends; your Jews dictate your foreign policy; and Mr. Shakespeare tries to embarrass us by pulling out of the Moscow Film Festival."

Actually, we talked about even more things in the next two hours, but now after that recital, Sagatelyan rubbed his hands together with glee, lifted a vodka and said—"We are going to talk turkey, as you say, because we have the same blood running in our ancient veins." Once or twice he became agitated, his voice rising above the din created by the Eurasian chaos nearby, but most of the time the give-and-take was in a civilized manner.

Some exchanges were brief, such as when he charged William Buckley with being "the ideological enemy of our people," and I corrected him—"not of your *people* but of your *regime*;" or on jamming when he asked—"Do you allow a hostile guest to slander you in your own home?" and I reminded him the so-called slander was news of Soviet making which the government kept from the people. I spoke of the huge imbalance of scholastic freedom, that is, the freedom of Soviet scholars to roam and lecture all over the United States and the police-state tactics to which American scholars were subjected in the Soviet Union.

His rebuttal to that was to denounce McKinney Russell's "illegal" contacts, on which I heaped scorn as not worth the mention in view of the fact that Russell was innocent of those concocted charges while Soviet diplomats were being caught red-handed every day in the United States. This form of debate of course got us nowhere.

But when he raised Solzhenitsyn, we had one of the most revealing exchanges. The eminent Soviet writer always seemed to evoke paranoia in my interlocutors, but with Sagatelyan the approach was pointed and realistic. I repeated to him the comment of TASS Bureau chief Melikyan—whom he knew—who had characterized Solzhenitsyn's work as "trash," and added my own view that "The First Circle" was a literary masterpiece, even in English.

"Melikyan is wrong," Sagatelyan said without hesitation, "Solzhenitsyn is a first-rate writer. I have read all three of his books and they are not trash. But they are anti-Soviet, in the sense that they reflect base elements in man's nature. His philosophy appears to be that man must survive at all costs. We find nothing noble in this; it is an insult to all those who died in the defense of the Fatherland, and to those who died in the camps."

I was startled to hear that, for Soviet officials did not so readily admit the existence of the camps, and pressed him—"Slave labor camps?"

Impatiently waving his hands—"Yes, yes, those camps. Now tell, me, Ed, what is so important about this man that the United States becomes his advocate?"

I was delighted at the opportunity to answer him—It seemed to us a colossal Soviet blunder not to have allowed Solzhenitsyn to go to Stockholm to accept the Nobel Prize because it revealed the deep insecurity and basic weakness of the Soviet system; it told the world that the seemingly all-powerful Soviet regime is afraid of one man, one book, one speech. In contrast, our media were full of intellectuals railing against the government, and we not only survived but felt a deeper commitment to our system which allowed such open dissent—something his newspaper did not seem to grasp.

Sagatelyan's face turned a deep red, he became angry and his voice began to rise—"Now listen to me, Ed, that's just what I might expect from one of Shakespeare's boys . . ." he stopped and seemed to recover, then said—"I just reminded myself that it was I who first raised Solzhenitsyn, and also that you are my guest."

Having recovered, he now jokingly referred to Nixon's policy toward China as Peking Poker; took a few swipes at American journalists, such as James Reston; and then worked his way around to the Jewish Defense League in what I realized shortly was a maneuver to table a pet peeve—

"You can thank not our Jews but yours for any rise in anti-Semitism in the Soviet Union. As for your State Department and your press, I can tell you that American Jews are well represented in Moscow. You have several in your embassy who are, naturally, pro-Israel. You shouldn't have any Jews in your embassy. And *The Washington Post!* It keeps sending us nothing but Jews. Look at the last three—Rosenfeld, Shub and now Astrachan. He will be leaving soon and you can be sure another Jew will take his place. And make trouble like all of them."

"For Christ's sake, Mike, talk about anti-Semitism!"

He took no offense and responded that he was "only being practical."

He had capsule comments on a variety of subjects:

"It was a mistake not to publish *Dr. Zhivago* in the Soviet Union. Not a good novel, but Pasternak could have been read without harm.

"The USIA version of the Angela Davis scandal was ridiculous.

"Shakespeare can pull out of our film festival all the time if he wants but our festival will go on and on."

Finally, we were sated with food, drink and talk, and arose and walked to his waiting chauffeured car. During the drive he was again very cordial and expressed gratitude for the "candid exchange of views." When his car stopped in front of the American Embassy, he helped me out, embraced me and shouting farewells, disappeared into the traffic, as the Soviet militiamen standing guard at the entrance watched. I enjoyed their perplexity as I breezed past them into the embassy.

On that, my last night in Moscow, the Russells and the Gilmores took me to the excellent Moscow Circus in its new quarters, an interesting building erected exclusively for the famed ensemble. As we sat and waited for the performance to begin, I looked around the huge audience packing the house and suddenly wondered what I would do if somewhere in that vast sea of faces I spotted the one face I had no desire to see. The thought was disconcerting and made me uncomfortable, but before I could dwell on it further, the band struck a lively tune and the show began. It was a wonderfully diverting evening.

The next morning on the drive to the airport, we were all in good spirits, each for his own reasons.

XL

T HE SUMMER AND AUTUMN OF 1971 PASSED WITHOUT
event, although anti-Soviet demonstrations instigated by the Jewish
Defense League erupted wherever and whenever Soviet cultural attractions appeared. Consequently, when the time approached late in 1971
that yet another Soviet exhibit would tour the United States, Jenks and I
expected the worst, because this exhibit, *Soviet Arts and Crafts,* culled
from many of the nationalities of the USSR—including Armenians—was
to tour six cities according to our cultural agreement, and we knew that
the JDL's impact on other ethnic groups was beginning to tell.

Although I shouldn't have been surprised, I was when one morning
Pavel Gevorkyan phoned me at USIA to announce his arrival in Washington as Deputy Director of the Soviet exhibit. He invited me to lunch
and we met at the Corcoran Gallery midst packing crates and general
confusion. It was a pleasant reunion and although the lunch was brief
because of heavy engagements for both of us, we caught up on chitchat
and families.

In the weeks that followed we met on and off, once spending an enjoyable evening at our home talking about Armenia, about mutual friends,
and most of all about his family and the severe medical problems of his
daughter, who had been born in New York. My wife offered to research
the specific medication at the National Institutes of Health for him and
find out what was available. Gevorkyan told us of the post-war years he
had spent with the Soviet delegation at the United Nations in New York
when he had been in touch with Armenian communities. He also told
many stories of his adventures during the Ethiopian assignment and of
his contacts in the Armenian community of Addis Ababa.

On this occasion and frequently when we were alone, I had the curious impression that he wanted to tell me something but hesitated—an
inflection in his voice, a questioning look in his eye, but whatever it was
hung in mid-air, much like a suspended chord awaiting resolution.

The exhibit opened at the Corcoran Gallery and the Soviet official present for the occasion was the Minister of Culture, Mme. Furtseva, a handsome figure of a woman and a close associate of former Premier Khrushchev. The Soviet Embassy was enormously pleased and Ambassador Dobrynin gave a huge reception to which Secretary of State Kissinger came, directly from the airport following an overseas trip. The lengthy and cordial *tete-a-tete* at the sumptuous buffet was the center of attention as a jovial Kissinger joked and chatted with a blushing, almost girlish Furtseva, normally a woman of austere presence. Dobrynin beamed.

Everything had been going well at the exhibit and the JDL's protest activities, despite earlier threats of violence, were low-key. One evening in January, as I was preparing to leave the office, the phone rang and an excited Gevorkyan pleaded with me to meet him as soon as possible because of a crisis. Since the Corcoran was just around the corner, I promised to meet him in ten minutes.

"I'm not at the Corcoran," he shouted, "I'm calling from the Soviet Embassy."

We met at the now-defunct Roger Smith Hotel bar, took seats in a quiet corner, ordered drinks, and Gevorkyan began, at first in English then continuing in Armenian. His excitement was not instigated, as I had suspected, by the JDL, but by something quite different.

"Dear Edward, this free press of yours is too much for me. This afternoon, just about two hours ago, I received a phone call from a man who identified himself as a Mr. Whitten and that he was an associate of columnist Jack Anderson. He asked me some questions— Who did I work for in Moscow? I told him the *Novosti Press Agency*. Had I always worked for *Novosti?* No, I was in New York at the Soviet UN Mission after the war. Did I work for some other agency while at the UN? No, I was at the UN from 1946 until 1951, and worked only for the UN. *Novosti* did not exist then. I asked Whitten why he was asking me all these questions, didn't he know that I was here as Deputy Director of the Soviet exhibit? Why did my past work interest him? Then, I found out."

He paused dramatically, looked tensely at me, and let it out—

"Whitten asked me if I am now in the KGB! Edward, I was paralyzed. I told him he had no right to ask me such provocative questions. Besides, I said, journalists don't interview other journalists. But if he intended to pursue this line of interrogation, I wanted him to talk to me face-to-face. I said he should meet me tomorrow at the Corcoran in the afternoon. He said he would come and hung up. I don't know what he's going to write about me. For all I know, he taped the whole conversation. As you can see, I'm very upset. I need your help."

The drinks came, he stared down into his for a few moments, then—

"I really believe in our cultural relations. Incidents like this can only destroy the good atmosphere we have now. You know, Minister Furtseva was so very pleased with her reception in the United States, and the exhibit is such a success. And soon, your president is going to Moscow. Edward, you must do something about this. If you know Jack Anderson, call him. Such a terrible man, always revealing government secrets."

That last comment made me do a mental double-take but I let it pass and instead replied that if Gevorkyan had learned anything from his five years in New York it should have been the independence of the American press. I asked if he was afraid that we in USIA would be prejudiced by charges against him or anyone else of secret police affiliations. If so, I continued, not waiting for his reply, he should not be concerned—

"At USIA, Pavel, we assume that all of you with the exhibit are KGB."

"You do? You really do?" he said, swallowing several times.

"Yes, we do. Just put yourself in our shoes. Wouldn't you also think so. Just reverse the roles and think it through."

After some silence he said meekly—"I guess you're right. I suppose so."

"That's why it really doesn't make any difference to us what any journalist writes about you. All we ask is that you do your job, the one you came for with the exhibit. You had no trouble getting a visa, did you? Of course not."

He became pensive, sipped his drink—"You know, I'll be with this exhibit for only its first half, until June. It really would be very unpleasant if Anderson publicly accused me of KGB connections."

I said we would review the matter, but knew we could do nothing. He in turn promised to phone if Whitten showed up.

"Incidentally, Pavel, why did you call me from the Soviet Embassy over an hour after Whitten phoned you and not immediately from the Corcoran?"

"Because I wanted to consult with my Soviet colleagues in the embassy. Actually, when I mentioned you and said I might ask your help, one of them thought it was a very good idea because, as he said—if there is any way to kill the story, USIA will know how."

I bristled at that and told Gevorkyan to tell his friend that USIA was not in the business of killing press stories, and Gevorkyan said ruefully—"Come on, Edward, I'm the one to be angry about this, not you." He said the problem had gotten to him because it came on top of new concerns for the health of his daughter which, he noted, was having a profound psychological effect on his wife in Moscow.

Whitten did not keep his appointment, as Gevorkyan told me later, but the item did appear in Jack Anderson's column, merely a brief comment, and although Gevorkyan was again dismayed, nothing further came of it.

I attended another opening of the exhibit in Los Angeles which went very well despite demonstrations by the JDL, Baltic groups and Ukrainians. Gevorkyan said he wouldn't have been surprised to see Armenians as well—"just to get a look at the Armenian KGB first hand," he said with a wry smile. In fact, some Armenians did picket briefly.

Whatever it was that Gevorkyan wanted to tell me remained a mystery, and soon after the Los Angeles opening, he returned to the Soviet Union. My guess is that he had a message from Aghayan and was seeking an opportune moment to deliver it. But when exposure of his own KGB affiliation was threatened and then came to pass, he decided to terminate his role of courier.*

---

*It is relevant to note here that in September 1985, when the British Government expelled thirty-one Soviet personnel from London who had been identified by the Soviet Embassy's defecting KGB chief as spies, six of them were journalists—two from Novosti and one from TASS, Melikyan's employer.

XLI

O F THE THREE OTHER ARMENIANS IN THE SOVIET Embassy in Washington, whom I had discussed with Aghayan, only Ashot Nanagyulian displayed more than casual interest in me. At embassy receptions he would work his way to my side and greet me somewhat shyly with *"Pari yerego, Hayrenagits,"* and I always wished him "Good evening" as well. Aghayan had identified the other two, Adamyantz and Assaturov, as consular officers, but about Nanagyulian he had said only that he worked "in the embassy." That had an intriguing ring to it and when Nanagyulian phoned me at home one night in March 1972 inviting me to lunch, I accepted.

Meeting at *Luigi's,* we both ordered large pizzas and I began by asking why he hadn't phoned me at USIA. He said he had, very often, but never found me in my office. I never got a message that he had called, I said, puzzled.

"Of course not, because I never left my name or number."

Why not? What did "of course" mean?

"For your protection, so you wouldn't get into trouble. Your people don't like you to have contact with us in the Soviet Embassy."

Shades of Rafael Aghayan! By telling me so little, he was telling me a lot. I couldn't suppress my laughter, but Nanagyulian was too busy furtively looking from left to right, suspicious of every newcomer. Once he settled back, however, his questions came one after the other.

He began with the Senate Foreign Relations Committee hearings on "Radio Free Europe" and "Radio Liberty" and wanted to know what might come out of them.* Without waiting for a reply, he underlined Senator Fulbright's position that the two radio stations were a contradiction of Nixon's policy of detente. He rushed on, as though his questions

---

*A pertinent question to be asking because at the time I was the USIA representative on an inter-agency committee chaired by State to determine alternate means of funding the two radios, although Nanagyulian couldn't have known that.

were making his points and my anticipated replies were irrelevant: would our relations with Communist China improve; would we open cultural centers there; would Shakespeare accompany Nixon to the Soviet Union; what happened when I made a recent trip to Romania to open our new cultural center in Bucharest; what was on Ceausescu's mind these days, and so on.

I asked him what he did in the Soviet Embassy, as though wiping his questions off the slate. He explained that when he had first arrived, he had been assigned to the Cultural Section but because of an increased work load and staff shortages, he had been transferred to the Consular Section.

"So many Americans are visiting the Soviet Union that Ambassador Dobrynin personally asked me to make the shift. I couldn't say no to the Ambassador, but anyway, my wife works there with me, and that is nice."

I asked what he had done prior to this assignment.

Nanagyulian said he had worked in the bureau in Yerevan which deals with Armenians abroad, directly responsible to the Armenian Foreign Ministry. This clarified his 'cultural' role—contacting Armenian communities in the United States. We discussed the centers of Armenian population, totaling almost one million—Boston, New York, Detroit, Philadelphia, Fresno, and, growing rapidly and larger than all of them, Los Angeles. Nanagyulian told me of a long trip he had made to California accompanying the Director of the Soviet Armenian Committee for Relations with Armenians Abroad, and spoke almost enviously of the prosperity enjoyed by most Armenians in the United States, "no poverty and very middle-class, bourgeois," he said, and seemed hugely impressed with the abundant flowering of Armenian churches and schools whose centers of learning were keeping alive the singular Armenian language as well as its history and literature.

In truth, Nanagyulian seemed well-informed about American-Armenians and their accomplishments, but it seemed to have been a rude awakening for him, as though he had come to the United States believing the Soviet propaganda that Armenian culture was dying in the West and surviving only in Soviet Armenia.

Nevertheless, he was aware of the eroding influence of other civilizations and wondered about communities elsewhere in the world, founded especially after the eleventh century invasion of the Seljuk Turks when Armenians dispersed to Bulgaria, Poland, Hungary and

Russia and other countries of Europe, to North and South America, to Asia. I asked if he were aware that Montevideo had an Armenian radio hour, as did most of the American cities, or that Translyvania had two completely Armenian towns, or that India had streets named after Armenians? He professed not to be familiar with communities beyond the United States, but whenever the subject of the Armenian diaspora came up, I found him to be genuinely emotional and he liked to say that maintaining the cultural heritage in the face of foreign assimilation was of prime importance.

When it came time to pay the check, we engaged in a small tug of war which ended when he pointed out, with considerable gravity, that it had been he who had extended the invitation, therefore, it was a matter of Armenian honor that he pay the bill. When we left the restaurant, his honor remained unsullied.

That was our first substantive conversation, but we were to have several more. The best of them took place in his apartment in Hyattsville, a suburb of Washington, when we were also introduced to his wife, a lively personality all her own. It was May 28, 1972 and President Nixon, who was in the Soviet Union, had just minutes before delivered an address over Soviet television which had been shown simultaneously in the United States. When we arrived at 3 PM, the Nanagyulians greeted us at their apartment door interrupting their extensive preparations, on which they blamed having missed Nixon.

An intense, nervous, energetic brunette, Mrs. Nanagyulian said she had been busy in the kitchen while her husband had been out in the woods behind the high-rise barbecuing the *shashlik*. She returned to the kitchen as we became comfortable and Ashot served Armenian cognac. He said it was their hope that Nixon had emphasized peace because that was what the Soviet Union wanted most. When I confirmed that Nixon had, a shrill voice from the kitchen rent the air—

"Then why doesn't he end the war in Vietnam if he loves peace so much!"

Not only we but Ashot too were startled, he more embarrassed and when he caught her eye she came into the living room and apologized for the outburst. But through the afternoon, it was she who took the initiative and obviously she who commanded the Nanagyulian household. Time and again, Mrs. Nanagyulian would interrupt our private political conversations with an ideological aside, indicating that even while attending to her chores, her ears were constantly alert to the chit-chat in the other room.

At the same time, it was the height of incongruity to hear her talk about American television and her favorite program—"I Love Lucy."

"I work half-days in the Consular Section and come home shortly after noon, and from that moment on, I can't wait to turn on 'Lucy' every day."

Despite her virtually non-existent English, Mrs. Nanagyulian seemed to catch all the nuances of the program and in fact, to the visible discomfort of her husband, re-enacted a "Lucy" episode involving a mink coat. As she performed some angular antics, I heard Ashot mumble something to me, but his wife's hysterical voice drowned it out. But when she finally finished, he tried again and I couldn't but marvel at the total absurdity of the scene—his wife behaving like a zany while he, pursuing his ends, was asking if progress had been made in Moscow on a US-USSR trade agreement.

I said it was not in my area of competence but that the settlement of the Lend-Lease debt appeared to be one of the obstacles. Ashot said softly, as was his manner, that the American terms were too high for settling the debt. From across the room, where she was still babbling on about television programs, Mrs. Nanagyulian cried out—

"It's not the terms, it's that you waited so long to open a second front in the war!"

She was proving to be a veritable firebrand, and I must admit, beginning to get my goat. I didn't want to let that go unchallenged and so we debated the origins of the Second World War, how we were thrust into it on a Sunday that shocked the nation and then had to fight a complex island war in the Pacific as we prepared to take on Europe. But she wouldn't give up—

"When you needed us, we came to your help in Japan."

I lost some of my control and shouted back—

"Sure, two days after we dropped the first atom bomb and six days before Japan surrendered. Some help you were!"

Roseann saved the situation by offering to help in the kitchen and so we moved on to dinner, our appetites now whetted slightly more by the lively colloquy. But after the delicious dishes she had prepared and Ashot's *shashlik,* the conversation became a free-for-all about civil rights, press freedom, minority problems and a host of other aspects of the American scene in which the Nanagyulians revealed themselves to be naive and simplistic. Their exposure to American society was limited to television, which they didn't fully understand, and distorted further by the prejudices of their embassy colleagues.

Repeatedly, Ashot drew comparisons with life in Soviet Armenia, as though the vastness and complexity of American society could be equated with that tiny republic. He cited statistics to prove the well-being of his fellow Armenian citizens and appeared to us almost pathetic in his convictions.

But suddenly, the conversation took an unexpected turn. My wife and I had avoided mention of children, aware of the sensitive nature of this subject to Soviet diplomats. But when Ashot began to rhapsodize about the homeland, his wife lost all of her nerve. She now became somber and silent. My wife asked her if something was wrong, and a completely subdued and transformed Mrs. Nanagyulian said in a whisper that she missed her three children who were in Soviet Armenia. From that moment on, there was no consoling her, and we all tried. Only Ashot succeeded, when he reminded her that their oldest daughter was coming soon to visit them, at which she did brighten slightly and said she was counting the days. Nevertheless, the vivacity of the earlier hours vanished and until our departure she sulked.

It was getting late and we too were missing spending this Sunday with our children. Just to change the subject and hopefully the atmosphere as well, I asked Ashot if he could clarify something that Artem Melikyan had raised when I had met Ambassador Dobrynin, namely whether there was some connection Dobrynin had with Armenians. Ashot smiled expansively and maybe even gratefully—

"Yes, there is and we are proud of the connection. When Dobrynin was put up for membership in the Central Committee of the Communist Party, long before he became Ambassador to the United States, he happened to be attending a conference in Yerevan. Consequently, his candidacy was sponsored by Soviet Armenia, and when he was elected, he always thereafter had a soft spot in his heart for Armenians. And he proved that when he gave a wonderful reception on the 50th anniversary of our republic."

I thanked him for the clarification but did not indicate awareness of the anniversary reception, nor did he pursue it.

It was the last time we were to see the Nanagyulians. The bureaucratic machinery of the Foreign Service had already been set into motion and we were soon to leave Washington. Driving back home to

Bethesda, we talked about this couple and Roseann expressed compassion for the mother of three, obviously a woman of considerable emotional volatility who must have been traumatized by having to leave them behind. It reminded us very much of Kohar Aghayan and her problem of always missing one child.

Roseann thought Ashot highly unsophisticated for the role that had been assigned him and asked if I thought he too were KGB in some capacity or other. I pointed out that while Aghayan was an out-and-out intelligence officer with a very specific mission, others like Ashot Nanagyulian simply spread their nets to catch what they could. In this instance, it was very probable that either Aghayan or Melikyan or Gevorkyan may have told Ashot that the highest ranking American-Armenian in the United States Government was located just a few blocks away, came often to the Soviet Embassy, and was approachable.

I couldn't blame Ashot for trying.

Athens
1972–1976

XLII

ONE MORNING EARLY IN JUNE, DEPUTY DIRECTOR Loomis phoned with the question—"How would you like an assignment in Athens?"

Speechless, I could only muster up one word—"When?"

"How about right now!"

I asked to see him immediately and went right down to his office. I anticipated the joy at home. In the Foreign Service, Greece was always a good post, and now with a military junta in power, for me it would be especially interesting. After all, I had known little else in my career other than totalitarian regimes. In Greece, I might feel at home.

In Loomis's office I expressed my pleasure at the prospect but pointed out that "right now" was out of the question for several reasons: the children were still in school; I never went anywhere without the entire family; we had a house to rent and a car to sell, and in any case, I had to have some Greek language training.

Jenks and I had always insisted on language training for Eastern Europe and I didn't see why Greece should be an exception, even though English was widely spoken there. Loomis listened to all this and agreed and said the assignment was mine. He said the incumbent, Abe Serkin, had been in Athens for five years and was leaving shortly and that Ambassador Henry J. Tasca wanted an overlap.

The overlap took place eventually, but not in Athens. Serkin returned as I was making final preparations to depart Washington and during several lunches got to know him well—an intelligent and thoughtful officer with a strong antipathy to the Greek colonels who had been in power during most of his tenure.

Meanwhile, USIA arranged for me to have private tutoring in Greek with a Cypriot student of international relations from American University, an explosive patriot named Elias Georgiades who had fought against the British in what they continue to this day to refer euphemistically to as "the troubles," otherwise known as the Cypriot struggle for independence. Elias would re-enact some of his most daring exploits in the Cypriot underground as I cringed in my chair hoping that despite the bombast of his performance I might extract one small nugget of Greek grammar. I did eventually learn the alphabet and some expressions, such as "Where is the toilet?" which served a universal need, and "Death to dictators!" which, as an American Embassy official accredited to the regime of the Greek colonels, I considered impolitic and promptly forgot.

As the day of departure neared, Frank Shakespeare called me to his office late in August for a final chat. He indicated that my background in communist affairs had weighed heavily in favor of being assigned to a country long the target of the Soviet bloc. By now, after three years of close association, Shakespeare knew me and my views, and that I could have little respect for the dictatorship in Greece. We talked about the Nixon Administration's support for the regime of Colonel Papadopoulos and the just instituted home-porting agreement for the Sixth Fleet—"An administration and an agreement which you represent and must support," Shakespeare said. He wished me well, said he didn't know if he would visit me, and we shook hands for the last time. I could not know that one year later, he would be leaving USIA.

We arrived in Athens early in September 1972 and the eager press, muzzled except when forced to parrot the Papadopoulos line, ran several stories speculating that in view of my experience in Soviet and East European affairs perhaps there was after all a communist threat and that Ambassador Tasca had requested me for that reason.*

Once we had settled into temporary housing and I had made my official calls on the Greek Government, we located the tennis club where we were to find some of our greatest hours of recreation and relaxation in the suburb of Kifissia, about thirty minutes from Psychico, the pleasant residential area where we lived.

---

*On the Saturday we arrived, Tasca had flown north for the opening of the Thessaloniki Fair. On Monday I joined him. Meanwhile, on that weekend a Soviet church delegation was making a first visit to Mt. Athos and the Athenian press engaged in the wild speculation that my objective was to arrange a secret meeting between Tasca and the Soviet churchmen in that isolated monastic retreat. Thus on my third day in Greece, I was introduced to the vagaries of the Greek press.

It was at the Kifissia Tennis Club one sunny afternoon that I first saw a short, blond athletic male frantically running down and retrieving impossible balls, accompanying his saves with exuberant shouts in Russian. From time to time he noticed us watching his game and when it ended he came over, gleaming in his sweat, extended his hand with a big smile—

"I am Ivan Pakhomov, Second Secretary, Soviet Embassy. You are new here?"

I looked into his friendly twinkling blue eyes and introduced myself, but the unspoken words running through my mind were on a quite different track—Ivan old boy, you've got KGB written all over you.

No one thing identified him as such, but after my own experiences still so fresh in memory, there was something about Pakhomov which set him far apart from those forbidding sullen Soviet diplomats for whom carrying on a conversation seemed to be a task worthy of Sysyphus.

As it emerged in the conversation which followed, it was not I who was new in Athens but Pakhomov. He had just arrived from Moscow and seemed anxious to tell me about his last post in Geneva, where he had spent four years with the Soviet United Nations Mission. As we chatted, Pakhomov would look away to ogle the tennis-clad Greek girls who abounded that day at the club and when I asked if he was enjoying the pleasures of Athens, looking with him at two budding Chris Everts, his smile disappeared as he replied somberly—"My wife joins me in three days."

We parted with the promise to play tennis and to "keep in touch on the situation," as he put it. We never did play, primarily because he never joined that club, but we did meet, and often, at various diplomatic functions over a long period of time.

Pakhomov's English and German were excellent so that communication with him offered no problems, and his innate sense of humor made conversation enjoyable. After the initial meeting at the tennis club, we found ourselves face to face next at the residence of the Mexican Ambassador who was celebrating his national day.

Pakhomov was in great spirits—

"If my sources are accurate, you are in charge of public affairs at your embassy, which includes press, radio, television and cultural activities. Is that correct?"

"That is correct, Ivan, and we have one name for that entire field, which is *information.* As opposed to your word *disinformation.* "

Pakhomov threw back his head and roared with laughter, then said—

"Now that I know what you do, I will look at all US-Greek news stories in a new light, because I personally know the dubious source which inspires them."

With this good-humored start, we plunged into a long exploration of events in far-away places on which he had capsule comments: on Chile— "Allende was not our man"; Czechoslovakia—"Dubcek was doing what we have been doing in the Soviet Union, only he went too fast"; China— "More basic than Soviet-Chinese ideological differences is the huge threat of the yellow peril—someday you will see."

But all this was parrying, for Pakhomov's major point of interest was Greece, to which he often turned and returned.

"Greece is in the American sphere of influence, we recognize that, so we in the Soviet Embassy play a very minor role here."

I teased him about that and said that a low Soviet profile simply meant standing in the wings waiting for the colonels to leave the stage.

"My dear American friend, you overestimate the effectiveness of Soviet diplomacy."

On another occasion he fired a battery of questions about a number of Greek government figures whose names were prominent at the time in the news. Thinking to pull his leg, I gave replies which obviously strained his credulity. Eyeing me with amusement he said—

"And you have the audacity to accuse us of disinformation."

But this too was good-humored. Occasionally, however, the steel beneath would flash for a split second. My career experience in East European affairs had been well publicized in the Greek press and the diplomats from those embassies always made a special effort to cultivate me. Further, when I had first arrived and Ambassador Tasca had held a large reception to introduce me, I had invited the press and cultural officers of all those embassies—except for Albania.

Consequently, whenever Pakhomov and I were in a corner deep in conversation and one of the East Europeans would sidle up, an expect-ant smile on his face, to join us, Pakhomov would turn on the hapless Czech or Bulgarian or Pole and bark at him in Russian. Once having chased the intruder away ruthlessly, he would become his amiable self and continue the conversation from where we had left off.

It was on one of those occasions that Pakhomov first alluded to "ethnic matters" and wondered if I had much contact with non-Greeks. It soon became evident that he was well-informed of my ethnic origin, although the press, in covering my background, had not as yet mentioned it.* Ever alert, Pakhomov said he remembered my wife once mentioning the upcoming birthday of one of our sons, in anticipation of which he wished to send a gift. A few days later a package arrived at my office containing a recording of music by Aram Khatchaturian and a bottle of Armenian cognac for me, attached to which was Pakhomov's card.

Soon thereafter, at a Hungarian function, he said—

"When you attend our October Revolution reception, I shall have a surprise for you."

I suppose my instinct should have by now made me wary of gifts and surprises, but events in Greece had put all of us in the American Embassy under great pressure, especially me.

Democracy had returned to Greece with the overthrow of the dictatorship and the arrival of Konstantine Karamanlis. The Communist Party, which had been legalized, organized massive anti-American strikes and demonstrations, parading up and down *Panepistimiou* Avenue where my offices were, shouting slogans and waving banners, paralyzing the already heavily-trafficked city. Even more in my domain were the unrelenting attacks of the largely left-oriented press on the United States and our policies.

Attending the Soviet Embassy anniversary reception was, by comparison, a peaceful respite from the turmoil outside.

---

*In 1975, however, I convinced our new Ambassador, Jack Kubisch, that he should invite the head of the Armenian Church in Greece, Archbishop Ayvazian to our Fourth of July Reception, duly noted by the Greek press which commented that I too was Armenian and made the connection. This was all to the good in the wake of the Turkish invasion of Cyprus, which Armenians had protested, the Archbishop's presence was taken as support for Greece and widely hailed.

XLIII

I VAN PAKHOMOV SAW ME ENTER THE SOVIET EMBASSY
on November 7, and as soon as I had congratulated Ambassador
Udaltsev, whisked me away from the one-man reception line with the
words—"That surprise I mentioned is here."

Preoccupied with the problems covered earlier, I had not given the
long chain of events which always seemed to contain Armenian links
any thought, but now as Pakhomov led my by the arm through the
crowded stag reception, a premonition gripped me. Did I even dare to
think that Rafael Aghayan was the surprise? But why not, I thought,
after all Athens is so much nearer to Moscow than Washington.

My speculation ceased abruptly. Facing me was a handsome smiling
Soviet diplomat, hand extended, as Pakhomov said—"I would like you to
meet our new Consul-General," and as we shook hands, Pakhomov
looked at me for its effect as he spoke the name—"Reuben Martikyan."

Neither could have guessed that my quick smile of pleasure was generated more by Martikyan not being Aghayan than by meeting yet
another Soviet Armenian diplomat. The camaraderie of the two, especially since Martikyan had only just arrived, indicated prior association,
and it required no lengthy deliberation to conclude that Pakhomov and
Martikyan had been colleagues before. So here we go again, I thought,
as Pakhomov smiled benignly at both of us like a godfather and disappeared into the mob. We of course immediately lapsed into Armenian,
with the usual questions about origin, background, family and career.

In his early forties, Martikyan was born in Tbilisi, as was his wife;
they had one daughter, 17 years old, studying languages, including
Greek, in Moscow, where both daughter and mother had been until she
had joined her husband a week before, leaving the daughter behind to
live with Martikyan's brother. Prior to his Athens assignment, Martikyan had served for three years in the Soviet Embassy in Nicosia. As

we talked, it emerged we had a number of mutual friends, one of them being the head of the Armenian community in Cyprus, Dr. Antranik Ashjian, a member of Parliament and perhaps the best dentist on the island, whose most prominent patient was the President of Cyprus, Archbishop Makarios.

"Ashjian fixed all of my wife's teeth, but none of mine because I'm afraid of dentists. They cause pain."*

As we chatted, a variety of his consular colleagues from other embassies came by to greet him in their own languages and he reciprocated in theirs. I commented on his linguistic ability and on the purity of his Armenian, which pleased him—

"But why not, dear compatriot, after all, I am a scholar of languages. I studied at the Moscow Institute for Foreign Languages and made sure I spoke my native language as best I could without the many accents we have in the Soviet Union. Incidentally, at the Institute, one of my close friends was Sergei Mikoyan, who has since become a fine journalist."

I mentioned the Armenians working at TASS, *Novosti* and *Izvestiya* and Martikyan claimed to know them all. He also maintained that composer Aram Khatchaturian was a distant relative.

As we spoke, prominent Greek political figures had been arriving and Martikyan, still inexperienced in spotting them, asked me to identify the more important ones which I did, pointing out Andreas Papandreou, the head of the newly-formed PASOK party, Foreign and Defense Ministers Bitsios and Averoff, and our own Ambassador Jack Kubisch.

I had pressing business back at the office and began to excuse myself when Martikyan said he wished to see me again soon, giving me his card. As he did, looking pointedly at me, he asked if I knew several people he named in the American Embassy. I shook my head and left. It was a strange note on which to depart because the people he had named were in the same line of work as Aghayan, Pakhomov and all the others in between.

As I left the Soviet Embassy, I wondered if Martikyan's move had been a deliberate attempt to send me a signal: either alerting me to his specific interests, or even testing me to see if I were associated with

---

*I recalled that Dr. Ashjian had told me during a visit that whenever he tended Archbishop Makarios' teeth, for days thereafter his office would be the focal point of interest by foreign embassies, "most notably the Soviet Embassy and an Armenian Consul." I realized now that that could only have been Martikyan.

those he had just mentioned. In any case, one thing was clear to me—I could dispel any doubts about his true status and duties.

I did not see Martikyan or Pakhomov for a period thereafter and, as it was, six weeks later a devastating event shook our embassy which made me studiously avoid such contacts.

XLIV

AMBASSADOR AND MRS. KUBISCH DECIDED TO HOST A large Christmas party in their residence that year and scheduled it for December 23. The invitees were a prestigious cross-section of Greek society from both the government and private life, and mixing among the throng one bumped into cabinet ministers, artists, writers, journalists, archeologists and a large contingent from our embassy.

One of my American colleagues at the party was Richard Welch, whose title was Special Assistant to the Ambassador. In fact, Welch was the CIA Station Chief, an officer of remarkable gifts when it came to knowing the Greeks—their history, psychology, and political vagaries. Welch was also the best Greek speaker in the embassy and his knowledge of the intricate language extended to the spoken *demotiki,* the written *katharevusa,* and the ancient language of Homer. Once at a staff meeting, Welch made a pun in Greek and seeing our blank reaction, had to explain that he had just punned. Dick Welch and I also played tennis whenever we could get away from our embassy duties, and consequently had become good friends.

On the night of the party, for reasons I have never been able to fathom, Dick and I had a long, searching conversation, about families, careers, and our very separate and individual missions. We had never engaged in such depth on the many other occasions we had been together, and it was with more than the usual warmth that we shook hands and left the party around 9:30 PM. The Welches lived only five minutes from the Ambassador's residence while we lived about twenty.

On arriving home, I heard the phone ringing inside as I fumbled with the key. When I finally entered and lifted the receiver, the excited voice of a colleague shouted—

"Dick Welch has just been shot and the Ambassador wants you at the embassy now!"

I rushed back to find the embassy lobby filling up rapidly with the Athens press corps, while every phone at the reception desk was off the hook, waiting for me. I answered each in turn—CBS from New York, NBC from London, ABC from Paris, and the European media which kept calling repeatedly, as for almost thirty minutes I fielded their questions, which always crystallized to the essential three: Was Welch the CIA station chief? Was he dead? Who did it?

Scores of local and foreign journalists, some of whom had been at the Christmas party and had seen Welch, shouted their questions even as I spoke on the phone, creating a scene in the embassy lobby approaching pandemonium and unlike any in my thirty years experience. But I knew the ambassador was waiting on the third floor and when eventually I was able to call him and explain why I was delayed, Jack Kubisch informed me solemnly that Dick Welch had died and that I should join him and the rest of the senior staff upstairs.

The remainder of that night was filled with despair, confusion and profound sorrow. Dick Welch had been an exceptional colleague and friend and our sense of loss was painful and deep. After drawing up a brief statement which I could use for the media, we sat around in the ambassador's office and talked long into the night, speculating on the identity of the assassins who had shot Dick as he had gotten out of his car to walk through the garage gates.

The range of possibilities extended from Cypriot leftists—Welch had once served in Nicosia—and Black Septembrists, to Greek junta Extremists and the KGB. We were certain though that somehow and somewhere they would be caught.*

The days that followed were heavy for all of us. I had my hands full, word-duelling with the Greek press, neither confirming nor denying Welch's true status in the embassy, which is standard public affairs policy in intelligence matters. When the press speculation finally became totally irrational, however, I held two press conferences for some fifty Greek journalists in my office. I explained the circum-

---

*We were wrong, for they are still at large. Shortly after the Welch assassination, a terrorist group called 'November 17,' named for the 1973 suppression by the Greek junta of a student revolt at Athens Polytechnic University, took credit for the murder. The same group also killed the U.S. Naval Attache in 1983, the U.S. Defense Attache in 1988, and bombed busloads of U.S. servicemen. None of its members has ever been caught.

stances of the tragedy, provided background details and arrangements the family had made, and described the procedures to be followed in the ceremonies at the airport where a flag-draped casket—the sole cargo of a giant Air Force C-141—would be flown to Andrews Air Force Base for burial on January 2 in Arlington National Cemetery. But despite my meticulous care in stressing all of this, the journalists distorted most of what I told them, preferring to wallow in mysteries and intrigues of their own making.

It was the most depressing Christmas and New Year for our embassy and the Kubisches, and hung like a pall over us even thereafter as some segments of the Greek press refused to let the story die, whipping up new twists and turns daily. The more responsible newspapers brought balance to their reporting and it was gratifying to see that reason could prevail in the country where reason was born.

Ambassador Kubisch instructed us to cancel all engagements and functions. For my part, I welcomed the opportunity to avoid discussing the Welch assassination with other diplomats, especially from the Soviet Embassy. But I knew this condition would not last, and when word came from Washington that I would be leaving Athens in the summer for transfer to our newly-established embassy in East Berlin, I began to measure everything I did by that yardstick.

I ran into Pakhomov often, either at one of the several tennis courts in Athens or on the street. I never knew how he found out but on one of those chance meetings he asked me point blank whether I was returning to the area of my chief interest, East Europe. I was noncommittal for some time, but apparently he wormed it out of an embassy colleague, and from that time on teased me about "our Germans and your Germans," in a manner reminiscent of Rafael Aghayan's needling.

Then one day, my secretary Dolly Moore buzzed on the intercom to say a Mr. Martikyan was on the phone. His first words boomed in my ear—

"Ed, for God's sake, where have you been hiding?"

He asked if I were going to take part in the annual Diplomatic Tennis Tournament at the Royal Tennis Club, as it was still being called despite the abolition of the monarchy. He said he would be accompanying Ivan Pakhomov to the tournament and hoped to see me there. Five months had gone by since the tragedy and a degree of social normalization in our embassy lives had been reached, so I told him that I would be participating.

During the first round matches, sure enough there was Martikyan to watch his friend Pakhomov lose. He spotted me soon as I entered and for some twenty minutes we engaged in light banter, both predicting that the finals would probably be a repeat of the previous year between a French military attache and my son Mark, who had since those early years in Berlin developed into a tennis player of professional calibre. Martikyan pressed me for a luncheon date and I gave in, knowing it would be our last.

In early June we met at *Zorba's Restaurant* in *Turcolimano,* a popular seaside area on the outskirts of *Piraeus.*

"Which Berlin are you going to, ours or yours?" was his first shot after he had ordered a dizzying variety of *mezedes* and shellfish.

I said it was not final and began a discussion of the archeological monuments of Greece and Armenia, comparing their age and condition. Martikyan elaborated on some of the sites in Armenia I had visited and said that he would shortly be going there on annual leave.

We were seated close to the water in the great curve of the shoreline and Martikyan said it reminded him of *Kyrenia* in Cyprus. He spoke nostalgically of his tour of duty there and of his Armenian contacts, especially of Dr. Ashjian. We compared notes on the dentist which produced an interesting fact, namely that when the Turks invaded in 1974 and it seemed to Ashjian that they would commandeer his house, he offered it to the Soviet Embassy, a gesture Ashjian had not told me of. I recalled only that he and his wife had "trembled with terror" on seeing the Turks enter his home, some sixty years after the Turks entered hundreds of thousands of Armenian homes in Turkey.

We went through a rapid tour of the Soviet horizon, Martikyan unwilling to discuss Khrushchev's reforms, and displeased when I corrected his evaluation of Mikoyan as a "great leader" to a "great survivor who did not do for Armenia what Stalin did for Georgia."

"Tell me about Ronald Reagan," he suddenly asked, referring to the election campaign in that year, 1976, "and explain how anyone can be against detente."

I replied that he had his facts wrong, because it was increasingly obvious that it was the Soviet Union which was against detente. I waved away his protests by pointing out that 15,000 Cuban troops in Angola and the Soviet naval build-up in the Eastern Mediterranean belied Moscow's talk of detente.

My manner was impatient and perhaps even aggressive, and Martikyan seemed displeased with the course of our conversation. I had no intention of seeing him again and as though reading my mind, asked me if Berlin was definitely my next post. I said that we all lived in an uncertain world and that in the Foreign Service, one could never be sure of an assignment until he was physically there.

"Berlin, Berlin," he muttered, abstractedly, but clearly an *idee fixe.*

I arose after he paid the check and we walked to our two cars parked next to each other. He took out a bottle of the ubiquitous Armenian cognac and said he would call me in August when he had returned from Soviet Armenia. I shrugged knowing I would already be in East Berlin.

My driver Kosta drove me back to the office, happily fondling the cognac I had presented to him. There I arranged to have sent to Martikyan the special Bi-Centennial issue of *Ameryka* magazine—the USIA Russian-language publication we distributed in the Soviet Union. Gift-wise we were even; I had seen the last of Martikyan; and ahead of me lay the German Democratic Republic.

PART THREE

East Berlin
1976–1979

XLV

THE CONTRASTS WERE MULTI-LAYERED: ATTITUDES, dress, color, architecture, traffic, even the climate seemed an element of the all-pervasive political systems—the one I was leaving behind in Athens and the one I was to struggle with for the next three years in East Berlin. Gone were the blue sky, the turquoise sea and the golden sun; gone were the devil-may-care Greeks with their mind-boggling hospitality, their gift for living—if not for driving!—with such a love for democracy that they almost loved it to death. Athens—a huge village surrounding the Acropolis.

And now, East Berlin: overcast, grey, somber, organized and controlled, its people grim and determined; the streets uncluttered with cars, the buildings richly adorned with political slogans. Outside of some new high-rise apartments, little had changed in the decade since I had last been there. East Berlin—a concrete and glass monolith trying so hard to match its opulent twin across the Wall.

In the flight time of three hours I had gone from one society, system and country to another as fundamentally different as *bouzouki* and Beethoven.

While the pre-war American Embassy on *Pariser Platz,* directly next to the Brandenburg Gate, had been bombed out, the Soviet Embassy on *Unter den Linden,* only slightly damaged, was built on the site of the old Russian Embassy. The largest in East Berlin, the Soviet Embassy was active with receptions, film showings and musical evenings. In my first week I had already been invited there and discovered that the Deputy Chief of Mission was none other than Anatoly Gromyko whom I had once met in Moscow at a luncheon hosted by the Beams. Remarkably similar to his famous father in both glum appearance and manner, Gromyko was the only Soviet official I knew at his embassy. That is, until five months later in January 1977 when I received an invitation to attend a function hosted by the embassy's new Counselor for Press and Information—Mikhail Sagatelyan! Well, well, I thought.

And there he stood, smiling, arms outstretched; when on good behavior, he combined the best traits of his Russian-Armenian heritage:

"Ed! How many years has it been?"

His greeting was very warm and he very attentive as we had a long chat and agreed to catch up with each other soon in a lunch. I was struck again, as I had been in Moscow eight years earlier, by his astonishing similarity in personality and inflection to the late film actor Akim Tamiroff (also an Armenian, originally Tamiriantz).

One of Sagatelyan's more intriguing mannerisms when disputing a point was to pronounce the first syllable of my name in tones an octave apart. Another was to make an outrageous statement accompanied by a knowing smile, as though to say—this is so obvious. For instance, once during a discussion of his Washington tour for TASS from 1959 to 1965, he mentioned having written a book entitled "Who Killed President Kennedy?" He claimed the book had been published in half a million copies in seven languages.

"There is even an English translation, ordered by none other than Aristotle Onassis, who owns all 300 copies. I had begun negotiations with Random House which were progressing well until the White House intervened. LBJ didn't want the book published. You know why? Because President Johnson and the Central Intelligence Agency conspired to kill Kennedy."

This was accompanied by his as-is-well-known smile but seeing me recoil, he encircled me in a bear hug and said—

"Ed" in three widely-spaced tones, "everybody knows it, calm down. By the way, when you visit our apartment, I'll show you an interesting photograph."

That invitation came soon thereafter and Roseann and I spent a long evening in the Sagatelyan apartment behind the Soviet Embassy. He scornfully dismissed the East German 'modern' furniture, saying their own was en route from Moscow.

Olga Sagatelyan turned out to be a stately Russian blonde who was by profession an endocrinologist, unable to practice while her husband was assigned abroad. A very pleasant woman, she was his second wife, he told me privately, he having divorced his first wife after a stormy marriage.

He led me to a wall on which hung four photographs of Senator Edward Kennedy with the Sagatelyans. "These were taken in Tbilisi," Sagatelyan explained, "and if you look closely you'll see that the Senator is holding in his hand a copy of my book about his brother's death."

Roseann and Olga got along somehow in that mystic communion that women of intelligence have despite the absence of a common language. Olga's few German words and Roseann's even fewer Russian were adequate for some areas but when a total breakdown would become imminent, Mikhail would leap into the breach and translate like the truly bilingual professional that he was.

He told me that just prior to his assignment to East Berlin he had served as Deputy Director of *Novosti*. I said that was a coincidence because at my last post, Athens, the new Soviet Ambassador had just come from *Novosti* where he had been Director. "Of course, Udaltsev, my old friend," Sagatelyan exclaimed joyfully, "that really *is* a coincidence."

I told Sagatelyan that it had been a surprise to learn he had been assigned to the Soviet Embassy in East Berlin since I had not been aware that he was in the Soviet Foreign Service. "My first assignment," he said in clipped tones, obviously eager to cut off any discussion of that subject. I wondered if I would ever know the true nature of his assignment.*

Sagatelyan loved to ramble on about his contacts in Washington and his talk was peppered with the names of the prominent, all of whom he claimed to know. For instance: "I asked Jim Hagerty one day why Eisenhower wasted so much time playing golf, and Jim replied that actually Ike did all his thinking about world problems on the golf course." Or: "I personally liked President Kennedy and spent much time with him. He didn't have enough opportunity to develop his potential."

Again: "I didn't like Bobby Kennedy's book on Cuba, full of lies. In the book I'm writing on Cuba, I'll tell all. For instance, how many people know that after the Bay of Pigs, Bobby and Ambassador Dobrynin cried together?" And, sneering: "John Scali! On the basis of one conversation which he inflated, Scali became a hero. How strange that your leaders pay attention to someone like that and ignore others. If you read the Pentagon Papers you will find my name too. Had your

---

*The diplomatic scuttlebutt in Berlin was that Sagatelyan must have botched his job at *Novosti* and been banished to Berlin because the post of Deputy Director of *Novosti* was at least the equal of Minister or Ambassador in the Foreign Service and Sagatelyan was neither.

government paid attention to my proposal, you could have saved over 35,000 lives in Vietnam."*

On and on it went about so many things, but all of which always revolved around Mikhail Sagatelyan. He spoke glowingly of Anastas Mikoyan—"A great man whom I knew well. You know, he predicted the downfall of Johnson whom he considered a weak President." I told him of having wanted to meet Mikoyan but never able to, and caught myself in time when, about to mention Mikoyan's visit to Berlin fifteen years earlier, I realized it would have injected Rafael Aghayan into the conversation. Instead, I switched to the bumbling Armenian diplomats at the Soviet Embassy in Washington. "Oh, those boys from the Armenian Foreign Ministry. They aren't very sophisticated. On the other hand, the correspondents, of course, are all my good friends.

He grew angry only once when the subject of human rights came up—at the time very much in the news coming out of Jimmy Carter's Washington. Leaning forward, face flushed and voice trembling, he barked at me—"Let me show you how important human rights are," and held his thumb and forefinger a quarter of an inch apart—"that much!" After quieting down, he suddenly asked—"Have you ever been in a submarine? I made a long trip in the Caribbean in a submarine which opened my eyes. For instance, do you know that in our submarines we grow vegetables in water under quartz lamps?"

The Sagatelyans were invited often and always came to the film showings I held at our embassy. Mikhail translated the dialogue for Olga who enjoyed the films, especially "One Flew Over the Cuckoo's Nest," saying as a medical person it had made a deep impression on her. When another time I told them I would soon be screening "The Russians Are Coming! The Russians Are Coming!" Mikhail exploded with enthusiasm telling Olga it was a marvelous picture.

As time went on, we saw each other frequently but without wives. Our conversations became more intensively political as now he began to probe

---

*In the Pentagon Papers, Gravel Edition, (pp. 375-377), Sagatelyan, then an official of TASS, met three times with Pierre Salinger during the latter's private visit to Moscow in May 1965 and proposed a peace plan entailing a bombing halt, Soviet intercession with the VietCong for a cease-fire, and a conference leading to a broad-based South Vietnam government to include elements friendly to the VietCong. Sagatelyan said he could fly to Paris and wait for Salinger to determine the U.S. Government's reaction to the proposal. Sagatelyan strongly implied that his proposal had Foreign Ministry backing, and it was so interpreted by Salinger. The proposal was rejected.

foreign policy matters. Always well-armed with information from the American press, especially the columnists and Joseph Kraft whom he often quoted, Sagatelyan insisted that not only was there a split between the White House and the State Department but that I surely would enlighten him further on the schism. I sensed that he was getting closer to the core of his duties as he pursued this theme at every meeting during the entire year. He also realized after awhile that he was getting nowhere with me and stopped seeking me out at diplomatic functions, on occasion acknowledging my presence by a mere wave of the hand from across noisy reception halls.

The diminishing contact allowed me to devote more time to pursuing my basic function of dealing with press and cultural relations with the East Germans and as we entered 1978 I was preparing for the most productive year of cultural presentations, having negotiated American programs in East Germany encompassing art exhibits, theatre seminars, film festivals and a string quartet tour of five cities.

These programs required total attention to countless details and occupied all of my time—until a certain day in February.

XLVI

ROSEANN HEARD ME DRIVE INTO THE GARAGE THAT evening and met me at the door with a curious smile—"Hello there, Edward."

Wives addressing husbands by their full first name are always sending a signal, but when I heard her thick Russian-Armenian inflection, I stared in disbelief, understood and cried out—

"*Nem! Az nem igaz!*" We frequently lapsed into Hungarian, especially this expression, and she responded in English with a firm nod of her head—"Yes, it is true. Rafael Aghayan is back in East Berlin."

We had a quick drink as she reviewed what had happened: Aghayan had phoned, asked about the family, then for me, rejected phoning me at the embassy, said he would call around 9 PM.

I found it difficult to believe. After all these years, after all that had happened, I didn't know whether to be annoyed or amused.

"What in hell do they still want?"

"You know very well what they want," Roseann replied, "you've got to either defect or work for them. Not much choice there. Of course," she added, looking up at the ceiling and walls, "you could also tell them to go to hell."

We laughed silently just as the phone rang. It was still early and Roseann answered it. Christian, our youngest, was calling from West Berlin to say he was sleeping over with a friend and that I should pick him up at Checkpoint Charlie the next morning. We had another drink, then had supper.

The phone rang again. Although only 8:30, I looked nervously at Roseann. She picked it up again. It was Sol Polansky, our Deputy Chief of Mission, proposing to pick us up if we were going to the same reception. We had declined, thanked him and waited some more.

At 9:05 the phone rang again. It had to be he, and it was. When I heard that same guttural, thickly-accented Armenian voice, it was as though the last fifteen years had never happened, and we were back to the beginning.

"My dear Edward! We are in touch once again. When can we meet?"

I had not decided in my own mind whether I would meet with him, but as he babbled on about being together again in the same city, it occurred to me that perhaps this was an opportune reunion, considering where we were, and that the time had come for a showdown. The charade, which I thought had ended some time ago, now had to be laid to rest forever.

"All right, Rafael, how about March 2, and you name the place."

This would give me two days to get my bearings and embassy approval.

Surprisingly, he proposed the *Johannishof*, an exclusive VIP hotel for special guests of the German Democratic Republic, actually diagonally across from the *Sofia*, where we always had met before.

"The *Johannishof*!" Roseann's eyebrows were raised. "Maybe he goofed up so badly that he got promoted. Sounds like Rafael's got status."

We retired early but I slept poorly, formulating over and over the things I wished to confront him with.

The next day I requested a special meeting of the embassy's senior staff and briefed them on the past history of this affair. All agreed that I should go ahead with it. Sol Polansky wanted me to be very careful and wished me well when on the following day I left the embassy.

I decided to walk rather than drive the fifteen minutes it took by foot. *Friedrichstrasse* was its usual busy self and walking over the *Weidendammbrücke* bridging the *Spree* was always pleasant. I reached the *Johannishof* and went through its revolving doors.

Rafael Aghayan was standing squarely before me smiling broadly and charged forward with outstretched arms. A number of guests stared as he embraced me, shouting exclamations in the language which to them was gibberish. He took my coat, checked it and led the way into the dining room. A respectful waiter stood by patiently as Aghayan ordered drinks in his pidgin German and—like old times—asked me to order the food. Once the waiter had written it all down he departed but not without a backward glance as the sounds of Aghayan's Armenian echoed through the half-empty dining room.

Perfectly at ease he took out photographs of his family and as I looked at them, I realized that Aghayan and I had known each other almost an entire generation. I did not recognize anyone in the pictures, either the children or the adults, and Aghayan had to explain quite proudly that the two young women were his daughters, Ina and Alla, both doctors now, and the little ones were their children, his grandchildren. He did not mention Edward his son, but when I asked about his wife, he said that Kohar was very content because she was again a practicing surgeon. He asked about my family and I merely said they were all well.

When the drinks and food arrived, he was already holding forth on a variety of things. He spoke of his trip to Washington as having disillusioned him about the United States; he complained of the sex films, pornography, crime, "muggings at the very door of the Soviet Embassy." I let him rant on, unwilling to engage in the debates of old, my mind focussing more on what I would say to him shortly. Enveloped in my own thoughts, I nevertheless was not unaware of what he was saying—at one point condemning the Germans ("our Germans and your Germans, all alike") and at another boasting of his connection with the foremost Armenian in the Soviet Union ("good old Mikoyan, 82 years old, I saw him last year, he is eating, drinking and enjoying life, like all Armenians").

Suddenly I realized that he had asked me a question. I looked up and he repeated it—"Why are you building this neutron bomb which kills people and spares buildings?" East Germany was inundated with slogans, banners and posters on the new weapon which the Carter Administration was considering, and whose whys and wherefores we in the Embassy were trying to explain at every diplomatic reception. But I took a different tack with Aghayan and baited him—"Rafael, you people are really envious of us, I think. You don't have anything so good, do you?" Aghayan snapped back sternly—"Anything you have, we have too!" I laughed at the innocent pride exposed by my needling but then could only shake my head in disbelief as he argued that if the United States gave the neutron bomb to its NATO ally Turkey, the Turks would use the bomb against the Armenians.

I diverted him from this stupid reasoning by asking how long he had been in East Berlin, adding sarcastically that perhaps he was not at liberty to tell me in what capacity. Aghayan said he had arrived only five days ago and would be leaving in another ten and that he had no reservations in telling me the purpose of this visit.

"I have come to do research in the archives of the German Democratic Republic on German attitudes towards the Turkish massacres of the Armenians in 1915."

"Come on Rafael, your German is terrible. You couldn't possibly know enough to understand those archives. For God's sake, every time we have been together, I have done the ordering in restaurants."

But he insisted that was the reason for his visit, and then said that he was now living nine months of the year in Soviet Armenia—"I am in charge of the Official Gazette of the Armenian Soviet Socialist Republic, publishing articles on foreign policy. That is why I ask you political questions"

As he said this, the reality of where we had been and where we were was brought home to me with impact. The austere manner with which he spoke and pronounced those words—"the Official Gazette of the Armenian Soviet Socialist Republic"—vividly recalled the scene by that lake, ironically not very far from where we were now meeting. It must have shown on my face for he was now watching me closely. Normally, Aghayan's expressions were either of evocative merriment, as though he always wished me to join in with his light banter, or of optimistic surprise, as though everything I said was of particular fascination for him. But now, his face assumed an expression of utmost gravity. My general demeanor must have signalled to him that the give-and-take of former times was not for this occasion. He leaned forward over the table, his face reflecting concern.

"What's wrong, Edward? Are you not feeling well?" It must be showing, I thought as I shook my head. "I'm fine, Rafael, just fine, but surprised to see you after all this time. Tell me, if you can, how did you know that I was here?"

"Very easy," he replied matter-of-factly, "I picked up the Diplomatic List of the Foreign Ministry and sure enough, there you were."

"That's a fantastic coincidence, isn't it?" I said, my voice sharply edged with sarcasm. He ignored the innuendo and nodded vigorously—"Somehow, our careers always seem to bring us together."

"And if not you, *friends of yours.*" I was now quite tense and aware that I was about to cross the threshhold. At first he pretended not to hear and took advantage of the waiter's arrival with the drinks not to reply. But when alone again, we looked at each other and I tilted my head expectantly, indicating I was waiting for a reply.

"What exactly does that mean, Edward, *friends of mine?*"

"Rafael, for the last fifteen years you have been playing a game with me. Maybe you felt I was a pawn and you were the queen, and when it was not you, here was a knight, there a bishop, sometimes a rook. They all had their missions, their instructions. In Washington, in Moscow, in Athens, here in East Berlin. How you ever missed me in Armenia . . . Budapest . . . ." He sat silently shaking his head as if incredulous. I sipped my drink and the food arrived. He beamed at me— "Isn't it great to be together again, like old times?"

"Don't change the subject" I replied sternly as the smile froze on his lips.

Now ostentatiously, he put his knife and fork down on his plate, bowing his head for added emphasis, looked at me with troubled eyes—"Edward, if you are referring to a certain incident not far from here, I thought all that was cleared up back in Washington. Didn't I explain everything to your satisfaction? Can't we forget it all happened? Can't we two Armenians be friends?"

"No, we cannot after what you asked me to do. Don't call yourself an Armenian. When you tried to get me to work for you and your organization, you desecrated Armenian honor. How you misjudged me!"

"Oh you are so wrong, wrong, wrong, Edward. I was trying to prove my friendship. I wanted to show you how you too could serve our people."

"*My* people are American, *your* people are Soviet. What in the hell are you talking about, Rafael, *that I should work for the Soviet Union?*"

"Oh, Edward, you have everything turned around. It is *you* who have misjudged *me.*"

"I don't know by what logic but all right, let's assume so for a moment. Can you explain how it is that every place I go, somehow, an Armenian from the Soviet Union is assigned there and contacts me?"

"Are you denying that we are a very talented people," he retorted, sitting up very straight. "The Russians give us opportunities. Why do you not see this as a positive phenomenon instead of looking for conspiracies?"

I smiled at his adamance but inside I felt a knot in my stomach. I had made a pledge to myself which I intended to keep, and the time was quickly approaching. I hoped my voice wouldn't quaver as I spoke the names of every Soviet Armenian who had crossed my diplomatic path over the last fifteen years. Aghayan watched me impassively as he chewed his food, and when I had finished, he smiled and said—"Our people are in every profession, everywhere."

"But with the same employer," I replied quietly, took in a deep breath and said—"The Committee." His eyes narrowed as an expression of hostility rearranged his features.

"And what is the Committee, if I may ask?"

I had used the term which my friends in Soviet Armenia had employed but realized that there was no way out of going the full route, even though I knew for certain that he had understood my meaning.

"The Committee for State Security, Rafael. You know very well what it is. Can you really have deluded yourself so much as to have thought I never suspected what you all were?" I was trying to avoid speaking the notorious letters themselves, as though Committee for State Security was an adequate euphemism and less incendiary.

His manner now became insolent and I felt my heart beating. I was as tense as when we had sat by that isolated lake in *Königswusterhausen,* and when he spoke I felt a shiver go down my spine:

"The Russian initials for the organization you mentioned are KGB. I assume that is what you are talking about." In Armenian and German, the letters were pronounced the same as in Russian and Aghayan, mindful of the few people nearby, lowered his voice at their mention.

I could hardly believe my ears. For the first time in our relationship, those three letters dangled ominously before us. At that moment I think he too was conscious that the secret was out. We looked at each other slightly surprised at this sudden turn in the conversation but I decided to pursue my advantage—

"Yes, Rafael, difficult as it has been for me to say, the truth is now out in the open, and you can see that I have had no illusions about you ever, or about your friends." I looked directly into his eyes and although I couldn't know what to expect, I saw the expression in them harden and I tensed as he began to speak:

"Since we seem to be seeking the truth, dear friend, why don't you tell me what is going on between your ambassador and his deputy? Or better still, how about what is going on between your ambassador and the State Department?" He leaned back and watched my ill-concealed astonishment with smug pleasure. He had fired a double-barrelled question at me.

"Nothing is going on, and even if it were, it's none of your business," I replied angrily, recognizing my comeback for the inadequate reply it was and annoyed that I had lost the initiative. I knew our personnel were careless, most of them never having served in a communist country and unaware of the countless techniques by which the host governments collect their information from inside foreign embassies. When conversations could be deciphered from vibrations on window panes monitored from afar, making even the tiniest of microphones obsolete, no conversation was secure. Additionally, our telephones in the embassy were wired to lines which ran through the German Democratic Republic so that phone calls between Berlin and Washington were vulnerable.

But there was the more painful other barrel in his question—the awareness of inner conflict. Every American Embassy in every country has its policy differences wherein the ambassador's staff presents him with options. But once he has made a decision, the options vanish—or should. In our case, they seemed to have an afterlife as we debated differing approaches to the GDR—a regime which in the eyes of Washington somehow could not come up with any virtues to match those of Hungary or Poland.

We had stopped eating now, he amused, I glaring. Then, his tones mellow and his manner gentle, Aghayan said—"You know very well there *are* problems, and now *you* know that *we* know too. But I don't think you are as surprised as you show. Edward, we are grown men, so let us not play any more games. I do not know when we shall meet again but let us at least part friends. In fact, I would enjoy another lunch while you are still here in Berlin."

I now sensed that we had arrived at the critical moment. Although he had impaled me with his two revealing questions, I knew also that their impact on me could not equal the impact on him of realizing not only my awareness of his true identity but of having drawn from his lips those three awesome letters which evoke fear inside and outside the Soviet Union. As far as I was concerned we had reached a stalemate in a game which had spanned fifteen years and which I had pledged to Roseann and myself to end. Nevertheless, I knew it to be a never-ending game which no one really wins; it goes on and on as more Abels and Powers and Philbys and Penkovskys and Aghayans do what they do.

"No more lunches, Rafael. This is our last."

"Well, then, I must now ask you a question I was saving for another time. Edward, *have you thought about it?*"

I felt a slight tremor go through me as I stared at him, except that it was as though a veil had been lifted from my eyes. So here it finally was, or as Hamlet put it—"So, Uncle, there you are." The two parallel lines had

converged. While the identity of the mysterious stranger—The Shadow—
was never to be known to me, Aghayan had become his surrogate. The KGB
had put it all together and for me, everything now fell into place.

I smiled benignly at him and stood up—

"I am glad we had this lunch. Most of the time I have enjoyed our
relationship, and you know when I haven't. *There is nothing to think about
any more, Rafael.* Give your wife and children our regards. You have a nice
family and we wish them well."

I extended my hand and for the last time looked into his brown eyes. They
were sad. He was about to embrace me but caught himself, aware that
diners nearby were looking at us, and merely gripped my hand with both of
his, pumping it vigorously, his face taut.

Turning around I walked out, feeling his eyes on me, picked up my coat off
the checkroom hook and went out to *Friedrichstrasse.* There was a chill in
the air. I didn't feel in the mood to returning quickly to the embassy so I took
a roundabout route back which lasted almost an hour.

I reviewed this ultimate lunch and the many things that had been said. To
my surprise I became aware of mixed emotions, of a certain lightness not
difficult to understand, combined with a certain melancholy which I
wondered about. Was I sorry to have seen the last of a KGB intelligence
officer? I laughed quietly at the irony. But I asked myself what harm had he
done, what harm had any of them done? None that I knew of.

True, Aghayan had tried to recruit me, directly and openly, another had
tried indirectly, but in Aghayan's loyalty to his government, he had found a
match in my loyalty to mine. Perhaps he had erred, blundered; most
assuredly he had misjudged. In the process which he had begun by that first
phone call in 1963, he had introduced me to a clandestine world. By virtue of
my professional career, ethnic heritage, and of having been in a certain place
at a certain time, I had been able to see behind the iron-grim facade of the
KGB and found not robots but people with emotions and some very human
problems: strained marriages, frustrated wives unable to practice their
professions, parents yearning for children held hostage back home, children
plagued by incurable illnesses, men working in hostile surroundings,
despising, and despised by their client populations, nostalgic for their
homeland, resenting having to place noxious duty before family.

But because they were human did not make their purposes humane.
There was nothing good or decent in trying to get a man to betray
his country, to commit treason. Fifteen years earlier I had continued to

meet regularly with Aghayan even though never entertaining any illusions about him. But I had not expected nor had I been alerted to the possibility that an elaborate scheme had been in preparation to recruit me into the most notorious of espionage organizations. It had stunned me when the plan had been revealed and its aftereffects clung to me through the years, making me wary of every Soviet Armenian I met. That is, until Soviet Armenia.

Strangely and ironically, I could thank Aghayan for the impetus to visit that small, sad, isolated, brave, ingratiating, ancient nation whose busy dedicated artists were creating literature, poetry, painting, sculpture, music and films, struggling within a cruel system to keep alive their unique language and culture.

I had walked the streets of Yerevan with them, dined with them, philosophized with them and reminisced about the Armenian past and present with them. In only five days, because of the common blood that bound us, they had opened their hearts and spoken their minds, and from them, true sons of the Armenian nation, I had learned the answers to some of the questions I had long entertained and which Aghayan couldn't or wouldn't answer: about the lingering vestiges of Stalinism, the attempts towards cultural pluralism, attitudes towards neighboring Soviet republics, the depth of emotion about Turkey, relations with the Russians, opinions of the Soviet leaders, and the seeds of nationalism; finally and simply, what it was like to be an Armenian living in Soviet Armenia.

As for the harsher realities, the truth was to come from an earlier generation, subdued survivors of dehumanizing camps now living with bitter memories, but content in the knowledge that their final years would be spent on the native soil of their ancestors. In the shadow of a Biblical mountain I had witnessed courage, integrity and a Job-like tolerance of extreme adversity.

Thanks to Aghayan, I had experienced both the serpent and the bees.

Wittingly and unwittingly, he had initiated this unique experience. Although I certainly did not feel grateful to him, neither did I bear him malice. All in all, he may not have been the KGB's best but he was also not the KBG's worst.

Looking around now at my surroundings, I discovered that I had walked almost the length of *Unter den Linden,* past Humboldt University and the *Staatsbibliothek,* over the *Spreekanal* and then back past the

Staatsoper and the *Bebelplatz* where the Nazis had staged their bookburn-ing, and was now standing at the corner of the *Komische Oper.* I looked down the linden tree-lined avenue, and back to the monumental dead-end which was the Brandenburg Gate.

My adventure had begun and ended here and though I knew that this historic half of the tortured city would linger long in my memory, over-laying it always would be a ghostly montage of faces, conversations and exotic places, the memories of which would haunt me for the rest of my life.

* * * * * * * *

PART FOUR

The Serpent and the Bees

XLVII

THERE CAN BE VERY FEW, IF ANY, ARMENIANS ON this planet whose lives have not been touched to some degree by either Turkey or the Soviet Union.

The generation which survived the 1895-96 massacres and the even greater cataclysm of 1915, all by Turkish decree, is still with us, and still obsessed in its twilight years by grisly scenes it cannot expunge. The offspring of that generation has grown up to a litany of those horrors, supplemented by eyewitness accounts compiled by historians.

Meanwhile, the acts of terrorism executed in order to attract the attention of a post-holocaust jaded world to the tragedy of a half century ago only compound and dichotomize the problem.

But how Armenians view the Soviet Union's role in their destiny, especially through the filter of Russian attitudes and policies *vis-a-vis* Soviet Armenia, is a story that remained to be told.

Mine has been an attempt to explore some aspects of that reality—a reality which even the most adamantly steadfast Armenians are beginning to accept as a viable alternative to the twin scourges of annihilation and assimilation.

The story I have related is primarily about Armenians, not a search for roots as much as an epiphany, about which some final thoughts after a few observations on the more sinister side of the story.

The Armenian nation represents a very special, perhaps unique case. Battered, humiliated, decimated, virtually annihilated, the Armenians keep rising up phoenix-like from the ashes, reborn and rejuvenated. Somehow, despair, even when present, has never overwhelmed them. They should long ago have been devoid of hope and faith, but it was precisely hope and faith in their religion and the culture with which it was inextricably entwined which helped them survive and transcend their fate. Thus, they entered the twentieth century, only to be confronted by the greatest horror of all in their long bloody history.

The Armenian tragedy of 1915 in Turkey, documented in full at the time in *The New York Times,* in diplomatic cables and later in history books, proved to be one of two massive counterweights to the small, harassed nation which in 1918 bravely declared itself an independent republic in a world where independence was and remains a highly tenuous condition. The other counterweight was the newly emerging juggernaut to the north, so that between the Turkish and Soviet threats to its well-being, Armenia reluctantly gave into the latter which, at least on paper, held out the hope that Armenian nationality might still be preserved.

In the seven decades since, the Soviet secret police—once known as the Cheka, later by other initials such as OGPU and NKVD and now universally notorious as the KGB—has foraged wide and far in the pursuit of two policies: publicly, enticing Armenians abroad to repatriate, and secretly, recruiting Armenians to work for the Soviet Union.

Repatriation proved to be thorny and ultimately unsuccessful. It introduced into the Soviet Armenian republic foreign attitudes and ideas which, as we have seen, had to be dealt with oftentimes in highly punitive terms, leading to dissidence and paving the way for the recent dramatic emigration—in some instances repatriating the repatriates.

Recruitment suffered even greater failure, especially in the United States. While plane-loads of tourists visit 'the homeland' every year, these same Armenians have not succumbed to the blandishments of the KGB, whose point of departure seems to be the premise that when Armenians attribute the salvation of their language and culture to the Soviet Union, a corollary commitment of their loyalties must necessarily follow. No doubt, here and there, certainly in the more volatile situations of the Middle East, the KGB has enjoyed some success, but the absence of Armenian names from the alarming list of traitors to the United States attests that Armenian-Americans have long since made a commitment of their loyalties.

Nor do Armenian-Americans betray this commitment when they express gratification that their ancient nation survives today, even if as one of the fifteen republics of the Soviet Union and dependent on the policies of bureaucrats who seldom if ever visit there. For even as they can appreciate the survival of their ancient culture, Armenian-Americans do not fail to recognize the trappings of tyranny, and that alone makes betrayal of their new homeland, where they have found not only refuge and security but liberty, odious and unthinkable. For such a people, whose history has been one gigantic tapestry of injustice, treason is out of the question.

How many Aghayans there are in the KGB, I don't know. There are enough Armenians dispersed throughout the world to warrant the use of Armenian-speaking intelligence officers by the KGB. Some are inept, "those boys from the Armenian Foreign Ministry," as Sagatelyan mockingly called them. But by and large, those whom I knew were smooth and sophisticated, having served mostly in the United States and the United Kingdom.

Occasionally, the talented among them rise to upper echelons, such as General Ivan Aghayants (sic). Until his death in the late 1960s Aghayants headed the KGB's Department of Disinformation and travelled widely visiting his outposts, one of which was *Karlshorst* in East Berlin, where he came in 1963, the same year of the KGB's initial interest in me.

If not always convinced at the outset, I was eventually that all of the 'diplomats' and 'journalists' with whom I consorted—Aghayan, Sagatelyan, Gevorkyan, Melikyan, Nanagyulian, Martikyan—were officers or agents of the KGB. Presumably, every one of them was convinced that I too was an intelligence officer. In us they see themselves. But how much can I find fault with those Armenians for allowing their services to be exploited for nefarious purposes? We too co-opt, we too recruit. In clandestine international operations, the paths of morality are twisted and labyrinthine.

The post-war history of Soviet intelligence activities bears sufficient witness to the ruthlessness and brutality practiced by the KGB. But in the era of *glasnost,* the KGB is attempting to humanize itself through a public relations campaign in which it denies ever having tapped phones or kept files on its citizens, much to the cynical amusement of wiser heads in the Soviet Union who now publicly proclaim the KGB to be an underground empire responsible for the imprisonment and torture of the cream of the nation. That course may continue, unless through *perestroika* a fundamental and genuine re-structuring of the dreaded agency is undertaken. But even so, the process of recruiting foreigners as potential spies cannot cease, whether through violence, blackmail or other forms of harassment.

In my case, the approach was different, depending more on intellectual and emotional persuasion. But through that experience, I also gained insight into the problems which confront KGB officers in service abroad.

Consequently, whether worldly or provincial, urbane or bumbling, the human beings who form the phalanx of the KGB, I learned, are no less subject to human pressures and no less immune to human frailties than the rest of us.

So much for the serpent. As for the bees . . . .

Undaunted, neither by the cruel past nor the precarious present, the prolific creative spirits of Armenia—writers, poets, sculptors, painters, composers—are assiduously seeking to repair the remnants of their embattled culture. That culture has always sprung from roots deeply entrenched in the native earth of Armenia, whose thousand legends inform every art form.

In the life of dogmatic systems it is often the case that politics infuse art. In Soviet Armenia today, that process has been reversed, for in reacting to the impact of an alien ideology, Armenia's native art has generated an all-pervasive national political consciousness.

Further, the atrocities inflicted on Armenians in neighboring Azerbaijan, which controls the enclave of Nagorno-Karabagh despite an overwhelmingly Armenian population, has galvanized the Armenians as no other issue and created a sense of ethnic unity in every corner of Soviet Armenia. (How prescient was Minas's comment two decades earlier that Azerbaijanis were merely Turks with another name!) Today, Armenian nationalism has done more than propelled one million Armenians into the streets of Yerevan—the first great challenge to Soviet authority in its seventy-year history and the precursor of all the demonstrations throughout Eastern Europe. It has inundated every layer of Armenian society with the symbols of its epic past.

Years after my visit, it overwhelmed me, first as a stunning surprise but then as eminently right, to learn that one of the nationalist movement's central figures was none other than the saintly, ascetic Minas. Another was the popular poet Barouyr Sevag. How strange that both should have suffered the same fate—death by hit-and-run drivers in the carless streets of Yerevan. Even the translator of Shakespeare, Khachig Dashdents, who had been absent during our visit, turned out to have been another of the underground nationalists.

Among those who provided new insights into Soviet Armenian life while I was there, it is sad to know that Mardiros Saryan and Yervand Kochar are dead, and of course Minas. But of the living, their spirit and their art continue to thrive, in the face of ongoing and new catastrophes.

1988 was for the Armenian nation a year of calamity. It began with the tragedy of Karabagh, and ended with the tragedy of a massive earthquake that not only devastated whole cities, towns and villages but rendered half a million Armenians homeless. The impact on Armenians world-wide of both these disasters—the ravages of which tragically continue—is having a unifying effect that no one could have predicted even five years ago. The artificial barriers erected over decades which divided the Armenian Church and Armenian political and social life are dissolving as Moscow, by virtue of *glasnost,* and Yerevan by virtue of a monumental need of aid, open the doors of the Soviet Union's smallest republic to the world outside.

Thus, while Armenians feel for Turkey an implacable hatred, they now view the Soviet Union in a more hopeful, if cautious, spirit. For if the former's policies signify extinction, the latter's hold out the hope that, at the price of curtailed freedom and sovereignty, the Armenian language, church and culture may be tolerated, and survive.

After all, the Armenian nation has survived for 2,500 years, whereas every tyranny which has assailed it has perished. And if the appeal for *collective strength* which Charentz invoked is heeded, then the perpetuation of the Armenian ethos is assured.

* * * * * * * *

Index

About the Author

Edward Alexander, a native of New York City, attended Columbia College and the Columbia University Graduate School of Journalism. During World War II, he served in Psychological Warfare in the European Theatre of Operations. In 1950, the State Department asked him to organize several of the Caucasian language units of the "Voice of America," and then appointed him chief of the Armenian Desk. Eight years later he transferred to the Foreign Service, where he dealt primarily with Soviet and East European affairs, on which he has written extensively for *The East European and Slavic Review, Problems of Communism, The Armenian Review, The Shakespeare Quarterly* and other scholarly publications. Since retiring from the Foreign Service in 1980, he has worked at the Board for International Broadcasting, which oversees RFE and RL; in the State Department's Freedom of Information Division; and at VOA. More recently, he has served as Public Affairs Advisor on the U.S. Delegation to Helsinki Human Rights Conferences in Ottawa, Budapest and Berne.